AF835741

161771

# HUNGER, APPETITE AND THE POLITICS OF THE RENAISSANCE STAGE

Hunger and appetite permeate Renaissance theatre, with servants, soldiers, courtiers and misers all defined with striking regularity through their relation to food. Demonstrating the profound ongoing relevance of Marxist literary theory, *Hunger, Appetite and the Politics of the Renaissance Stage* highlights the decisive role of these drives in the complex politics of early modern drama. Plenty and excess were thematically inseparable from scarcity and want for contemporary audiences, such that hunger and appetite together acquired a unique significance as both subject and medium of political debate. Focusing critical attention on the relationship between cultural texts and the material base of society, Matt Williamson reveals the close connections between how these drives were represented and the underlying socioeconomic changes of the period. At the same time, he shows how hunger and appetite provided the theatres with a means of conceptualising these changes and interrogating the forces that motivated them.

MATT WILLIAMSON is Senior Lecturer in the Department of Literature, Area Studies and European Languages at the University of Oslo.

# HUNGER, APPETITE AND THE POLITICS OF THE RENAISSANCE STAGE

MATT WILLIAMSON

*University of Oslo*

CAMBRIDGE
UNIVERSITY PRESS

**CAMBRIDGE**
**UNIVERSITY PRESS**

University Printing House, Cambridge CB2 8BS, United Kingdom

One Liberty Plaza, 20th Floor, New York, NY 10006, USA

477 Williamstown Road, Port Melbourne, VIC 3207, Australia

314–321, 3rd Floor, Plot 3, Splendor Forum, Jasola District Centre,
New Delhi – 110025, India

79 Anson Road, #06–04/06, Singapore 079906

Cambridge University Press is part of the University of Cambridge.

It furthers the University's mission by disseminating knowledge in the pursuit of education, learning, and research at the highest international levels of excellence.

www.cambridge.org
Information on this title: www.cambridge.org/9781108832069
DOI: 10.1017/9781108937672

© Matt Williamson 2021

This publication is in copyright. Subject to statutory exception
and to the provisions of relevant collective licensing agreements,
no reproduction of any part may take place without the written
permission of Cambridge University Press.

First published 2021

*A catalogue record for this publication is available from the British Library.*

ISBN 978-1-108-83206-9 Hardback

Cambridge University Press has no responsibility for the persistence or accuracy of URLs for external or third-party internet websites referred to in this publication and does not guarantee that any content on such websites is, or will remain, accurate or appropriate.

# *Contents*

# *Acknowledgements*

This book began as a thesis completed at Queen's University Belfast, and countless thanks are due to Edel Lamb and Mark Thornton Burnett for their advice and guidance. Invaluable feedback was also provided at many stages of the project by Ramona Wray. It was supported by funds from the Department of Employment and Learning in Northern Ireland. Thanks are due to many at Queen's, but especially to Romano Mullin, Sonja Kleij, Mia Hewitt, Simon Statham, Denise Mulgrew, Sheila McWade, Stephen Millar and Liz DeYoung.

At the University of Oslo, I have benefited from the support and advice of numerous colleagues, in particular Elly McCausland, Juan Pellicer, Stuart McWilliams, Rebecca Sherr, Ragnhild Eikli, Bruce Barnhart, Mia Brunelle Jønnum, Cristina Gomez Baggethun and Tom Zachary Bradstreet.

At King's College London, thanks to Gordon McMullan for first introducing me to the work of John Fletcher, and to Lucy Munro for her invaluable feedback on the initial thesis. Many of the ideas in the book were elaborated during my work on Massinger, as part of a Read not Dead season at Shakespeare's Globe. Thanks are due to Patrick Spottiswoode, Frances Marshall and all the other staff and practitioners working with Globe Education.

Numerous others have contributed with their friendship and support over the years, but especially Theo Merz, Will Tregear, Tyler McNally, James Hart, Rob Kiely, Hesham Zakai and Lukas Kudic-Gloster.

Many thanks to Emily Hockley and all the staff at Cambridge University Press for their support throughout the publication process.

Thanks to my mum, my dad and my sister. And above all, thanks to Erin, for her love and support.

Chapters 3 and 6 include material previously published as 'Imperial Appetites: Cannibalism and Early Modern Theatre' in *To Feast on Us as Their Prey: Cannibalism and the Early Modern Atlantic*, edited by Rachel B. Herrmann (Fayetteville: The University of Arkansas Press, 2019).

# *Introduction*

I live with bread like you, feel want,
Taste grief, need friends: subjected thus,
How can you say to me, I am a king?

William Shakespeare, *Richard II* (III.ii.175–7)

Sooner or later, everyone needs to eat. This is the realisation which enables Shakespeare's increasingly impotent King Richard II to acknowledge his own mortality. On one level, Richard's bread constitutes the basis of a more general recognition of his implication within a material situation beyond his control. He has returned from Ireland, faces a superior force of rebels, and is rapidly discovering the inefficacy of a supposedly divinely ordained power. Eating, in this sense, is an index of the limits of authority. For all the power of kings and courtiers, they cannot escape the material restraints of the flesh: of which none is more significant than the need to consume food. Eating emerges as a fundamental element common to all humanity. It is an indicator of bodily equality which gives the lie to 'respect, / Tradition, form and ceremonious duty' (III.ii.172–3). The need for food, like the approach of death, is inescapable. Food is also, as many critics have noted, the basis of conviviality, and it is therefore unsurprising that, for Richard, to live by bread and to need friends are allied concepts. Indeed, bread was a fundamental constituent of that central ritual of Christian conviviality, the Eucharist. Richard consequently appears to be elevated to a Christlike status at the very moment that he acknowledges his own humanity. Yet the bread which Richard invokes here is an ambiguous property. For it was also, as Diane Purkiss has noted, 'the food of the desperate': a foodstuff associated with the poor and a traditional gift bequeathed to the needy (Purkiss, 2010, p. 13). Richard's speech has the potential to invoke a paradox. Of all drives, hunger and appetite are perhaps the most universal. But they are also profoundly determined by social and economic forces. What we eat, how we eat and whether we can eat have always been dependent on our position within society. The historical Richard's court was a space of consumption and excess, producing *The Forme of Cury* (*c.* 1390), the first cookbook written in the English language. His invocation of a fundamental kinship with his subjects is arguably disingenuous. He may well require food, but at this point in the play, he has never gone without it. Others in his realm are not so lucky. And while a modern audience may have little awareness of this fact, few amongst the spectators in early modern London would have shared this complacency. Then, as now, everybody needed to eat, yet many starved.

This fundamental opposition constitutes the driving force behind this book. It is also, I will argue, one of the most significant material and ideological oppositions of the early modern period, and one which acquired a particular resonance in the plays and playhouses of early modern London. The drama of the period manifests an obsession with those who eat and those who do not. Hunger and appetite recur as a means of characterisation, with servants, soldiers, courtiers and misers all repeatedly defined through their relation to food. The two drives are deployed as a comment on sexual desire, with culinary images pervading the speeches of both elite lovers and lower-class prostitutes. They are integral to the representation of empire, hospitality and revolt. Attention to the opposition and interrelation of these drives is required in the first instance because it provides a perspective on an abiding concern of the early modern period. But it also furnishes a means to move forward with the culinary emphasis which has recently emerged in critical studies of the literature of the Renaissance.[1] It enables an escape from the 'soup-pot of nostalgia' which, as the historian Ken Albala has noted, occasionally defines critical interest in food and food-ways, in favour of an approach which stresses the forces of polarisation and expansion which defined early modern society (Albala, 2003, p. xv). Hitherto, the sheer force of want has remained remarkably peripheral to critical analyses of food.[2] The representation of those who lack has been largely confined to those who engage in armed

[1] Early work on the history and literary representation of food in the early modern period includes Albala (2002), Appelbaum (2006) and Fitzpatrick (2007). More recent work includes Goldstein (2013) and Goldstein and Tigner (2016). There have also been significant special issues of the *Shakespeare Jahrbuch* (2009), *Early Modern Studies Journal* (2013) and *Shakespeare Studies* (2014) which explore the role of food in Shakespeare and related authors. Although all these works are fundamentally concerned with the relationship between food and issues of gender, class and nation, the critical trajectory has been from an emphasis upon individual food choice, towards an emphasis on food 'from the point of view of community' (Goldstein, 2013, p. 3).

[2] Significant exceptions to this tendency include Burnett (1995); Gutierrez (2003); Angel-Perez and Poulain (2008); Knowles (2009); and Mukherjee (2015).

resistance. In criticism, as in much of society today, hunger is visible only when accompanied by violence. But the playwrights and audiences of early modern London did not have this element of distance. There were few amongst them that could say, definitively, that they would never experience unsatiated hunger. And this basic material fact lends a pronounced significance to the manner in which the need and desire for food were represented.

In order to scrutinise these oppositions and interrelations, this book adopts a bifocal approach, considering the representation of both hunger and appetite. The relationship between these concepts is a matter of some complexity, as the two are closely related, both on and off the stage. For this reason, it is productive to draw on Stephen Mennell's research charting the 'tangled connections' between them (Mennell, 1985, p. 20). Hunger is a physiological state, defined by Mennell as 'a body drive which recurs in all human beings in a regular cycle' (Mennell, 1985, p. 20). But on the early modern stage, it is visible primarily in the context of lack, as a hunger which cannot be satisfied. I will therefore supplement Mennell's understanding of the hunger drive with the *OED*'s definition of hunger as 'The uneasy or painful sensation caused by want of food' and 'the exhausted condition caused by want of food' (*OED*, 'hunger', def. 1a). Appetite, by contrast, is merely a 'craving for food', with broader associations of 'desire, inclination, disposition' as well as a 'Capacity for food, feeling as regards food; relish' (*OED*, 'appetite', def. 4a, 1a, 5). As Mennell has argued, it is driven by the 'appestat', by which is meant 'a *psychological*, not simply physiological, control mechanism regulating food intake' (Mennell, 1985, p. 21). Although it may indeed be stimulated by hunger, it is also a product of 'psychological processes in which social pressures can play a considerable part' (Mennell, 1985, p. 21). It is therefore necessary to consider the specific social and environmental phenomena which determine these processes in early modern England, exploring factors as diverse as the pattern of good and bad harvests, the period's relations of production, the level of technological advancement and the country's imperial capabilities. Whereas hunger implies necessity, appetite is simply the desire for food. But the relationship between them is always historically determined.

This book will argue that the act of representing these drives in the early modern English theatres was inherently political. More precisely, it will show that when hunger and appetite were placed on stage, the resulting performances were not merely determined by socio-economic forces, but also supplied a means of reflecting on them. In order to understand this relationship, it is necessary to draw on the resources of Marxism. Existing critical analyses of food have elicited a wide range of evidence for the extent to which taste and appetite are implicated within the construction of identities. Issues of class, gender, race and nation determined what foods were accessed by particular individuals, and the representation of foodstuffs was consequently integral to the manner in which these groups were perceived. Yet while this is undoubtedly true, the resulting research tends to mask what in practice constitutes a relatively static conception of society. Great care has been taken to explore how the patterns and perceptions of consumption associated with distinct groups changed in the period. But the dominant critical distrust of grand narratives has prompted a tendency to focus on the particular at the expense of the totality. This constitutes a problem of especial significance for an understanding of hunger and appetite, because their representation is intimately related to social change. What and how specific groups ate cannot be detached from more general changes in the production and distribution of food. It is not enough, for instance, to consider shifts in the representational strategies at work in the depiction of the hungry poor. Rather, it is necessary to acknowledge that the society in which the poor existed was itself fundamentally dynamic and that their role within it was therefore implicated in a more general process of change. In order to understand the representation of hunger and appetite, it is necessary to adopt a dialectical approach which relates the parts to the whole, situating these changing identities within a society conceived as a complex and contested totality.

Indeed, recognition of this dynamism is essential for a study of hunger and appetite, because the two drives repeatedly operate within contemporary discourse as a means of understanding emergent forms of social organisation. They provide a way of conceptualising the changes affecting early modern society, while allowing the depiction of imaginary solutions to the problems which those changes produced. Moreover, because hunger and appetite almost invariably operate as drives associated with particular groups or individuals, they also tend to focus attention on the agency of specific classes. In this manner, consideration of these twin concepts provides a mechanism to avoid reification of the basic transition from feudalism to capitalism. Attention to the representation of hunger and appetite reveals the frequency with which contemporary texts associate the destructive impulses of an emergent capitalist system with specific class forces in early modern society. Concern with excess, with want and with self-inflicted hunger recurs in the theatre, but the precise inflection which is placed on these issues varies enormously. A pervasive fear of uncontrolled appetite dominates the stage. But it is an appetite which can be ascribed to the poor, to the aspirant middle classes and the aristocratic elite in more or less equal measures. As a result, these texts can be productively interpreted as a series of hegemonic acts, whereby 'the development and expansion of [one] particular group are conceived of, and presented, as being the motor force of a universal expansion' (Gramsci, 1971, p. 181). They reflect upon the fundamental class struggle of early modern society, but they also constitute acts of intervention in that struggle, comprising a key means by which contemporaries conceptualised it, 'for the purpose of *fighting it out*' (Mészáros, 1989, p. 11).

The parameters of this ideological conflict can only be understood by grounding analysis of hunger and appetite in the material and discursive factors which defined their representation in the Renaissance theatre. Chapter 1 therefore begins by considering the factors which defined the lived experience of hunger and appetite in early modern England, situating these issues in the context of a Marxist understanding of the transition from feudalism to capitalism. The theatrical representation of hunger constitutes a means of reflecting on fundamental changes in the mode of production which defined the period's class struggles. The Marxist approach enables understanding of hunger as not simply an unfortunate side effect of the period's sweeping social changes, but as the driving force behind them. Yet the capacity of hunger and appetite to conceptualise these changes was a product not simply of material change itself, but also of the complex discursive connotations which those drives had accrued. For this reason, it is necessary to engage with both medical and religious texts, in order to define the precise nature of early modern attitudes to hunger and appetite. Attention to these broader ideological frameworks reveals the utility of these drives in conceptualising socio-economic change. Finally, the chapter concludes by considering the practical and theoretical implications of staging hunger and appetite on the Renaissance stage. It focusses on the theatres as places devoted to the sale of both plays and food, and considers the complex and multifaceted relationships of the period's various audiences with the lived experience of hunger and appetite. If representation of these drives is situated in the context of the material base, ideological structures and specific factors which determined the staging of contemporary plays, it becomes possible to demonstrate their vital importance as a mechanism for the theatre to engage with the central political issues of the period.

Chapter 2 explores the stereotype of the hungry servant. This character type appears in plays of a wide range of genres, throughout the early modern theatre. It provides a means of considering the relationship of hunger and appetite to dramatic form and highlights the ambiguity of the dividing line between hunger and appetite on the Renaissance stage. It is of fundamental importance for understanding the complexity of audience response to the representation of these drives. The chapter begins by considering John Lyly's *Campaspe* (1584), a text which embodies many of the broader characteristics of the hungry servant type. Here, the representation of hungry servants serves to mystify the actual conditions of the average servant's existence, representing hunger resulting from deprivation as an inalienable characteristic of the servants and figuring that hunger as an insatiable appetite. Yet once detached from the material conditions of hunger, the servant's appetite increasingly acquires metaphorical connotations which ensure that it can function as a means of conceptualising broader drives of profit and acquisition within early modern society. The second section will therefore scrutinise a range of plays, in which the servant's appetite is deployed to explore features of England's nascent capitalist system. Lastly, the chapter will consider the relationship of the hungry servant type to gender. Although female servants are rarely driven by appetite to the same degree as their male counterparts, the figure of the hungry servant constitutes a significant trope through which the theatre explored the complex relationships between husbands, wives and their servants. The final section will consider these issues through analysis of Massinger's *The Picture*, in which the character Sophia deploys hunger as a means to chastise not only her servant, but also her husband.

In the depiction of the domestic servant, appetite is predominantly a constant, in a manner which figures it as a characteristic of specific classes. But contemporary texts could also portray hunger and appetite as temporal states, subject to change. This is particularly apparent in the representation of food gifts. Chapter 3 therefore considers the representation of the food gift in plays such as William Shakespeare and George Wilkins's *Pericles* (1607), Shakespeare and Middleton's *Timon of Athens* (1607) and Massinger's *The Unnatural Combat* (*c.* 1626). It argues that attention to hunger enables recognition of the role played by use value in gift exchange, and places this in the context of the declining significance of traditions of hospitality in the period. It considers the recurrence of figures such as the discharged soldier, and suggests that the soldier's hunger constitutes a key means by which contemporary texts commented on the policies of pacifism carried out by monarchs such as James I. It emphasises the nostalgic dimension to representations of hospitality, but also argues that this nostalgia frequently marks the system itself as fundamentally untenable. It demonstrates that towards the end of the period it is possible to discern narratives of restraint and moderation which embody emergent bourgeois ideologies. Of especial interest is the extent to which these plays manifest anxiety not simply at the scarcity and want which was produced by the nascent capitalist mode of production, but also at the problems of plenty and excess.

Chapter 4 considers how the early modern theatre deploys the elision of appetite and desire. This can be related to a more general tendency, evident in a wide range of periods and cultures, to use food as a surrogate for sexual activity. Yet this chapter will argue that the early modern theatre is distinct in two significant ways. Firstly, contemporary medical theory placed a strong emphasis on the literal, rather than merely metaphorical, nature of the connections between sexual and culinary consumption. Secondly, appetite acquires a particular utility as a means of conceptualising desire at a time when theological debate increasingly acknowledged the legitimacy of moderate, but not of excessive, sexual intercourse. Above all, the elision of the two drives serves to lend a gustatory logic to the theatre's depiction of excessive desire, in a manner which lends it a profound political significance. The chapter will begin by exploring the extent to which this serves to associate desire with the excessive appetites unleashed by material excess and tyranny. But it will also emphasise the vulnerability which the culinary logic instils in representations of desire. The second section will consider the extent to which the simple subject–object relationship of consumption generates a profound ambiguity regarding who, precisely, is being consumed in the context of a sexual relationship. It will focus on Thomas Dekker and Thomas Middleton's *The Bloody Banquet* (*c.* 1609). The third section, meanwhile, will emphasise the extent to which the imagery of appetite foregrounds the potentially debilitating consequences of sexual desire, at a time in which humoral theory asserted a model of the body as porous, and potentially vulnerable.

Chapter 5 develops a number of these concerns, through attention to the representation of female food refusal in the period. It argues that although the refusal of food is not confined solely to women, it resonates in the early modern theatre as a gendered mode of resistance. In order to explore these issues, it begins by considering the contemporary phenomenon of 'miraculous maid' pamphlets, which recounted supposedly factual accounts of prodigious acts of religiously motivated food refusal. It then turns to Thomas Heywood's *A Woman Killed with Kindness* (1603) and George Chapman's *The Widow's Tears* (1604). It places these plays in the context of changes to religious practice, contemporary understandings of the female body, and the space of the household. It argues that in the context of female food refusal, hunger has the capacity to function as a form of parodic obedience to the norms of contemporary gender ideology. By carrying dictates of privacy and closure to a point of often terminal excess, these texts query or satirise the double standard within early modern English society. While Heywood's text approaches this dynamic in tragic mode, and Chapman's in an overtly comic fashion, in both plays the literal process of embodiment inherent in the dramatisation of food refusal threatens to carry prevailing gender norms to the point of collapse.

In Chapter 6, I turn to the depiction of hunger, appetite and imperialism. Food comprised an integral component of colonial discourse in the period, and the representation of hunger and appetite therefore provided a significant means by which the theatres could legitimise or critique England's overseas expansion. The chapter focusses on Fletcher's *Bonduca* (*c.* 1613) and Fletcher and Massinger's *The Sea Voyage* (1622), two plays in which hunger and appetite occupy positions of particular significance as a means of conceiving the problems and advantages of colonial settlement. Through an emphasis of the interrelation of hunger, appetite and empire, it becomes possible to acknowledge the role played by imperial expansion in the elimination of hunger in England, while simultaneously figuring that expansion as a product, rather than a cause, of the country's wider social changes. The chapter focusses on the use of hunger and appetite as a means to critique or endorse emergent bourgeois ideologies of imperialist expansion, with emphasis on how colonial adventures are constructed as both a solution to the problem of hunger and the object of new and occasionally unnatural appetites. It considers the cultural significance of cannibalism as an act which at this time is associated not only with subaltern native populations, but also with the expansive appetites of European colonisers, in a manner which can be deployed to express anxiety at the potential consequences of imperial expansion.

Chapter 7 considers the interrelation of hunger, appetite and armed resistance to the state. It focusses on texts such as Shakespeare and Marlowe's *2 Henry VI* (1590), the anonymous *Life and Death of Jack Straw* (1594) and Shakespeare's *Coriolanus* (1608), in which hunger and appetite emerge as grounds for rebellion.[3] It explores how the initial causes of revolt are represented in these plays, stressing the interrelation of the hunger of the poor with the appetites of the rich. But it also emphasises the

[3] For recent debates on the authorship of *2 Henry VI*, see Craig (2009), Vickers (2011) and Segarra, Eisen, Egan and Ribeiro (2016).

degree to which these onstage revolts are represented as processes, which move from depictions of an initial grievance, to representation of the appetites which can be unleashed by the act of rebellion. Lastly, it stresses the utopian possibilities of presenting these rebel appetites onstage, arguing that discernible in the most radical of these texts is a proto-communist emphasis on the potential creation of a society in which all are equal, in which the excesses of the rich are moderated so that all may have enough. The depiction of hunger, appetite and revolt emerges as the subject of a pronounced interpretative instability, rooted in the legitimation of the contemporary status quo, but permeated, nevertheless, by insurrectionary possibilities.

This range of topics and texts is, of necessity, partial. Attention to the representation of hunger and appetite in the early modern theatres reveals, almost immediately, a vast surplus of material. In adopting the thematic approach, I aim to highlight the primary trends within this corpus, and to explore the fundamental dynamics at work within the representation of these drives. The approach, of course, raises the issue of teleology. The conventional critique of the Marxist analysis is that it enacts an anachronistic model of history, uninterested in the motivations of the original participants. Yet to argue that the representation of hunger and appetite in the later sixteenth and early seventeenth centuries is intertwined with social forces which would cause a civil war and revolution a few decades later, is not to suggest that the revolution was inevitable. On the contrary, to disregard these underlying causes is to reduce the study of history and literature to little more than a descriptive account of what happens, with scant ability to outline alternative possibilities. To ignore the fact that England descended into conflict is to risk attributing an excess of permanence to structures and hierarchies which at many historical moments in the period were palpably unstable. The depiction of hunger and appetite provided a means for the writers of early modern England to conceive of widespread and threatening social changes which they had limited means of understanding, but which for the modern critic can be identified as constituting the emergence of capitalism. The complex ramifications of these changes would eventually drive England into civil war and revolution. But in the late sixteenth and early seventeenth centuries, they found focussed expression primarily in the literature of the period, and rarely more so than in the representation of hunger and appetite.

CHAPTER 1

# *Thinking through Hunger and Appetite in Renaissance England*

In order to understand the depiction of hunger and appetite correctly, it is necessary to explore the historical conditions surrounding their representation; for the apparent universality of these drives masks the complex ways they both determine, and are determined by, social formations. Hunger, as Ernst Bloch notes, may constitute 'the oil in the lamp of history, but even this primary need looks different according to the changing ways in which needs are satisfied' (Bloch, 1995, p. 69). The precise significance of hunger varies depending on a vast range of material and ideological factors. This is not simply a matter of distinguishing between the passing pangs experienced by all and the profound hunger which affects those who starve. There are also significant differences in terms of both cause and perception, between a peasant who starves alongside their entire village and the outcast who is famished in the midst of plenty. To comprehend what is at stake in the representation of hunger and appetite, it is therefore necessary to consider the material factors governing the lived experience of these drives in the early modern period, and the ideological framework within which they were understood.

Grasping the material dimension to the existence of hunger and appetite involves acknowledging the power which these drives exert over society. In the first instance, they are defined by disruptive potential. Hunger, for example, constitutes a key manifestation of the power exerted by lived experience to challenge dominant ideologies, so that, as E. P. Thompson has argued, 'old conceptual systems may crumble and new problematics insist upon their presence' (Thompson, 1995, p. 11). When people starve, 'their survivors think in new ways about the market'; when they are imprisoned, 'they meditate in new ways about the law' (Thompson, 1995, p. 11). Yet hunger and appetite also play a significant role in the production and reproduction of social formations. Keith Wrightson notes that in this period 'agriculture was the dominant sphere of economic activity and levels of agricultural production governed the growth opportunities of the economy as a whole' (Wrightson, 2000, p. 160). If, as Terry Eagleton has argued, 'in the production of human society some activities are more fundamentally determining than others' (Eagleton, 1989, p. 169), then few spheres of the English economy were more important than the production of food. In a very real sense, hunger is not simply a drive which might be compared to any other form of need or desire, but instead constitutes the primary drive in this period. A correct understanding of hunger and appetite thus requires an engagement with the economic sphere. This is not a matter of identifying a single, unambiguous mode of production since, as Perry Anderson has argued, 'societies are nearly always a mixture of forms, and change in them is more usually the result of an expansion of one of them at the expense of others' (Anderson, 1992, p. 238). Instead, it is necessary to assert the contested, contradictory nature of the economic base at a time of sweeping socio-economic change. Attention to the material factors dominating the representation of hunger and appetite has the potential to reveal the complexity of their political significance. Certainly, they are implicated in moments of crisis, when the lived experience of ordinary people threatens to overturn the existing social order. But they also play a fundamental role in the processes of expansion and polarisation which defined the early modern period.

The representation of hunger and appetite is therefore determined by the material base of early modern society. But, as Raymond Williams has emphasised, the concept of determination should be understood not as 'an external cause which . . . totally controls a subsequent activity', but rather as 'setting limits, exerting pressures' (Williams, 2005, p. 32). The material activity of human beings defines the contemporary lived experience of hunger and appetite. But in order to understand their complex ideological function, it is necessary to consider the diverse ways in which contemporaries understood these drives. The playing companies and audiences of early modern London had inherited a wide range of interpretations of, and perspectives on, the issue of hunger and appetite. There exists an extensive body of religious, medical and popular texts which explore the practical and moral significance of these drives. Of course, this ideological framework is also, like the material base, dynamic. It responds to the prevailing material conditions, attempting to resolve contradictions at the base. But it also determines how instances of hunger or appetite might be interpreted, establishing a series of images and assumptions governing the political significance of these drives on the early modern stage. Through attention to these contemporary perspectives, it becomes possible to discern those characteristics imbued in hunger and appetite which lent them utility as a means of conceptualising the rupture between lived experience and ideology which defined the period.

Lastly, however, it is necessary to acknowledge that these more general ideological structures are subject to a specific inflection in the context of the playhouses. To understand the dramatic significance of hunger and appetite, it is vital to move beyond the legacy of Cultural Materialist and New Historicist criticism, with its tendency to treat all forms of text as indistinguishable. The early modern theatres constituted specific superstructural entities, engaged in the production of both profit and ideology.[1] The theatre functions to make sense of lived experience, to lend it form and structure, and to query or legitimise the element of disjuncture which invariably exists between dominant ideological structures and individual lived experience. This act of definition makes possible a degree of intervention into ideological conflict, providing a rationalisation of social contradiction which invites praxis, rather than simply contemplation. In order to assess this process of intervention, it is necessary to explore the practical and theoretical implications of staging hunger and appetite. In doing so, it becomes possible to discern the role played by the representation of hunger and appetite in the ideological conflicts of a period defined by sweeping processes of material change and increasingly overt class struggle.

As such this chapter will move from the general to the particular. The investigation will begin with the seismic socio-economic changes which were both motivated by, and determined, the material reality of hunger and appetite in early modern society. It will draw on the vast body of medical and theological understandings of these drives, to outline the complex ideological significance which could be attributed to them. And it will define the characteristics of these drives in the context of the theatres. In each of these areas, hunger and appetite emerge as topics of profound political significance. Their existence is rooted at every level in the processes of social, economic and ideological change which developed in early modern England. But perhaps more significant is the extent to which these drives also constituted a medium for debate. By historicising hunger and appetite, it becomes possible to discern their profound utility for ideological conflict. The representation of these promotes a form of analysis which, like the society which produced them, is fundamentally dynamic.

[1] In this, I differ from critics such as James Holstun and Gabriel Egan, who in practice tend to equate superstructure and ideology. Instead, I will follow Eagleton in reading superstructural forms as material, while using ideology to describe immaterial concepts. This enables a critic to avoid a liberal opposition of determined base to undetermined superstructure. Like the material base, superstructural forms are contested. It is for this reason that the representation of hunger and appetite on the early modern stage is defined by such ambiguity.

They provide a series of images and motivations which contain an unparalleled capacity to comment on a social formation in the grip of profound change. It is for this reason that the study of hunger and appetite in the early modern theatres constitutes a topic of pressing significance.

## Profit and Polarisation

The availability of food, the specific types of food on offer and the degree of inequality in diet, exerted a determining influence over how hunger and appetite were experienced and represented. Of particular importance is the degree to which early modern England escaped the generalised subsistence crises which had tended to restrain population growth for much of human history. In previous centuries, European society had been characterised by a steadily increasing population, followed by periods of demographic crisis, in a pattern which broadly accords with a Malthusian belief that 'the power of population is indefinitely greater than the power in the earth to produce subsistence for man' (Malthus, 1959, p. 5). As Robert Brenner has noted, 'This two-phase cyclical pattern prevailed in the economy of most of Europe in the later medieval period (1100–1450) and continued to predominate over large parts of it into the early modern period (1450–1700)' (Brenner, 1985b, p. 217). Famine, defined by Roger Appleby as 'a crisis of mortality caused by starvation and starvation-related disease . . . measured by the increase in the number of deaths' (Appleby, 1978, p. 1), played a significant role in these demographic crises. Yet the sixteenth century in England was defined by socio-economic change which was to culminate in what Brenner has described as 'the final disruption of the Malthusian pattern and the introduction of a strikingly novel form of continued economic development' (Brenner, 1985a, p. 24). The period was defined by a marked increase in agricultural productivity coupled with sustained demographic growth.[2] England's population rose from 2.98 million in 1561, to 4 million in 1601 and 5.23 million in 1651 (cf. Wrightson, 2000, p. 159). In the face of these increases, inflation was high and periods of dearth were frequent.[3] But by contrast with the generalised demographic

[2] Wrightson notes that 'Shipments of grain to London from the Essex ports of Colchester and Maldon rose from roughly 1,000 quarters in 1565 to almost 13,000 in 1624, while those from the specialist grain-producing districts of north-east Kent grew from 12,000 quarters in 1587–8 to over 57,000 in 1638' (Wrightson, 2000, p. 173).

[3] Appleby has demonstrated that between 1593 and 1596 wheat prices doubled, and he has argued that in 1597 the impact of shortages 'was substantial throughout all England' (Appleby, 1978, p. 2). A. L. Beier reports that 'Rises in food prices averaging about 4 per cent a year [were] sustained for nearly 150 years and had serious consequences' (Beier, 1985, p. 20). Wrightson notes that 'by the

crises of the thirteenth century, outbreaks of outright famine were localised, and never applied the same restricting pressure on population growth, even if they continued to exert a considerable psychosocial influence on contemporary society.[4] Hunger remained a constant in the lives of the mass of people in early modern England, but the country as a whole had escaped the Malthusian trap. It is only by exploring the causes and consequences of this shift that it is possible to contextualise onstage representations of hunger and appetite in the contemporary theatre.

In the first instance, increasing agricultural productivity and the resultant elimination of demographic crisis were predicated on technological development in the agrarian sector. Historians have differed extensively on the degree to which changes in agricultural production in the period might be termed 'revolutionary'.[5] But there can be little doubt that the period was defined by a sudden and pronounced interest in putting land to more efficient use. This involved not only an expansion in the acreage under cultivation, but also an increased intensity. Keith Wrightson has noted that there is 'much evidence of increased manuring to raise the fertility of the land by spreading and ploughing in muck, lime or marl' (Wrightson, 2000, p. 162). Perhaps more importantly, the period also saw increased use of convertible husbandry. Whereas before, farmers had in general adopted a three-year rotation of grain, peas and beans, and fallow, in order to allow the soil to regain its fertility, convertible husbandry involved keeping a larger acreage under pasture, allowing it to rest for longer and receive

1570s, the price of a hypothetical "basket of consumables" constructed to reflect most of the basic needs of a typical household was more than three times what it had been at the turn of the century' (Wrightson, 2000, p. 116).

4 Since the work of Appleby in the late '70s, most historians have acknowledged that the counties of Cumberland and Westmorland were struck by famine in 1587–8, 1597 and 1623 (cf. Appleby, 1978, p. 1). However, the fear of famine was far more wide-ranging. Mandrou has noted that one of the defining features of early modern Europe was 'the obsession with starving to death' (Mandrou, 1975, p. 26). Braudel argues that famine 'recurred so insistently for centuries on end that it became incorporated into man's biological regime and built into his daily life' (Braudel, 1992, p. 73). Mennell claims that 'what could not immediately disappear with general famines was the fear of going hungry engendered by centuries of experience' (Mennell, 1985, p. 27).

5 Prior to the 1960s, the historical consensus situated the agricultural revolution in the eighteenth and nineteenth centuries, and tended to present it as a product of parliamentary enclosure. However, a range of revisionist historians have emphasised the extent to which productivity increased prior to this point. Eric Kerridge, for instance, argues that 'the agricultural revolution took place in England in the sixteenth and seventeenth centuries', and asserts that the most significant changes in practice were established by 1673 (Kerridge, 1967, p. 1). Eric Jones, by contrast, stresses a slightly later period, emphasising the significance of the Commonwealth and Restoration periods (Jones, 1965). More recently, Robert Allen has identified a range of overlapping revolutionary periods in English agriculture, but argues for the existence of a 'yeoman's agricultural revolution' in seventeenth-century England, which was 'marked by a doubling of corn yields' and a consequent rise in England's national income (Allen, 1992, p. 21).

manure from livestock for greater fertility. The results were dramatic. Wrightson notes that 'evidence from five counties in eastern and southern England suggests that cereal yields rose by around 12 per cent in the second half of the sixteenth century and by a further 4 per cent in the early seventeenth century' (Wrightson, 2000, p. 163). John Walter similarly argues that agrarian innovation 'perhaps doubled gross yields between the early sixteenth and mid seventeenth centuries' (Walter, 1991, p. 80). Without these technological advances, it would have been impossible for England to produce enough food to feed its growing population, and they can therefore be said to exert a profound influence on the lived experience of hunger and appetite.

Nevertheless, the precise reasons for these sudden changes to agriculture have been the subject of wide-ranging debate. For many, technological development should be read simply as a consequence of demographic pressure. The contours of this argument were succinctly summarised, in an early article by H. J. Habakkuk, as a model of history whereby 'the long-term movements in prices, in income distribution, in investment, in real wages and in migration are dominated by changes in the growth of population. Rising population: rising prices, rising agricultural profits, low real incomes for the mass of the population' (Habakkuk, 1958, p. 487). An increase in population generates inflation, which provides an incentive for technological development. Yet as historians including Brenner and Wrightson have noted, similar trends in population growth across Europe manifested very different effects. Brenner, for example, notes that while in France increasing population prompted 'fragmentation of holdings, rising rents and declining productivity . . . the parallel growth of population in England in this same period has been used to explain precisely opposite developments' (Brenner, 1985a, p. 24). It should therefore be acknowledged that 'whatever population growth in England and Wales had in common with most of Europe in terms of its origins, it was being sustained by factors which were more peculiar to the English and Welsh situations' (Wrightson, 2000, p. 160). If population growth was a necessary cause of technological development, it was far from a sufficient one. To understand the material and social basis for the contemporary lived experience of hunger and appetite, it is necessary to move beyond demographic change and scrutinise the specific social characteristics of early modern England.

One significant perspective is provided by the work of Political Marxists such as Robert Brenner and Ellen Meiksins Wood, who emphasise the role played by class struggle as the determining factor in the diverse results of population change across the European continent. As Brenner has noted, many of the period's agrarian innovations had been in existence for a considerable time.[6] But the feudal model of landownership had acted as a fundamental bar to their wider dissemination. The unfree nature of the peasantry within the feudal system had meant that 'the lord's most obvious mode of increasing income from his lands was not through capital investment and the introduction of new techniques, but through squeezing the peasants, by increasing either money rents or labour services' (Brenner, 1985a, p. 31). Not only this, but 'the surplus-extraction relations of serfdom tended to lead to the exhaustion of peasant production *per se*', since the peasants were left without any incentive to innovate for themselves (Brenner, 1985a, p. 33). They also lacked resources, such as animals for ploughing and as a source of manure, prompting a deterioration of the soil which would eventually lead to a loss of soil quality. In other words, as Brenner has argued, 'the breakthrough from "traditional economy" to relatively self-sustaining economic development was predicated upon the emergence of a specific set of class or social-property relations in the countryside – that is, capitalist class relations' (Brenner, 1985a, p. 30). For Brenner, the English peasantry occupied an ambiguous position in the wake of the class struggles of the late medieval period. Unlike the peasantry of Eastern Europe, they had resisted the re-imposition of serfdom. Unlike those of much of Western Europe, however, they had failed to establish freehold rights to their land. In this context, landlords were able to pursue aggressive processes of enclosure and the consolidation of holdings, marginalising the poorer peasantry in favour of large-scale tenant farmers.[7] These more extensive farms enabled 'the displacement of the traditionally antagonistic relationship in which landlord squeezing undermined tenant initiative, by an emergent landlord/tenant symbiosis which brought mutual cooperation in investment and improvement' (Brenner, 1985a, p. 51). In conjunction with inflation, the increasing capitalisation of agriculture worked to drive poorer farmers off the land. The result was 'the emergence of the "classic" landlord / capitalist tenant / wage-labourer structure which made possible the transformation of agricultural production in England' (Brenner, 1985a, p. 49). Furthermore, these parallel social changes contributed to each other, creating a cycle that fuelled the

[6] Convertible husbandry, for example, had been 'systematically adopted on Battle Abbey's manor of Marley from the early fourteenth century' (Brenner, 1985a, p. 32).

[7] Wrightson has noted that, between 1600 and 1650, '40 per cent of the manors of Leicestershire and 18 per cent of the land area of Co. Durham were enclosed, while the period 1575 to 1674 saw the enclosure of some 17 per cent of the land in the south-midland counties, the heartland of open-field farming' (Wrightson, 2000, p. 162).

polarisation and marketisation of English society. As previously self-sufficient peasants were driven onto the market, they increased levels of demand for corn, which increased prices, which further increased the incentive for more efficient farming methods. The consequence was the creation of an ever more capitalised form of agricultural production alongside a surplus population which was highly vulnerable to market fluctuations.

This process of agrarian transformation provided the impetus for substantial shifts in the economy, prompting a growth in levels of expansion and consumption, constituting a factor of critical importance for the contemporary understanding of appetite. Greater profits for gentry farmers and increased lower-class reliance upon the market prompted a substantial rise in demand. Before long, 'urban economies were responding to a quickening of internal trade and the growth of rural demand for their products', in what Wrightson has characterised as a 'reciprocal relationship between agricultural development and urban growth' (Wrightson, 2000, pp. 165–6). The effects were dramatic. Wrightson has noted that the country's national income 'more than doubled in real terms between 1566 and 1641' (Wrightson, 2000, p. 181). Contemporaries were well aware that the economy was expanding, with John Hawkins claiming in 1584 that 'the substance of this realm is trebled in value' since Elizabeth's accession (Hawkins, 1888, p. 44). The consequences for overseas trade were no less significant. Brenner stresses the extent to which the 'remarkable secular rise of domestic demand for imports in England' prompted the 'extraordinary long-term growth and continuing high profits' of emerging merchant companies focussed on the Levant and the East Indies (Brenner, 1993, p. 5). Demand for luxury comestibles such as currants, for instance, was such that the Venetian Ambassador reported in 1628 that the English 'consume a greater amount of currants than all the rest of the world', desiring them so much that 'men have been said to hang themselves because they have not enough money to buy them' (Calendar of State Papers, 1916, XXI, p. 553; cited in Brenner, 1993, p. 43). England's hunger was fuelling its rapidly expanding economy. The result was the creation of new and, from the perspective of contemporary observers, frequently troubling appetites.

At the same time, there existed a number of impediments to the further expansion of England's economy. For the Political Marxists, the market is the primary force driving the period's process of class differentiation, so that, as Ellen Meiksins Wood has argued, 'the market dependence of economic actors, was a *cause*, not a result, of proletarianisation' (Wood, 2002, p. 60). Indeed, it is in large part this emphasis on the impersonal force of the market that has prompted figures such as Chris Harman to condemn their conception of history as 'class struggle without any element of class consciousness' (Harman, 2008, p. 187). Yet, as Henry Heller has argued, 'it is a mistake to assume, as Brenner apparently does, that an already rational and competitive market imposed a strict market rationality on the emerging rural capitalists' (Heller, 2011, p. 95). While it is true that, as Wrightson notes, the very existence of agrarian specialisation and intensification implies 'the existence of larger and more integrated markets for agricultural produce', this process was far from complete at this time (Wrightson, 2000, p. 184). As Jane Whittle has noted, early modern England was defined by 'an economy in which market relations were taken for granted, and in which land was regarded as an investment as well as a livelihood, but it was not market-dependent' (Whittle, 2000, p. 315). On the contrary, 'the initial profitable windfalls of the sixteenth century, reinforced by unprecedented inflationary pressures, cannot be thought of as the way "normal" or established markets based on competition operate, but rather describe a process of market formation' (Heller, 2011, p. 95). In particular, the early modern state worked to restrict the market in a number of key ways. Institutions such as the Star Chamber, High Commission and Court of Wards, as well as practices of purveyance and feudal tenure, constituted a clear barrier to the further development of capitalist relations and marketisation. Issues of hunger and appetite were often central to these conflicts, with the state repeatedly acting to restrict a free market in grain, particularly in times of dearth. As Heller argues, 'until the English Revolution helped to sweep away many of these restrictions, there was nothing approaching a competitive market' (Heller, 2011, p. 95). Late sixteenth- and early seventeenth-century England can consequently be understood, in orthodox Marxist terms, as defined by a tension between an economic base increasingly dominated by nascent capitalist forces, and a state which, while initially conducive to their development, increasingly operated as a restraint on the further development of these forces.

Naturally, the ability of the population of early modern England to understand these tensions was fundamentally compromised. But as Wrightson has noted, 'if they were only dimly aware of the underlying causes of economic and social change, they were acutely aware of the more pathological symptoms of the process of change' (Wrightson, 1982, p. 157). Hunger and appetite were bound up with the contemporary experience of these 'pathological symptoms'. Most importantly, hunger was intimately related to the growth of what Wrightson has defined as 'structural poverty', or poverty that is:

> Derived not so much from individual misfortune or default as from the fact that for a growing proportion of the population periodic hardship was inevitable, for the demand and rates of payment for their labour were such as to mean a diminishing capacity to meet their households' needs. (Wrightson, 2000, p. 197)

Extensive historical, Cultural Materialist and New Historicist work has testified to the severity of the threat which the period's new mass of landless poor was perceived to constitute to the status quo of early modern England, and the wide range of measures which the state adopted to deal with them.[8] Hunger was a defining feature of the lived experience of this section of the population and constituted an issue of central importance for the attempts of the early modern state to control them. The period saw a marked decrease in the quality of the average diet and left many at risk of starvation at times of harvest failure. The representation of lower-class hunger in the early modern theatre is inseparable from these wider issues of order and control. The possibility of violent resistance exerts a defining influence upon even the more ostensibly benign depictions of the hungry poor.

Moreover, if hunger was central to the life of the poor, considerations of appetite played a similarly significant role in changes at the top of society. Numerous critics and historians have emphasised the importance of conspicuous consumption as a fundamental constituent of ruling-class ideology in the period. Socio-economic change exerted a major disruptive force upon these groups, precisely because inflation 'threatened to erode their incomes and undermine their living standards' (Wrightson, 1982, p. 138). The most influential treatment of this pressure is Lawrence Stone's *The Crisis of the Aristocracy,* a text which argues that over the course of the sixteenth and seventeenth centuries, the peerage declined politically, economically and socially, in large part as a result of the pressures which inflation placed upon their traditional patterns of spending. Stone's more general conclusions have been widely criticised, particularly by revisionist

[8] Seminal work in this respect includes A. L. Beier's *Masterless Men* alongside essays by Paul Brown, Steve Carroll, Stephen Greenblatt and Linda Woodbridge. Beier emphasises the severity of the punishments meted out against the masterless poor, noting that 'a statute of 1572 ordered [children aged 5 to 14] to be stocked and whipped. Those over 14 were to be gaoled, whipped and burnt through the ear; after 1597 children under the age of seven were exempted from prosecution' (Beier, 1985, p. 10). The literary accounts suffer from their emphasis upon subversive forces, with Greenblatt, for example, characterising vagabonds as the 'very types of Elizabethan subversion' (Greenblatt, 1994, p. 30). But their exploration of the manner in which texts embody and comment upon state action, including the 'regular modification and reissuance of the Poor' has productively highlighted the implication of contemporary texts within wider attempts at social control (Carroll, 1996, p. 4).

historians who emphasise continuity rather than rupture. Nevertheless, the underlying significance of rising prices has rarely been dismissed entirely.[9] Even beyond inflation, the changing nature of English agriculture contributed to a wider sense of crisis amongst the aristocracy, for as Corrigan and Sayer have argued, 'the growing commercialisation of landlord/tenant relationships and Tudor state centralization itself had progressively eroded specifically feudal bases of aristocratic power and authority' (Corrigan and Sayer, 1985, p. 74). As I shall demonstrate in Chapter 3, the consumption and distribution of food had always had a crucial role in the maintenance of these traditional, hierarchical structures of control. Appetite assumes a position of privileged visibility in the plays of the period, in large part because it enables the theatre to conceptualise these changes, becoming both a literal and metaphorical means of depicting those sections of the elite increasingly compromised by consumption.

For all that these changes caused suffering for some, for others they presented an opportunity. As Sir Francis Bacon noted, 'The improvement of the ground is the most natural obtaining of riches; . . . but it is slow; and yet, where men of great wealth do stoop to husbandry, it multiplieth riches exceedingly' (Bacon, 1985, p. 166). At the same time, the question of precisely who benefited from the increasing capitalisation of agriculture is an open one. For Brenner, the active agent in the process was undoubtedly the landowner class. As such, his work can be situated within a more general tendency within recent Marxist thought to marginalise the rise of a distinct bourgeois class, and to assert in its place what James Holstun describes as 'the internal transformation of the English ruling class' (Holstun, 2000, p. 121). According to this view, the period's process of polarisation is part of 'the reality of bourgeois revolution in England – a story of centuries-long embourgeoisement of England's dominant classes (and proletarianisation of the ruled, the two being inseparable) complexly facilitated by the protracted making of a nation state' (Corrigan and Sayer,

[9] D. C. Coleman, for instance, disputed the economic basis of Stone's claims (Coleman, 1966). Barry Coward expanded upon this critique to dispute the extent to which the aristocracy was defined by a crisis 'of its political and social power and influence' (Coward, 1982, p. 54). Arguably, however, the tendency of more recent historians to eschew Stone's conclusions stems not so much from his specific argument, but rather from a wider acceptance of revisionist beliefs about 'the impossibility of ever *demonstrating* a strong enough link between society and politics to convince the sceptical reader' (Burgess, 1990, p. 611). In fact, as Karin Coddon has argued, although it is unwise to assert a 'direct causality between aristocratic excesses and the development of a revolutionary movement', it is nevertheless clear that 'the nobility's profligate expenditures and conspicuous consumption served to weaken the aristocracy both economically and in terms of cultural perception' (Coddon, 1993, p. 312). Likewise, J. A. Sharpe acknowledges that 'the period 1580–1620 does seem to have been one of financial difficulties for the peerage as a group' (Sharpe, 1997, p. 161).

1985, p. 11). To a degree, this perspective is supported by contemporary sources. Faced with rising costs, and in the absence of traditional routes to preferment, it was natural that many amongst the gentry and nobility turned increasingly to the profits of the newly capitalised agriculture. Sir Thomas Wilson, for example, noted in 1600 that gentlemen who previously were 'wont to addict themselves to the wars' now increasingly focussed on husbandry, and 'know as well how to improve their lands . . . as the farmer or countryman, so that they take their farms into their hands as the leases expire, and either till themselves or else let them out to those who will give most' (Wilson, 1936, p. 18). At the same time, it is surely questionable to what extent processes of innovation and the capitalisation of agriculture were led by this group. Marx himself noted that the model of property of large-scale English landowners in the period was 'in perfect harmony' with the bourgeoisie, and was in fact 'not feudal but bourgeois property' (Marx and Engels, 1975–2004, X, p. 254). But he also stressed the agency of tenant farmers, who, as a consequence of both inflation and the prevalence of long-term copyhold leases, 'grew rich at the expense both of their labourers and their landlords' (Marx and Engels, 1975–2004, XXXV, pp. 732–3). More recently, Terrence Byers has emphasised the importance of processes of differentiation amongst the peasant class, arguing that wealthy tenant farmers were not 'passive recipients' of change, but rather 'active agents in the process of transformation' (Byres, 2006, p. 27). Indeed, as Heller notes, it is significant in this respect that 'agricultural capitalism developed in areas where lordship was weak and peasant property rights were strong' (Heller, 2011, p. 122). The formation of an English bourgeoisie can consequently be read as a twin process of *embourgeoisement*, encompassing not only the elite but also the middling sort. In the literature of the period, patterns of consumption are bound up with this process of transformation. Appetite recurs as a means to encapsulate not only elite excess, but also the unrestrained expansive capacities of an emergent capitalist class, which appeared ready to swallow up what remained of the poor's property and rights.

The significance of socio-economic change for representations of hunger and appetite in the theatre is therefore multivalent. In the first instance, the way these drives are understood is contingent on how the food was produced, distributed and consumed. The types of food available, and the specific ranks and classes of people who were able to consume them, were governed by the basic processes of a society in change. But the role of this shift in the representation of hunger and appetite also extends beyond this. For hunger and appetite emerge with a stark clarity in this period as both driving forces and symptoms of these underlying changes. Representations of these two drives constitute a central means through which the theatre conceptualised the widespread consequences of more general shifts in the socio-economic structure of early modern England. They play a fundamental role in the articulation of change and continuity in areas as diverse as service, hospitality, sexuality, empire and revolt. For this reason, the two drives assume a privileged ideological position. Ideology is conceived by István Mészáros, following Marx, as 'the imperative to become *practically conscious* of the fundamentals of social conflict – from the mutually exclusive *standpoints* of the hegemonic alternatives that face one another in the given social order – for the purpose of *fighting it out*' (Mészáros, 1989, p. 11). It is precisely this element of practical consciousness which is inextricably bound up with the representation of hunger and appetite on the early modern stage. To represent hunger and appetite is almost invariably to discuss the forces of social change which produced them. Attention to the ways in which these drives were depicted is therefore invaluable for an understanding of the period's politics.

## The Humoral Body

The early modern period was defined by what Ken Albala has described as an 'immense outpouring of dietary literature' (Albala, 2002, p. 1). The ideas of humoral theory permeated contemporary conceptions of the body and its drives, providing, as Michael Schoenfeldt has argued, 'a near-poetic vocabulary of corporeal experience', which contributed to 'a particularly physiological mode of self-fashioning' (Schoenfeldt, 1999, pp. 3, 12). In the first instance, it is therefore necessary to relate the depiction of hunger and appetite to contemporary ideas regarding consumption and the body. As Albala has noted, 'all dietary literature in this period depended on a common theoretical framework based on the work of Galen' (Albala, 2002, p. 5). It was argued that the body consisted of four humours: blood, which was hot and wet; phlegm, which was cold and wet; yellow bile, which was hot and dry; and black bile, which was cold and dry. An imbalance of these fluids was believed to affect both temperament and health, so that an excess of black bile might cause melancholia, while an excess of yellow bile could lead to aggression. The characteristics of hot, cold, wet and dry were believed to correspond to the properties of specific foods, so that diet constituted one of the most significant means by which the humoral balance was regulated. Black pepper, for instance, promoted yellow bile, while cold and moist foods like lettuce encouraged phlegm (cf. Albala, 2002, pp. 11, 13). Central to this model was the belief that, as Fitzpatrick has noted, 'careful consumption might correct moral as well as physical shortcomings' (Fitzpatrick, 2007, p. 3). Cogan, for example, argued that 'meates and drinkes doe alter our bodies, and either temper them or distemper them greatly' (Cogan, 1636, p. vi). The theory, as Michael Schoenfeldt claims, possessed 'a remarkable capacity to relate the body to its environment' (Schoenfeldt, 1999, p. 3). By contrast with the post-Cartesian assumptions which dominate modern thought about the body, the population of early modern England was accustomed to thinking in terms of the interrelationship of body, mind and the surrounding world.

These theories also dominated contemporary understanding of hunger and appetite. As Albala has observed, 'The first stage of the entire [eating] process was thought to be the attainment of a sufficient appetite.' But the precise relationship between hunger and appetite was a matter of some scrutiny (Albala, 2002, p. 54). An early translation of the seminal dietary the *Regimen Sanitatis Salerni*, for example, distinguishes between 'very hunger' and 'feigned hunger', arguing that the former 'is whan a man nedeth meate: But fayned hunger is an appetite to haue meate thoughe the bodye hath no nede therof' (de Mediolano, 1528, sig. D2$^{v}$). Humoral balance was central to determining the existence of these necessary or unnecessary desires for food, although the precise nature of these effects was a matter for debate. Thomas Elyot declares that 'the cholerike stomake, doth not desyre so moch as he may digeste, the melancholye stomake may not digeste so moche as he desyreth: for colde maketh appetyte, but naturall heate concocteth or boyleth' (Elyot, 1539, p. 17). Ruscelli, by contrast, gives advice on how to 'remedie the yexings of the stomacke and vomitings, & losse of appetite, occasioned through cold humors' (Ruscelli, 1569, sig. A4$^{v}$). The properties of foods were likewise bound up with the regulation of appetite. A key component of the dietaries' numerous lists of food types is their effects on the appetite. Elyot argued that lettuce 'doth set a hote stomake in a very good temper, & maketh good appetite' (Elyot, 1539, p. 23). The 1607 translation of the *Regimen Sanitatis Salerni* claimed that vinegar 'lessens *sperm*, makes appetite to rise' (de Mediolano, 1607, sig. B4$^{r}$). In particular, as Albala has noted, 'complex sauces and elaborate presentations were also thought to overstimulate the appetite, provoking it beyond the stomach's natural capacity' (Albala, 2002, p. 55). Although the precise claims made regarding appetite vary substantially, the unifying theme of these texts is the attempt to understand the dissociation between hunger and appetite. In this manner, dietary literature raised the possibility of unnatural appetites, which extended beyond the simple requirement of feeding the body.

Of especial significance for an understanding of the politics of the Renaissance stage is the extent to which these ideas intersected with the issue of class. Fitzpatrick notes that 'early modern dietaries make clear the view that food and drink are not mere necessities but also indices of one's position in relation to complex ideas about rank, nationality, and spiritual well-being' (Fitzpatrick, 2007, p. 3). Albala argues that in the early modern period 'the social connotations of food are perhaps the most powerful determinant of dietary preferences' (Albala, 2002, p. 184). In particular, there is a pronounced tendency to associate the working classes with food that is 'difficult to digest' (Fitzpatrick, 2010, p. 22). Brown bread, for example, was considered 'good for labourers' (Cogan, 1636, p. 28), while bacon was believed to be 'good for carters and plowmen, the whiche be ever labouringe in the earth or dunge' (Boorde, 1547, sig. $F2^{v}$–$F3^{r}$). Thomas Cogan asserts that 'husbandmen and labourers are nothing hurt by eating of Onyons, but rather holpen both in appetite & digestion' (Cogan, 1636, p. 65). Puddings, which as Fitzpatrick has noted were constructed from the 'stomach or one of the entrails of an animal mixed with ingredients to bind it such as suet and then seasoned' (Fitzpatrick, 2010, p. 345), were believed by Philip Moore to be bad for the digestion, but he nevertheless acknowledged that 'labouryng men maye often use them without any great hurt ensuing, by meanes of their great bodily laboure & vehement exercises' (Moore, 1564, sig. $C7^{v}$). Albala has argued that these tensions increased as a consequence of England's changing society, so that 'as demographic pressure, economic specialisation and social stratification advanced, dietary prejudices based on class intensified' (Albala, 2002, p. 187). The resulting culinary anxieties were in no small part a consequence of a nutritional theory which assumed 'the literal incorporation of a food's substance and qualities into the consumer' (Albala, 2002, p. 184). Both on and off the stage, these ideas raised the possibility of upwardly and downwardly mobile appetites. A taste for a certain food might imply degeneration on the part of the elite, or aspirational desire on the part of the lower classes.

Contemporary understanding of appetite was also intertwined with the construction of gender. The dietaries argued that male and female bodies were characterised by differing humoral balances, with William Bullein, for example, declaring that 'as menne be hote & drie, so be wemen colde and moiste' (Bullein, 1595, p. 13). This could at times influence dietary choices. Thomas Cogan, discussing rue, declares that 'Because the nature of women is waterish and cold and Rue heateth and drieth, therefore (say they) it stirreth them more to carnall lust, but it diminisheth the nature of men, which is of temperature like unto the aire, that is, hot and moist' (Cogan, 1636, p. 44).

Fruits, widely considered to be bad for the health, were treated with particular anxiety in the case of women's bodies, with William Vaughan urging caution in their consumption 'least their effects appear to our bodily repentance, which in women grow to be the greene sicknesse' (Vaughan, 1612, sig. E4$^{v}$). The consumption of food could also be associated with the attempt to attain physical beauty. Bullein comments that certain foods were favoured by those women who 'would fayne be fayre: they eate peper, dried corne and drinke vinegar, with such like baggage, to dry up their bloude' (Bullein, 1595, p. 74). The consequences could be severe, he argued, noting that 'a great nomber though not all, fal into weakenes, greene sickenes, stinkinge brethes, and oftentimes sodaine death' (Bullein, 1595, p. 74), prompting Albala to argue that it is 'quite possible that he is referring to a form of anorexia in the modern sense' (Albala, 2002, p. 152). Furthermore, the period's more general tendency to elide food and medicine is particularly apparent in the case of women. The dietaries highlight specific foods which were believed to stimulate the production of milk, regulate periods and enable the 'deliuerance' of women 'hauing the child dead within their bodyes', likely a covert reference to supposed abortifacients (Bullein, 1579, sig. B1$^{v}$). Appetite, therefore, becomes a means by which the particularity of women's bodies could be categorised and defined by the predominantly male cultural and medical authorities of the period. Yet it also provides a way of imagining transgressive forms of consumption, through which women evaded or confronted the regimens which were imposed upon them.

Furthermore, food constitutes a significant means by which national identity could be defined. Albala notes that 'dietary authors had a strong sense of nationally based stereotypical eating habits and increasingly they warned against strange tastes and customs of neighbouring countries' (Albala, 2002, p. 224). Often, this sense of national identity was rooted in analysis of the climate of a country. Thomas Cogan, for example, began his text *The Haven of Health* by resolving 'first to declare the situation and temperature of this our countrey of England' (Cogan, 1636, p. ix), noting its relatively cold and moist climate, and arguing that 'this is the cause why Englishmen doe eate more, and digest faster than the inhabitants of hotter countries (*videlicet*) the coldnesse of aire enclosing our bodies about' (Cogan, 1636, p. xii). William Bullein argued that:

> Englishmen being born in a temperat region, enclyning to cold, may not without hurt eate raw herbes, rootes, and fruits so plentiful, as many men which be borne far in the South partes of the worlde, which be moste hoate of stomacke. (Bullein, 1579, sig. B2$^{v}$)

Analysis of the climate was combined with patriotic insistence on the country's fertility. Cogan links the comparatively large appetites of the English not simply to the climate, but also to the 'plenty which our country yeeldeth' (Cogan, 1636, p. xii). He insists that 'we have as good Wheat in England, both red and white, as may be found in any Countrey in all Europe' (Cogan, 1636, p. 24), while in a similar fashion Bullein declares that 'the goodly fyeldes, and fruitfull groundes of England do bring forth to mans vse, as good Hoppes as groweth in any place of the world' (Bullein, 1579, sig. B6$^{v}$). Foreign foods and forms of eating, by contrast, were perceived as a dangerous source of corruption. Cogan gives an account of 'a gentleman who had beene a traveller in forraine countryes, and at his returne, that he might seeme singular, as it were despising the old order of England, would not begin his meale with pottage, but instead of cheese would eate pottage last' (Cogan, 1636, p. xiii). As I shall demonstrate in Chapter 5, these fears were particularly pronounced in the case of colonial expansion.

Humoral theory provides the early modern theatre with a complex range of properties and associations through which to depict hunger and appetite. The two drives are intimately connected to issues of class, gender and nation. While in modern society particular foods undoubtedly retain many of these associations, these tendencies are understood as largely socially constructed. In the early modern period, by contrast, they are seen as inherent properties of the foods themselves. At the same time, the humoral method provides the theatres with an overtly material understanding of the connections between sustenance and temperament. Indeed, at times, food can emerge as a source of vulnerability. Different understandings of the body undoubtedly reinforced perceptions of social difference, but the underlying understanding of the body as porous left open the possibility that the consumption of certain foods might destabilise these categories. As such, humoral theory has the potential to invert the conventional hierarchy of plenty and want, with hunger constituting a state of self-sufficiency, while the indulging of appetite is a source of profound weakness. This complex range of social connotations means that the representation of hunger and appetite can be deployed to conceptualise a complex combination of both similarity and difference. Different members of society might be expected to lead different lives, and to eat different foods in different ways, but they were all believed to operate within the same basic model of consumption. That ambiguous combination lends a profound political resonance to the representation of hunger and appetite.

## Religion

Contemporary understandings of hunger and appetite were also defined by religious ideas, with texts ranging from ballads to sermons interrogating the moral stakes of issues of famine, charity and greed. Indeed, the centrality of food to the practice of Christianity, and of religion more generally, has been widely acknowledged. Food, as Jean Soler has noted, is mentioned 'in the very first chapter of the first book' of the Bible (Soler, 1997, p. 56). The consumption of food was central to the fall of man, and in the early modern period, as Albala has noted, gluttony 'was actually the first of the seven deadly sins, thanks to Eve's apple' (Albala, 2011, p. 43). Food was central to a number of the miracles which Jesus performed, and the Eucharist privileged the consumption of bread as the central ritual of Christianity. In the wake of the Reformation, these issues become one of the key sites of tension in a broader conflict between variant forms of Protestantism and Catholicism. Albala, for instance, argues that 'at the grass-roots level, fasting and feasting issues played just as great a role [as theological disputes] in fermenting anticlerical sentiment' (Albala, 2011, p. 42). Within this culinary context, it is possible to discern key ways that religious ideas both drew upon and determined the cultural construction of hunger and appetite in the period.

Without doubt, the key culinary issue of the period was the debate over the Eucharist, or the Lord's Supper. Within Catholicism, the doctrine of transubstantiation had asserted that the bread was literally and miraculously transformed into the body of Christ. Caroline Bynum notes that in the late medieval period, this belief prompted an increasing emphasis upon veneration, with contemporary texts describing various miracles in which consumption of the Eucharist was accompanied by sensory effect, including 'smelling sweet, ringing with music, filling the mouth with honey' (Bynum, 1987, p. 77). Protestantism marked a significant change in this respect. Luther introduced the concept of consubstantiation, whereby the bread was at the same time both Christ's body and bread. And the Calvinists had gone further, asserting the purely metaphorical nature of the rite. The consequences of these debates were complex. The centrality of the Lord's Supper to the practice of the reformed English Church lent a special significance to issues of commensality. Food was not simply a way, but the principal way, that people could be united in a single religious community. Indeed, Protestants criticised the Catholic tendency to prevent Communion for the masses, with John Foxe, for instance, declaring 'Christ took bread and dealt it to his apostles: the Priest because he is an apostle himself, taketh bread and eateth it every whit alone' (Fox, 1844, II, p. 953). At the same time, the debates surrounding the precise significance of the rite introduced a degree of tension to considerations of hunger and appetite. An excessive emphasis on the latter might imply a potentially idolatrous veneration for the sacrament. But the consistent Protestant focus on the consumption of bread as a symbolic act of remembrance also enabled a relatively experiential emphasis. As Foxe noted, 'Christ gave it to be eaten: the priest giveth it to be worshiped' (Fox, 1844, II, p. 953). Indeed, perhaps the most significant consequence of the Reformation for the understanding of hunger and appetite was that it facilitated scrutiny of how and why food might function symbolically. Huston Diehl notes that 'the sacrament depends on the correspondence between earthly bread and Christ's body, between physical eating and spiritual nourishment' (Diehl, 1997, p. 106). Calvin, for instance, asserted that 'bread and wyne are signes, whiche represent vnto vs the inuisible foode, whiche we receyne of the fleshe and blood of Christ' (Calvin, 1561, IV, p. 119). But he also emphasised the precise symbolic significance of the food, noting that 'bread nourisheth, susteineth, and mainteineth the life of our body: so the body of Christ is the onely meate to quicken & geue lyfe to oure soule' (Calvin, 1561, IV, p. 119). Foxe, meanwhile, memorably declared that 'it feedeth, it tasteth like bread, it looketh like bread, the little silly mouse taketh it for bread, and, to be short, it hath all the properties and tokens of bread: ergo, it is bread' (Fox, 1844, II, p. 954). The repeated debates surrounding the Lord's Supper left early modern England with a marked degree of awareness of the extent to which a simple, readily available foodstuff such as bread could enshrine a complex range of symbolic associations.

A similar emphasis can be discerned in the contemporary representation of Carnival and Lent. As Bynum has noted, for the Christianity of antiquity, 'feast and fast defined the church' (Bynum, 1987, p. 33). In medieval Europe, this pattern had remained visible in the annual cycle of feasts and fast days and was at its most overt in the opposition of Carnival to Lent. In the days prior to Lent, the population engaged in what Albala describes as a 'riotous orgy of indulgence', culminating in a mock battle between personifications of Carnival and Lent, the latter frequently depicted as 'a scrawny woman armed only with a herring, some vegetables and dry bread' (Albala, 2003, p. 195). By the early modern period, these traditions were undoubtedly under threat. The rise of Protestantism introduced a series of restraints on traditional festivities. Albala goes so far as to argue that in Protestant Europe as a whole 'the cycle of feast and fast was definitively broken' (Albala, 2003, p. 202). While this is perhaps an oversimplification in relation to England, it is undoubtedly the case that the nation's material move beyond the Malthusian trap is mirrored in a gradual ideological shift away from communal patterns of feasts and fasts, towards an emphasis on individual moderation. At the same time, numerous forms of both feasting and fasting persisted in the period, and the battle of Carnival and Lent recurred as a cultural trope, often imbued with overtly political implications. As such, it might be argued that as their specifically religious element became marginalised, the residual traditions of Carnival and Lent increasingly functioned as a means of providing a poetic and experiential vocabulary through which to conceptualise the opposition of hunger and appetite.

Furthermore, attention to the broader deployment of hunger in contemporary theological texts reveals its recurring metaphorical role within early modern religious thought. It constituted a key metaphor for the desire for scriptural knowledge. Bernard Gilpin deploys the comparison of material and spiritual hunger when he warns that God, in punishing a nation, may 'threat[en] hunger, not of breade, but of hearing Gods word' (Gilpin, 1581, p. 62). Thomas Cooper makes use of an extended culinary metaphor, declaring that, in order to feast at the Lord's table in the afterlife, it is necessary to have 'both a desire to eate stirred by a sense and feeling of true repentance, and also an assured faith to receiue and digest this wholesome and comfortable medicine of our soule' (Cooper, 1580, sig. B2 r). In a similar manner, Robert Bolton compares religious knowledge to a sumptuous feast, declaring that here 'the hunger is more importunate and important; the Feast-maker more faithfull and sure of his word; the fare more delicious and ravishing' (Bolton, 1631, p. 411). Likewise, John Donne uses the imagery of appetite and taste as a means to conceive of 'spiritual diet', noting that just as 'every man hath his *Appetite,* and his *tast* disposed to some kind of *meates* rather then others', so too 'man may have a particular love towards such or such a book of Scripture' (Donne, 1649, p. 159). In part, the recurrence of these metaphors might be interpreted as a consequence of the residual significance of practices of fasting, seeming to mimic the logic of chastising the flesh in order to encourage spiritual reflection. The metaphorical invocation of hunger simultaneously relies upon the invocation of the drive, and marginalises its significance. It has the potential to function as a tool of legitimation, asserting that bodily hunger is insignificant, compared to the pressing need for religious satiation. At the same time, however, the relationship between material hunger and spiritual hunger is complex. The demand for one can be read as the demand for the other, and vice versa. Indeed, this is a tension which appears in the Bible itself, most notably in the conflicting accounts of the Beatitudes in Matthew and Luke. Where in the former Christ states 'Blessed *are* they which do hunger and thirst after righteousness: for they shall be filled' (Matthew 5:6), in the latter he says simply 'Blessed *are ye* that hunger now: for ye shall be filled' (Luke 6:21).[10] It might be argued that the continuing, if restricted, role of fasting within contemporary faith encouraged this tendency to read the metaphorical invocation in a relatively literal manner, with the potential consequence that the poor might be interpreted as obtaining a closer connection to God than the rich. The metaphorical invocation of hunger can never be entirely detached from its material presence within society.

Theological texts not only drew upon contemporary constructions of appetite, they also influenced culinary practice. Gluttony, in particular, was treated with suspicion. The *Book of Homilies* declared that 'surfetting and drunkennesse bites by the belly, and causeth continual gnawing in the stomacke' (Church of England, 1571, p. 208). Humoral theory was deployed to assert that 'he that eateth and drynketh vnmeasurablye, kyndleth ofte tymes suche an vnnaturall heate in his bodye, that his appetite is prouoked thereby to desire more than it should' (Church of England, 1571, p. 206). Appetite could be created not simply by hunger, but also by excess. Indeed, one of the most significant images of appetite within both the theatre and the wider culture of the period is this notion of exponential increase, of appetite as a drive which cannot be satisfied. This element of uncontrolled consumption could rapidly be transferred to other forms of desire, prompting a turn towards 'whoredome and lewdenesse of heart, with daungers vnspeakable' (Church of England, 1571, p. 208). Moreover, excessive appetite could be identified as the cause of hunger in others, since consumption might prompt indifference to the plight of the poor. The 'Homily Against Gluttony and Drunkenness' declares 'Had not the riche glutton ben so greedely geuen to the pamperyng of his belly, he woulde neuer haue ben so vnmercifull to the poore Lazarus, neyther had he felt the tormentes of the vnquenchable fire' (Church of England, 1571, p. 204). It even ascribes the fall of Sodom and Gomorrah to the like indifference, declaring 'was it not their proud banquetting and continual idlenes, whiche caused them to be so lewde of lyfe, and so vnmercifull towardes the poore?' (Church of England, 1571, p. 204). Appetite thus renews itself by ensuring the continuing hunger of the excluded. It

[10] Quotes from the Bible are to the King James version throughout (Carroll and Prickett, 1997), except where otherwise stated.

constitutes the fundamental Renaissance image of consumption in the face of need. As such, it constitutes a motif of profound political significance.

Nevertheless, self-inflicted hunger was also treated with a marked degree of unease. As Fitzpatrick has argued, 'excessive fasting was associated with the monastic life and was by some considered as indulgent as gluttony' (Fitzpatrick, 2007, p. 3). The 'Homily Against Gluttony and Drunkenness', for example, endorses 'abstinence and fasting', but does so in the context of an endorsement of 'sobrietie and moderate dyet' (Church of England, 1571, p. 212). The 'Homily of Good Works' notes Christ's condemnation of fasting by the Pharisees, who 'put a religion in theyr doyngs and ascribed holynesse to the outwarde worke wrought, not regardyng to what ende fastyng is ordayned' (Church of England, 1571, p. 177). Fish days were imposed by the government primarily for economic reasons and because a large fishing industry was believed to strengthen England's navy. They appear to have been particularly unpopular. Edward Jeninges, in a pamphlet on the fishing industry, comments that many declared them to be 'made and used in the time of Papistrie, and by ancient authoritie of the Pope, who we should not in anything imitate, but rather in all thinges by contrarie', although he himself asserted the potential economic benefits of secular fish days (Jeninges, 1590, sig. $D3^r$). The same opposition may underlie Kent's claim, in *King Lear*, that he will 'eat no fish' (I.iv.17), which as Gordon Williams has noted implies a resolve to 'avoid the ways of Roman Catholics' (Williams, 1994, p. 126). Throughout the period, religious texts tend to advocate moderation, stressing the need to avoid either the excessive indulgence of appetite, or a papist cultivation of hunger.

Hunger produced by famine and dearth is scarcely less troublesome in the eyes of many contemporary authorities. Here, hunger is inscribed within a providential discourse which operates across a wide range of sermons, pamphlets and providential tales. These texts ostensibly identified sinful behaviour as the cause of famine. Yet as Ayesha Mukherjee has noted, the purely religious explanation invariably intersected with 'social, political and literary arguments about the organization of resources' (Mukherjee, 2014, p. 29). A key example is the work of William Gouge, a puritan preacher and fellow of Cambridge University. Famine, for Gouge, is 'a judgement', one of 'three sharp mortall arrowes of the Lord which he useth to shoot as judgements against children of men' (Gouge, 1631, pp. 133, 134). Yet it is a punishment sent to afflict not individuals, but 'the wickednesse of a sinfull nation' (Gouge, 1631, p. 149). Consideration of sin consequently entails consideration of the state of the nation. Certainly, Gouge is at pains to make clear that the fault need not lie with the authorities, since even 'The best Governours have many times most impious subjects under them' (Gouge, 1631, p. 147). But his recurring concern with the need for 'Moderation in diet', 'fasts' and care for 'the poore, the maimed, the lame, and the blind' implies a desire to redress the symptoms of socio-economic change in early modern society (Gouge, 1631, p. 142). The political dimension to these providential ideas intersected with the rise of apocalyptic thought within radical Protestantism. As Alexandra Walsham has noted, 'The Gospels of Matthew, Mark, and Luke . . . listed false prophets, wars, earthquakes, famine, pestilence, and empyreal sights among the forerunners of Christ's Second Coming', and the regular outbreaks of famine and dearth in this period came to be read as signs of the coming apocalypse by sections of the Protestant community (Walsham, 1999, p. 169). Once again, this had a profound political as well as religious dimension. Walsham demonstrates that 'Daniel and Revelation, along with the apocryphal book of 2 Esdras, insisted that occult phenomena would prefigure the overthrow of the present earthly order, the annihilation of Antichrist, and the vindication of the elect' (Walsham, 1999, p. 170). Indeed, it was precisely in the service of overthrowing the earthly ruling order that apocalyptic ideas would come to be used during the English Civil War and subsequent revolution. Religious ideas produce a tendency for the outbreak of famine to prompt questioning of social changes. The sheer breadth of famine's effects lends a political dimension to its association with sin.

This emphasis upon the social dimension to hunger and appetite is particularly pronounced in the popular literature of the period. Ballads such as 'A Looking Glasse for Corne-hoorders' (1631), and 'A Warning-Piece for Ingroosers of Corne' (1643) consistently place the suffering of famine and dearth in the context of the 'poore being abus'd / by the rich' ('Looking Glasse', 1631). Attention to these texts seems to substantiate the claim of writers such as Engels that, in this period, 'The sentiments of the masses, fed exclusively on religion, had to have their own interests presented to them in a religious guise in order to create a great turbulence' (Marx and Engels, 1975–2004, XXVI, p. 395). Claims that 'God will not let these long / alone, that doe his wrong, / Though ne'r so rich and strong / that are agressors' articulate a message of social and political change through a medium that is both popular and religious in nature ('Looking Glasse', 1631). Certainly, the message of these texts appears to endorse passivity, since God will avenge the crimes of the poor. But, as Alexandra Walsham has noted, 'the timing of such ephemera deserves particular scrutiny: many coincide with moments of agrarian crisis and riot like the Midland Revolt' (Walsham, 1999, p. 107). These texts served to turn the scrutiny of vice typical of periods of famine away from the population as a whole and focus it instead on the actions of the rich. This was of particular significance in times of dearth and famine.

Religious difference exercised a central influence over contemporary constructions of hunger and appetite. At this time of profound theological conflict, both within and beyond the Church of England, food was a crucial issue. In the first instance, this was a period in which debates surrounding the Eucharist ensured that food emerged much more visibly as a sign and symbol. Residual traditions of Carnival and Lent provided a repertoire of images through which to personify the basic drives of hunger and appetite. And this tendency was accentuated as English society moved from the temporal experience of want to a more overtly class-based inequality. Indeed, the overt emphasis upon moderation to be discerned in most contemporary religious texts might be understood as manifesting an underlying recognition of the need to reconcile the constituent elements of an increasingly polarised society. Likewise, the focus of so many sermons on the need to satisfy the population's spiritual hunger testifies both to the absolute significance of the hunger drive within early modern society, and to an anxious wish to depreciate the significance of such issues, in a period of widespread want. At the same time, if religion provided a means of legitimation, or model of reconciliation, it also functioned as one of the key means through which oppositional class interests could be expressed. Puritan attacks upon the sinfulness of a nation retained the potential to function as a critique of its government. And popular ballads reveal a repeated tendency to imagine the providential application of God's wrath to the rich and powerful. Like the theatre, religious debate both manifested emergent contradictions within early modern society and provided one of the key spheres within which the resulting conflicts could take place.

## Staging Hunger and Appetite

On the Renaissance stage, the representation of hunger and appetite was determined not simply by how these drives were constructed in society, but also by the specific characteristics of the contemporary cultural field, as it was manifested in the various institutions of the theatre. Playing companies were accountable both to upper-class patrons and to the interests and desires of their audiences. The former had been made necessary by the 1572 Act against Vagabonds, which as Janette Dillon has noted 'made it mandatory for players to be attached to a noble patron', without which 'they were liable to be treated as vagrants and subject to the rigours of punishment routinely meted out to masterless men' (Dillon, 2000, pp. 1–2). Recent research on theatre history has emphasised the extent to which patrons could deploy their connections with playing companies for political capital and the dissemination of specific ideological material.[11] However, ordinary ticket sales represented a significant source of profits for the playing companies. Although critics have disputed the precise class make-up of early modern audiences, few would deny that they were in general defined by a pronounced heterogeneity.[12] The cheapest tickets in the public theatre cost one penny, approximately a tenth of an average day's wages in the period (Oates and Baumol, 1972, p. 152). Critical and historical work on the early modern theatres has increasingly acknowledged the diverse effects which this element of commercial reliance could have on both the content of the plays produced and a particular playing company's choice of repertoire.[13] Throughout this book, I consider the theatres as superstructural

11 The Queen's Men, for instance, as Sally-Beth Maclean has noted, made annual tours of England in order to perform 'plays informed by moderate Protestant ideology in the service of the Crown's interests during an unstable political era' (Maclean, 2009, p. 41). Roslyn Knutson, drawing on evidence from Record of Early English Drama (REED), argues that touring players were 'particularly welcome when their shows offered political advantage to the local VIPs such as looking good to the company's patrons' (Knutson, 2009, p. 65). The theatre could also be deployed for more oppositional ends, such as when the Essex faction commissioned a performance of a play, probably by Shakespeare, which depicted the fall of Richard II, as a means to inspire support for their own unsuccessful uprising (Knutson, 2009, p. 61).

12 Early controversy regarding the class composition of the early modern audience centred on the work of Alfred Harbage and Ann Jenalie Cook. The former argued for an audience composed primarily of artisans, while the latter emphasised the comparatively privileged nature of much of the contemporary audience, even in the public playhouses. Gurr tends to reject both approaches, arguing that 'citizens were the staple, at least of amphitheatre audiences' (Gurr, 1987, p. 64). More recent research has built upon Gurr's insights. Levin, for example, claims that 'among those paying guests in the audiences there were many women', and argues that as a result they may well have been regarded by authors and playing companies as 'a constituency whose interests and feelings should be considered' (Levin, 1989, p. 165). Whitney draws on evidence from the commentary of early spectators and readers of Renaissance plays to assert the multifaceted nature of audience response, focussing in particular on the notoriety of characters such as Tamburlaine and Falstaff (cf. Whitney, 2006).

13 As regards repertoire, Knutson, for instance, notes that 'in addition to acquiring multi-part plays, the Admiral's Men often marketed these serials by scheduling them in tandem', and hypothesises that a similar strategy may have been adopted in the performance of Shakespeare's first tetralogy (Knutson, 2009, p. 68). In terms of content, Cartelli sees the drive towards the fulfilment of the audience's subversive fantasies as being in tension with the structural boundaries enacted by the plots of the period, and claims that this prompts the creation of a 'theatrical economy of engagement and resistance', which is 'coordinated (though not finally controlled) by the choices the artist makes in the disposition of his fantasy material' (Cartelli, 1991, p. 27). Fitter argues that the complex class basis of the audience contributes to the generation of 'concealed ideological flexibility', with the result that 'the plays' stagecraft secrets harboured dissident subtextual dimensions that were readily triggered in the conditions specific to the public playhouse, with its distinctive horizons of expectation' (Fitter, 2012, p. 36).

phenomena, which act 'as a support to the exploitative or oppressive nature of social relations' (Eagleton, 1989, p. 174). But it is also necessary to acknowledge the extent to which the theatres constitute sites of struggle, with plays produced by the desires of their diverse audiences and the restrictions enforced by the early modern authorities. Hunger and appetite are not merely exterior to these issues but intertwined with them. The sale of food, the practicalities of staging and the role played by the lived experience of hunger and appetite for both actors and audience constitute factors which exert determining influences upon the representation of these drives in the theatre, in a manner which embodies the wider social and commercial forces operating on the London theatre scene. Attention to hunger and appetite provides the definitive instance of how the theatre 'responded to the market, even as it sprang from it' (Bruster, 1992, p. xi).

Indeed, the representation of hunger and appetite furnished a key means by which the theatres reflected upon these competing imperatives. This is evident in the recurrent tendency for prologues and epilogues to figure the act of watching a play as akin to the consumption of food. Farah Karim-Cooper has argued that this tendency is particularly characteristic of Ben Jonson's work, but similar examples can be found across the gamut of early modern theatre, from early work by Lyly, to Jacobean and Caroline dramas by John Fletcher and Philip Massinger (cf. Karim-Cooper, 2013). In Lyly's *Sappho and Phao*, for example, the prologue to the court provides a means of negotiating the unsettling necessity of appealing to the tastes of both the court and the first Blackfriars theatre. It expresses the hope that the Queen may 'resemble the princely eagle who, fearing to surfeit on spices, / stoopeth to bite on wormwood' (Pro. 6–7). Beyond the standard, self-deprecating tone characteristic of the prologue form, the image betrays anxiety at the notion that dramatic offerings might be served up to both the monarch and the comparatively less privileged attendees of the Blackfriars. In a similar manner, Ben Jonson's *Epicene* (1609–10) opens with the claim that 'Our wishes, like to those make public feasts, / Are not to please the cook's taste, but the guests' (Pro. 8–9). The image distances the playwright from the work produced, embodying Jonson's more general anxiety at his dependency upon the dramatic appetites of the public. The imagery of hunger and appetite becomes a characteristic strategy of the Renaissance prologue, a means to stress the particularity of taste and the playing company's purported distrust of excessive luxury, as well as delivering self-deprecating acknowledgements of the humble nature of their own dramatic fare. Above all, these prologues highlight the opposed imperatives of the theatre itself. Although they ostensibly compare these plays to either delicacies or rough fare offered up to a courtly patron, the recurring emphasis on the theatre as feast announces its nature as a product for mass consumption.

Furthermore, hunger and appetite were connected with the competing imperatives of the theatre at a material as well as a metaphorical level. Eating 'proved a vital part of the theatre-going experience', with playgoers at both the public and private theatres enjoying 'ample opportunity to purchase food during performances' (Nunn, 2013, p. 101). The evidence suggests that selling food was considered a lucrative business. The grocer John Cholmley paid Philip Henslowe £102 a year for the right to sell food and drink at the Rose Theatre (Nunn, 2013, p. 101–2). Thomas Platter, a Swiss traveller who reported on a 1599 performance at the Curtain, noted that 'during the performance food and drink are carried round the audience, so that for what one cares to pay one may also have refreshment' (Platter, 1937, p. 166). The distribution of these foodstuffs raises issues of gender, for as Natasha Korda has argued, their sale in London 'was predominantly performed by market women' (Korda, 2011, p. 146). Excavations of the Rose Theatre revealed the presence of 'hazelnut shells, walnut shells, plumstones, figs, cherrystones, grape pips, remnants of apples and pears, elderberry seeds, plus seeds of blackberry, raspberry and sloeberry, along with remnants of rye, oat and wheat bread and marine and freshwater oyster shells' (Gurr, 2009, p. 161). Of the 138 pottery utensils unearthed at the Rose dating from the period 1587–92, 40 per cent were for cooking or serving food, while for the period 1592–1603 the figure is 35 per cent (Bowsher and Miller, 2009, p. 147). In the case of touring companies, the tendency to perform in inn-yards meant that an even wider selection of food might be available, since they sold 'a strikingly aromatic mixture of buns, cakes, and bread (which were often served toasted and steeped in ale), bacon, all sorts of salt meat, pottage, and roast meat' (Templeman, 2013, p. 82). The preponderance of fruit in the public theatres is significant, since as Albala has demonstrated, contemporary dietaries evince 'a fear of fruits bordering on the pathological' (Albala, 2002, p. 8). Elyot, for example, declares that 'all fruites generally are noyfulle to man, and do ingender ylle humours, and be oftetymes the cause of putrified feuers, yf they be moche and contynually eaten' (Elyot, 1539, p. 19). These foods may consequently have been the object of an illicit attraction, a contemporary equivalent, perhaps, of the modern cinema's popcorn and carbonated drinks. The sale of food marked the early modern playing space to no less an extent than did the sale of the tickets. The theatre's ability to satisfy, for a price, the appetites of its audiences constituted a visible indication of its implication within a market economy.

It can even be argued that the theatre's emphasis on the sale of food exerted a defining influence on the representation of appetite within the plays. Hilary Nunn claims that the theatre, particularly in the case of comedy, actively seeks to awake the appetites of its audience. She demonstrates the extent to which early modern writers believed that 'the mere sight of food ... held the power to stimulate a viewer's appetite and provoke gluttonous indulgence' (Nunn, 2013, p. 106). As a consequence, 'watching actors feign hunger, and viewing the plays' tempting presentations of food, sets into motion the visual dynamics understood to cause increased appetite, drawing playgoers to a more immediate, bodily understanding of the struggles unfolding on-stage' (Nunn, 2013, p. 117). Nunn's essay persuasively argues for the interaction of playhouse practice and playtext content, but her tendency to equate on- and offstage foods seems to efface the disruptive potential of encouraging these appetites. Nunn argues that 'The similarities between the foods appearing on- and offstage allowed the plays and audience members to consider, together, profound questions about the nature of hunger, temptation and human desire' (Nunn, 2013, p. 117). Yet it could equally be argued that the luxurious feasts and elaborate banquets of the early modern stage threaten to awake in the audience appetites for foods which they could rarely have encountered. The relationship of individual audience members to the staging of appetite is influenced to a great extent by their material circumstances, in a manner which broadly conforms to the class make-up of an audience.

The issue of class is also of absolute significance in considering the relationship of the audience to hunger. Critics have tended to stress the satiation of dramatic audiences. Michael Dobson, for example, argues that the sheer quantities of food available means that the experience of the audience is liable to be defined by revulsion. He claims that:

> an audience that isn't hungry is liable to be distractingly sickened by the spectacle of eating. In practice, on-stage feasts exclude and repel spectators; they are meals which aren't appropriate to us, marking the action of the scenes in which they occur both as elsewhere and physically troubling[.] (Dobson, 2009, p. 64)

In a similar manner, Angel-Perez and Poulain highlight the 'well-fed' nature of the theatre audience, but introduce a moral dimension, noting that the opposition of satiated spectator to onstage hunger situates the former in the position of an 'uncomfortable voyeur' (Angel-Perez and Poulain, 2008, p. ix). However, the satiated nature of the early modern audience is surely far from a foregone conclusion. The intersection of hunger and appetite in the audience is governed in the first instance by the temporal dimension to performance. Dobson argues that food is 'bound up with our perception of passing time', and emphasises the probability that performances in the public theatres would have 'taken place in the remaining daylight after a mid-day meal at a Southwark ordinary' (Dobson, 2009, p. 62). Yet the consequence of this is surely that the audience's experience may well have been defined by a progressive increase in hunger as the play was performed. Furthermore, while the privileged elite of the rear sections of the public theatres may well have experienced a sense of satiation which distanced them from the plight of the onstage hungry, the situation of the groundlings was necessarily more complex. If they did not directly experience hunger in the moment of performance, there is no guarantee that they did not experience it as a relatively frequent occurrence in their day-to-day lives.

Similar factors govern the staging of hunger and appetite. As Pascale Drouet has argued, dramatising hunger tends to raise the problem of representation, since 'hunger can only be successfully staged if the social field and the theatrical field interact, i.e. the discourse of experiencing hunger must be validated by the actor's thin and weakened body' (Drouet, 2008, p. 3). Although this argument tends to ignore the wider representational strategies of the early modern theatre, there is evidence to suggest that certain actors within the playing companies were renowned for their thin physique and that they specialised in the performance of hungry characters. Fitzpatrick notes that 'it seems that a single actor in the Chamberlain's/King's men took the role of the "thin man" in Shakespeare's plays, which suggests dramatic exploitation of a recognizable stereotype' (Fitzpatrick, 2007, p. 6). Baldwin Maxwell has similarly argued that during the later period of the company's existence, the actor John Shanke was given the task of playing the character of the 'hungry knave' in plays by John Fletcher (cf. Maxwell, 1926). If hunger is 'mere lack', the practicalities of drama ensure that its absence is frequently an embodied one. Furthermore, this has potential consequences for how hunger is represented. The very fact that a single actor might specialise in the performance of hungry characters tends to detach the depiction of hunger from lived experience, constituting the drive as a characteristic, rather than a temporary state. At times, therefore, the theatre has the potential to essentialise the problem of hunger, figuring it as an inherent characteristic, rather than a specific configuration of social or physical forces.

On the other hand, actors might experience hunger themselves. As Richard Helgerson has noted, there was 'a strong popular element in both the play's production and reception. Its author was a commoner, its actors were commoners, the greater part of its audience were commoners' (Helgerson, 1992, p. 196). As such, it is unwise to stress the distance between actors and the hungry poor, without also acknowledging the parallel distance between the majority of the players and the onstage fictional elite that they frequently represented. The average wage for a hireling in Henslowe's companies appears to have been six shillings a week (cf. Oates and Baumol, 1972, p. 157). This was broadly equivalent to the average wage in London in the period, and as a consequence left these low-level actors and musicians in much the same situation as other Londoners in a period of rising food prices and periodic outbreaks of dearth. Hunger, indeed, could on occasion be specifically associated with actors. Thomas Rawlins's *The Rebellion*, for example, describes those audience members who 'exercise their dexterity, in throwing of rotten apples whilst my stout Actor pockets, and then eates up the injury' (Rawlins, 1640, sig. C1$^{r}$). The same was true of many playwrights; for example, Thomas Dekker frequently faced bankruptcy and spent large amounts of time in debtors' prisons. Dekker's writings on his own incarceration dwell heavily on the issue of food (Dekker, 1620). It might be argued that the process of ventriloquism applies as much to the representation of a satiated elite as it does to hungry characters.

Moreover, hunger and appetite are also portrayed by means of juxtaposition, in ways which have the potential to stress the social dimension to these drives. In the first instance, the staging of both hunger and appetite is, unsurprisingly, intimately connected with the representation of food. Evidence for the staging of food is, as with many stage properties, relatively sparse.[14] But research by Chris Meads has exposed the extent to which food was represented through a mixture of actual and replica comestibles. Stage directions, for example, are replete with references to trenchers, plates and covered dishes, prompting Meads to argue that 'given the visual splendour of the costuming in Elizabethan, Jacobean, and Caroline theatre and the many references to table furniture, it seems safe to assume that sundry items were present on the table itself' (Meads, 2001, p. 47). Occasional references to the use of stage properties in dramatic texts and manuscripts imply that onstage food could be constructed from a variety of materials.

[14] As Douglas Bruster has noted, 'where a play can easily contain thirty or more hand properties, a playhouse inventory will list only a fraction of these, an account or illustration of a production fewer still' (Bruster, 2002, p. 71). Even texts such as Henslowe's diary are of limited use, since clothing, as a 'more valuable' resource, 'largely supplants notice of other theatrical objects throughout his diary' (Bruster, 2002, p. 72).

Brome's *The Antipodes*, for instance, contains a description of properties in a theatre which includes reference to 'Our pasteboard marchpanes, and our wooden pies' (III.294).[15] Meads suggests that bread would have constituted a useful substitute for many onstage foods, and also argues that 'when they were available, it is not unreasonable to assume that actual common fruits were placed upon stage tables when unequivocally required by the story-line' (Meads, 2001, p. 61). Beyond the literal representation of onstage food, both hunger and appetite are conveyed through exteriorisation. The states are portrayed linguistically, through extensive, hyperbolic lists of food which frequently efface the distinction between appetite and hunger.[16] In both cases, however, these techniques tend to stress the relational nature of hunger and appetite, in a manner which implicitly accords with wider popular tendencies to stress the connections between want and plenty, hunger and unrestrained appetite.

The early modern theatre can therefore be said to embody many of the wider tensions surrounding hunger and appetite in the material and cultural life of early modern England. The theatre is a space of sale and profit. Yet it is also a contested space, where class difference becomes manifest and where the significance of this difference can be digested. The positions of audiences, patrons and playing companies with regard to their varying lived experiences of hunger and appetite exert a defining influence on the form and content of these plays. But that influence is, of necessity, both contested and multivalent, so that individual depictions of hunger or appetite frequently produce multiple, equally legitimate readings. The plays of the early modern theatre do not simply exemplify these tensions, but are simultaneously aware of them, and as a consequence the representation of hunger and appetite is frequently marked by a heightened reflexivity, providing the playing companies with a means of exploring their own implication within the processes of social change which they depict and conceptualise. The theatre must be understood as a space which creates performances that simultaneously reflect, and reflect upon, the changes taking place within early modern society, and it is for precisely this reason that the plays' myriad representations of hunger and appetite assume a specifically political significance.

[15] As Meads has noted, the former term 'could be artificial marchpane constructions fabricated in pasteboard . . . or two separate items of stage property, namely pasteboards and marchpanes' (Meads, 2001, p. 65).

[16] This is particularly characteristic of the recurring character of the 'hungry servant'. See Chapter 2.

## Conclusion

Hunger and appetite can therefore be read as drives which permeate every level of early modern society, assuming far greater significance than they retain in the developed countries of the modern world. They are inextricably linked to the processes of socio-economic change which determined England's transition from a feudal to a capitalist mode of production and are bound up with the contradictory nature of that transformation. On the one hand, an increasing population could only be sustained through widespread marketisation and increased levels of productivity. On the other, these very processes were in large part responsible for the systematic hunger and episodic subsistence crises to which the country was subjected. The cost of economic expansion was the creation of a new layer of landless unemployed labourers, subject to the whims of the market and consequently at risk of both long-term malnutrition and starvation. The development of England's productive capabilities was necessary to feed its growing population, but this would have been impossible to achieve without the processes of centralisation and polarisation which accompanied it. Hunger was the cost of these developments, but it was also their driving force, both creating demand which stimulated the production of grain for profit, and acting as a motivating force driving newly landless labourers to work for cash wages. Hunger and appetite are thus both root cause and overt symptom of the period's processes of change, and this imbues them with a profound significance as the subject of ideological struggle.

Moreover, the significance of hunger and appetite extends beyond this, for the two drives constitute the means as well as the matter of political debate. Attention to the ways hunger and appetite were conceived in the period reveals their unique capacity to function as a mechanism for conceptualising social change. The representation of hunger and appetite constitutes a form of political contestation which is enacted within the framework of a series of common assumptions determined by the period's medical and religious beliefs. The two drives therefore provide a significant example of the degree to which belief in society is challenged. They can be understood with reference to the concept of the ideologeme, defined by Fredric Jameson as 'the smallest intelligible unit of the essentially antagonistic collective discourses of social classes' (Jameson, 2002, p. 61). Concern with excess, with want and with self-inflicted hunger recur in the theatre, but the precise inflection which is placed on these ideologemes is hugely diverse. In particular, a fundamental pervasive fear of uncontrolled appetite dominates the contemporary stage. But it is an appetite which can be ascribed to the poor, to the aspirant middle classes and the aristocratic elite in more or less equal measures. Only by identifying the diverse means by which this central theme is situated in the period's various social discourses is it possible to discern the complexity of the cultural conflict over the basic human drives of hunger and appetite.

By rooting these ideas in the practice of the contemporary playhouse, it becomes possible to acknowledge the degree to which the early modern theatre was implicated in the very dynamics which it sought to represent. The nature of the audience, operating as a heterogeneous collection of classes and genders, serves to recreate the wider struggles of early modern society. The theatre's intervention into the cultural conflict of the period can only be understood by acknowledging the ways in which the playtexts engage with these various audiences, producing multiple and frequently conflicting readings. Yet the existence of this balance of forces is also significant for the extent to which it distinguishes the theatre from other forms of text. It is, therefore, necessary to qualify the traditional Cultural Materialist injunction to treat dramatic works as simply interventions into a generalised textual discourse, to assume 'the historicity of texts' and 'the textuality of history', in favour of an approach that asserts the specificity of the early modern theatre as a space in which wider historical forces were embodied according to a particular dynamic (Montrose, 1989, p. 20). The representation of hunger and appetite in the Renaissance theatre is both qualitatively different from that to be found in other texts of the period, and simultaneously a specific embodiment of the wider forces at work in contemporary society which, as a consequence of the peculiar characteristics of the theatre business, emerge in this context with particular clarity.

CHAPTER 2

# *Service*

Servants, on the early modern stage, are obsessed with food. They sing songs in its praise, abandon their masters in the hope of a better meal and list, repeatedly, the many delicacies upon which they wish they could dine. The hungry servant constitutes a recognisable character type which recurs in the plays of the period. It spans genres, appearing in the courtly drama of Lyly, the city comedies of the Jacobean period and the tragicomedies of Fletcher and Massinger. Although it has antecedents in the plays of classical Rome and bears numerous parallels to characters in the theatres of early modern Italy and France, it acquires a particular significance in the changing economic and social practices of sixteenth- and seventeenth-century England. When embodied in the onstage servingman, hunger and appetite provide a means of questioning the tenability of the period's residual ideologies of service as love or duty. They have the potential to both legitimise and critique underlying structures of class difference. They offer a way of exploring the role played by material self-interest within a society increasingly dominated by the fluidity of the market. The servant raises questions regarding the relationship between the material reality of hunger and its dramatic representation and highlights the comic potential of appetite in the period. But the character is also defined by ambiguity, standing as a symbol of the contradictory nature of the changes taking place in service and in early modern society. It is of central importance for understanding the complex interactions of hunger, appetite and politics as they are manifested in one of the period's major ideological forms.

Yet despite this evident importance, the role played by the 'hungry servant' in the early modern theatre has received relatively little critical attention. When the servant's appetite has been considered at all, the recurrent nature of the character has prompted a tendency to treat it as indistinguishable from other historical incarnations of the stereotype. Christian Biet, for example, equates the servingman with the slaves of classical Rome and the Zanni of the Italian *Commedia dell'arte*. His consequent decision to 'laugh quickly, with the servants' before moving on to more serious material undermines the insights which he provides (Biet, 2008, p. 56). More usually, hunger and appetite are ignored altogether. This neglect is unfortunate, because attention to hunger and appetite provides an invaluable perspective on the competing material and ideological emphases which have defined critical attention to service.[1] Early accounts situate the representation of servants in the context of contemporary exploitation and oppression, defined within a broadly Foucauldian paradigm.[2] But in 2005, a series of monographs were published which emphasised wider conceptions of service as an 'affective relationship' and generalised ideal.[3] This new wave of material attacked the dominance of materialist theoretical frameworks, asserting the role played by 'personal volition' and 'love' in contemporary service relationships (Evett, 2005, p. 7; Schalkwyk, 2008, p. 9). Critics such as David Evett and, later, David Schalkwyk proclaimed the need to 'treat service at all social levels as, in many respects, intrinsically the same' (Evett, 2005, p. 30).[4] More recent work has problematised the tendency to assume a uniform ideology of service, and has increasingly stressed its contradictory nature.[5] Laurie McKee, for instance, has identified a conflict between the ideal of selfless service, and the expectation that servants earn their own position within society (McKee, 2013). Amanda Bailey highlights the competing imperatives at work in attitudes to livery, which simultaneously established the status of a master through the number and accoutrements of their retinue, while constituting a site of anxiety regarding the unruly potential of allowing servants to dress too finely (Bailey, 2004). At times, there remains a relatively idealist dimension to these accounts. Recognition of the differing imperatives of upper- and lower-class service is often marginal, and critics have been inclined to consider the conflicting imperatives of contemporary ideology at a solely ideological level.[6] But the overwhelming

[1] For a more extensive summary of these critical positions, see Rivlin (2015).

[2] See Burnett (1997) and Neill (2000).

[3] See Anderson (2005); Evett (2005); Weil (2005); and Schalkwyk (2008).

[4] In a similar manner, Schalkwyk declares that 'the most important aspect of service in medieval and early modern England, systematically overlooked in a class-obsessed post-Marxist environment, is the fact that it transcended class barriers' (Schalkwyk, 2008, p. 20).

[5] See Bailey (2004); Rivlin (2012); McKee (2013); Maitra (2013).

[6] Bailey, for instance, is undoubtedly correct in identifying an ideological clash between a model of aristocratic identity which encouraged extensive retinues, and contemporary anxieties regarding excessive luxury in the dress of servants. Yet these tensions surely emerge with particular significance in this period as a consequence of the fact that expensive retinues were increasingly difficult to maintain within the context of the late sixteenth century's rampant inflation.

tendency, as Elizabeth Rivlin notes, is towards a perspective which seeks to resituate 'the disjunction between idealist and materialist critics as one inherent to early modern service' (Rivlin, 2015, p. 27).

Attention to hunger and appetite provides a useful perspective on these issues precisely because they provide a means to articulate the complex combination of similitude and difference which defined the opposition of upper- and lower-class types of service. As Michael Neill has argued, this was a period in which 'the notion of what it meant to be a "servant" was progressively narrowed and specialised until it came to refer almost exclusively to a form of domestic wage-labor' (Neill, 2000, p. 46). Contemporary texts frequently deploy issues of sustenance as a means of distinguishing between these variant forms. In a translation of an Italian source, *The Civile Conversation of M. Steeven* (Guazzo, 1581), the speaker notes 'you will not say that Gentlemen, and common Seruingmen, serue with one mynde, or propose to themselues one selfe ende of theyr seruice', and throughout the text insists upon a fundamental distinction between the 'golden chaynes' of upper-class service for love, and 'iron chaynes' of lower-class service rooted in necessity (Guazzo, 1581, p. 47). As A. L. Beier has demonstrated, domestic servants were dependent upon their masters for food, clothing and lodging and there is 'considerable evidence' that breakdowns in the master–servant relationship occurred, with 'disagreement over food and clothing' an issue of central importance (Beier, 1985, p. 25). Contemporary accounts declare that the lot of the servingman is to be 'as hungrie as a Horse, and as greedye as a Dogge' (Saker, 1580, p. 111). Jest books mock 'miserly masters' with revenues large enough 'to starue a thousand persons' (Copely, 1595, p. 138). Buchanan Sharp has noted that during the Oxfordshire rising of 1596, the ringleaders planned to recruit help from the servants of the local gentry, and 'felt sure of success because they believed the servants were kept like dogs and would welcome the opportunity to rise and cut their masters' throats' (Sharp, 1980, p. 39). Hunger and appetite are characteristics of the onstage servant precisely because of his lower-class status. Yet while the service of the lower classes is far from 'intrinsically the same' as that of their upper-class counterparts (Evett, 2005, p. 30), it is nevertheless the case that hunger and appetite can function as an index of similitude. Masters on the early modern stage are frequently depicted in thrall to appetite, whether literal or metaphorical. The universality of the hunger drive lends it utility as a means of enabling comparison between differing forms of service. Indeed, attention to the depiction of service in the early modern theatre reveals a pervasive concern that the ruling class might be reduced to the same basic material compulsions as those of the male domestic servant.

The precise significance of this dynamic varies according to the dramatic context in which it is employed. It is therefore necessary to explore the specific social, dramatic and historical forces operating upon the various texts in which the hungry servant appears. To this end, I will begin my discussion with consideration of John Lyly's *Campaspe* (1584; Lyly, 1991), a play which establishes the basic parameters of the class dynamic which defines every incarnation of the hungry servant. By detaching the hunger of his servants from the lived conditions of which it is a product, Lyly converts it into appetite. The consequent representation of that appetite embodies changing attitudes to the body and consumption which make visible the class dynamic, while simultaneously legitimising it. In other texts of the period, appetite can be read as an index of broader material interests, at a time in which wage labour was becoming increasingly dominant, and the ordered hierarchies implied by ideologies of service were disrupted by material change in early modern society. The second section therefore explores a range of texts in which the servant's appetite is inscribed within a society defined by market forces, becoming a means to conceptualise processes of acquisition and self-interest. Lastly, the combination of similitude and difference is deployed with particular frequency in the context of texts depicting hungry servants with both male and female masters. The chapter therefore concludes with attention to the significance of gender for the representation of the hungry servant. In all these texts, the depiction of hunger and appetite is implicated in the intersection of class and ideology, at a moment when the residual traditions of service are in tension with the material practices of a society in the process of change.

## Normative Appetites

The central role played by hunger and appetite in enforcing class identity can be demonstrated through attention to the servants of John Lyly's *Campaspe*.[7] Performed in the first Blackfriars theatre and at court, the text assumes an elite audience whose full bellies distanced them from the

[7] Critical analysis of the play has frequently focussed on generic issues. Janette Dillon argues that Lyly is the first playwright to introduce many significant tropes of the stage comedy into early modern drama, including 'the musings of lovers on their own feelings, the mockery of their folly by others, the careful plotting of the game of love' (Dillon, 2002, p. 51). Michael Pincombe, by contrast, asserts the 'tragi-comical credentials' of *Campaspe* (Pincombe, 1996, p. 24), and Andy Kesson notes that 'the idea that his plays were comedies has encouraged scholars to see happy endings where there are instead major challenges for early modern audiences and modern readers' (Kesson, 2014, p. 218). Critics have also scrutinised the play's relationship to royal patronage. Although early works such as Pater Saccio's *The Court Comedies* (1969) situated Lyly's drama as attempts to secure patronage,

predicament of onstage servants.[8] The representation of the servants' appetites functions as a means of exploring tension between these two basic groups. In Act I, Scene II, the servant Manes speaks seventeen times and discusses hunger or food on ten different occasions. He repeatedly rails against his master's failure to provide him with what he considers to be sufficient sustenance, claiming to serve 'instead of a master a mouse, whose house is a tub, whose dinner is a crust and whose bed is a board' (I.ii.1–2). Appetite is presented as a property common to all men. His master's suppression of that appetite reduces him to the level of a mouse, implying timidity and inhumanity. The name Manes, which means spirit or ghost in Latin, implies almost mortal thinness, serving to emphasise the extremity of his hunger. *Campaspe* can therefore be said to embody what Stephen Greenblatt describes as power's tendency to 'record other voices, permit subversive inquiries, register at its very centre the transgressions that will ultimately violate it' (Greenblatt, 1994, p. 26). It provides the audience with access to grievances which they might not have heard from their own servants but which, in an era increasingly sceptical of the servingman's sincerity, they may well have suspected were being voiced behind their back. The text registers lower-class resentment, but does so within the resolutely upper-class settings of the Blackfriars and the Court. In doing so, it tacitly acknowledges the capacity of hunger and appetite to function as a means of critiquing the elite.

Yet if *Campaspe* provides a window onto these grievances, it does so with a marked air of scepticism. The appetites of Lyly's servants are defined by appetence as much as necessity and are frequently figured through the description of food rather than assertions of hunger. They sing songs in praise of 'a plump fat leg of mutton / Veal, lamb, capon, pig and coney', declaring that 'None is happy but a glutton' (I.ii.103–5). In the song's chorus, they claim that even the pleasures provided by 'wine' and 'girls' are second only to those produced by the consumption of 'brave victuals' (I.ii.107–8). This emphasis on appetite and pleasure rather than hunger can productively be considered with reference to the work of Christian Biet, who has noted the degree to which the servant's hunger is typological:

Pincombe has asserted the significance of the '"non-courtly" or "counter-courtly"' elements to the work (Pincombe, 1996, p. 1). In a similar manner, Marguerite Tassi notes that 'While it is certainly the case that Lyly desired a position at court, it cannot fail to strike the reader of *Campaspe* that Lyly expressed ambivalence about the constraints and dangers to artistic independence entailed by patronage' (Tassi, 2005, p. 71).

[8] Evidence regarding the first Blackfriars theatre is scarce. But, as Gurr has noted, the early boys' companies 'had an air of respectability which set them in contrast to the adult companies', and which consequently made them particularly popular with the elite and at court (Gurr, 2009, p. 46).

a 'dramaturgical mark', detached from the lived experience of contemporary servants and a product of dramatic tradition as much as the social reality (Biet, 2008, p. 56). The text dramatises appetite, but obscures the conditions which have produced it. As a consequence, deprivation assumes a comic significance which ostensibly has little to do with the hardship which early modern servants experienced. The result is that their appetites embody a Hobbesian conception of laughter as 'nothing else but sudden glory arising from some sudden conception of some eminency in ourselves, by comparison with the infirmity of others, or with our own formerly' (Hobbes, 1981, p. 125). Its purpose, above all, is to bind audience members together as a homogenous group, united in their ridicule of a lower class which, almost by definition, is excluded from the privileged space of the private theatre's audience. The representation of the servant can therefore be read as an example of what Sartre described as 'interiorised scarcity', the process by which the upper classes:

> which are perpetually in danger of liquidation because they are the absolute Other (living off the labour of Others), interiorise this ambivalent alterity and behave towards individuals either as if they were Other than man (positively, as gods) or as if they alone were men in the midst of a different, sub-human species. (Sartre, 2004, p. 150)

The servant is dehumanised in order to legitimate the basic inequality which exists between the material situations of the audience and those of the masses outside the space of the private theatre. Appetite is significant here primarily for the distinction which it establishes between these two groups.

However, although Biet recognises the existence of this basic dichotomy between audience and character, it should be acknowledged that *Campaspe* is not merely a product of that divide, but actively comments upon it. For the denigration of the servant's grotesque appetite is reliant, above all, on the opposition of the servingmen to their elite counterparts. Where his master, the philosopher Diogenes, derives sustenance from contemplation, Manes declares 'I had rather fill my guts than my brains' (I.ii.55–6). Psyllus, meanwhile, claims that his master, the painter Appelles, 'feedeth me as Diogenes doth Manes, for at dinner the one preacheth abstinence, the other commendeth counterfeiting' (I.ii.57–9). Instead of food, he presents Psyllus with paintings, providing 'dishes to feed the eye but not to fill the gut' (I.ii.62–3). In staging this opposition, the play provides a key example of the tendencies outlined in the work of Gail Kern Paster, who has demonstrated that in this period the representation of resistance to or subjection to bodily impulses is increasingly implicated within 'the production and maintenance of gender and class difference' (Paster, 1993, p. 7). Where the elite are constructed as self-contained subjects, superior to their bodily impulses, lower-class and female characters are invariably depicted as 'leaky vessels' in thrall to their bodies (Paster, 1993, p. 23). The repression of hunger can be situated as part of this more general 'suppression and silencing of the body's functions' (Paster, 1993, p. 16). While Appelles 'tells of birds that have been fatted by painted grapes in winter' (I.ii.67–8), his servant Psyllus enacts the opposite operation, declaring his hunger 'maketh me, when I should begin to shadow a lady's face, to draw a lamb's head and sometime to set to the body of a maid a shoulder of mutton' (I.ii.76–8). The masters not only insist on their ability to survive without what Manes and Psyllus believe to be adequate sustenance, but also enforce that diet on their servants. The master demonstrates through an act of will his ability to transcend his own bodily instincts. Appetite is a force which primarily affects the lower classes.

Nevertheless, it should be noted that Paster's emphasis on the role of shame in this process prioritises the depiction of excretion over consumption. I would argue that appetite assumes a special role within this more general shift in attitudes towards the body and that this is largely a consequence of sixteenth-century England's rampant inflation. Although this process contributed to changes in the depiction of appetite more generally, it is nowhere more evident than in the representation of the servant. For this was a period in which rising prices were forcing many aristocrats to reduce the size of their retinues. Beier has noted that 'between 1520 and 1700 the numbers of living-in workers fell by something like 50 per cent: from perhaps 20 per cent of the total population to just 10 per cent' (Beier, 1985, p. 23). While these increasing costs were widely acknowledged to lie at the root of a general crisis in service, they were often associated not with inflation so much as the excessive appetites of the servingman. The Commonwealth writer John Hales, for example, describes those who, 'seeing the charges of householde encrease so much', resolve to move from the countryside to the city, where they 'spende their time some of them with a seruant or two, where he was wont to keepe thirty or forty persons daily in his house' (Hales, 1581, p. 33). But the text argues that 'one great cause of the greater charge of householde' is the unrestrained desire of the servingman for both apparel and food, in overt contrast to those of previous generations who were content to survive on 'a piece of biefe or some other dishe of sodde meate all the weeke longe' (Hales, 1581, p. 33). *Campaspe*, by translating hunger into appetite, participates in this attribution of blame, characterising the decline of service as a consequence of the servingman's propensity to consume without restraint.

At the same time, it should be acknowledged that appetite within the play is never solely the province of the lower classes. Indeed, the text depicts Alexander's love for Campaspe as the product of an appetite gone awry. Hephestion, his adviser, tries to persuade him to reject his romantic inclinations, declaring that 'time must / wear out that love hath wrought, and reason wean what / appetite nursed' (III.iv.136–8). The effect of Alexander's initial inability to conquer that appetite is presented as disastrous for his people as a whole. In the absence of further wars, decadence spreads, with Diogenes declaring 'You build as / though you should live for ever and surfeit as though / you should die tomorrow' (IV.i.49–51). Nevertheless, these are clearly presented as undesirable exceptions which derive their satiric power precisely from the unambiguous association of the common servingman with appetite. To be a servant is to be defined by that appetite, and thus to allow oneself to be governed by appetite is to be reduced to the level of the servingman. This is significant, because the period was defined by a general shift in elite patterns of consumption. In earlier periods, across Europe, power was displayed through acts of excess. Roy Porter, for example, has argued with reference to early modern Italy that 'Eating well was more important than being rich, famous, or of high status – conspicuous food consumption in fact stood as the very proof of all these attributes' (Porter, 1980, p. 9). But the greater influence of market forces and inflation on the economy of England prompted a tendency to detach power from excessive ingestion. Mennell notes that class difference was increasingly manifested not in the quantity of food consumed but in the 'invention and elaboration of . . . ever more refined and delicate dishes' (Mennell, 1985, p. 33). The servant thus functions as a means to enforce upon the ruling class what Christopher Hill has described as 'bourgeois qualities necessary to success – thrift, industry, readiness to rack rents and watch markets, moderate consumption and reinvestment of profits' (Hill, 1967, p. 48). *Campaspe* reveals the extent to which the depiction of unrestrained appetites was not only implicated in the ridicule of the lower classes, but also provided a means of governing the behaviour of the elite.

Attention to Lyly's servingmen reveals the complex roles of hunger and appetite in the depiction of the period's class divide. In the first instance, it shows the weakness and instability in the political superstructure. Depicting the insatiable appetites of the lower classes provides a means of understanding the collapsing power of the traditional nobility. Their resources are quite literally being eaten up by their retainers. In this sense, the text can productively be read in the light of Holstun's claim that the ruling classes 'move even more strongly toward binary schemes at moments of class discord, redirecting their taxonomic energies toward the dyke holding back the many-headed monster' (Holstun, 2000, p. 101). But more significantly, analysis of these servingmen reveals the extent to which appetite provides Lyly with a way to urge restraint. The Other that is the servant is a didactic tool to enforce a series of moral principles rooted in restraint and moderation which, although irreducible to, are nevertheless in the final instance determined by, underlying changes in the mode of production. The class dynamic is employed to influence ruling-class behaviour, in a manner which can be broadly situated in what Corrigan and Sayer have described as the 'centuries-long embourgeoisement of England's dominant classes' (Corrigan and Sayer, 1985, p. 11). *Campaspe* therefore reveals the extent to which the depiction of hunger and appetite inclines towards the political. It reacts to material change within society, but does so in such a way as to endorse a specific praxis.

## Naked Self-Interest

For all the tensions which surround its representation of service, it should be acknowledged that *Campaspe* depicts the relationship between master and servant as stable. The servant Manes and the philosopher Diogenes maintain a relationship of reciprocity. They 'dine one upon another', with the cannibal metaphor implying mutual dependence (II.i.56). The audience learns that Manes is known for the frequency with which he 'runnst away' (I.ii.28), but the repetitive nature of this act of rebellion serves to erase any sense of the threat which it might pose to the existing social order. Indeed, that repetitive pattern of rebellion and reconciliation is further reinforced by the classical context of the piece. The grievances of the servingmen undoubtedly resemble those of many servants across England, but the fact that the masters they serve are famous philosophers implies an element of universality which normalises the existence of the basic divide which the text represents. The dichotomy of appetite and restraint is, by implication, one which defines both the classical and contemporary worlds. Certainly, it is true that tensions within wider ideologies of service and consumption make necessary the visibility of a basic class dynamic. But there is little sense that this opposition is truly threatened by these changes. The interrelation of well-fed master and appetite-driven servant is presented as both stable and universal. Appetite is implicated in the depiction of class identities, but simultaneously works to normalise them, effacing the historically specific material changes of which it is a product.

However, in the late Elizabethan and Jacobean period, that opposition begins to look increasingly unstable. Appetite emerges as a force which threatens, rather than legitimises, the class dynamic of early modern society. Where the servants of *Campaspe* merely grumble, those of the late Elizabethan and Jacobean period take action to improve their situation. And this active dimension is invariably accompanied by depictions of the servingman's predilection for vice and the implied possibility that his appetite may prompt him to abandon service entirely. By contrast with classical examples of the hungry servant, who, as Burnett has noted, are invariably motivated 'by their fidelity to their masters', hungry servants from the 1590s onwards display a markedly undiscriminating attitude towards whom they should serve and how (Burnett, 1997, p. 80). In this manner, legitimation of an inequitable society becomes in this period increasingly associated with a pronounced anxiety as to the tenability of existing modes of exploitation. Whereas in *Campaspe*, appetite served to reinforce a class divide within wider ideals of service, in the late Elizabethan and Jacobean period it becomes a means to assert its instability.

In large part, this can be situated as a product of emergent tensions regarding the decline of service. Evett argues that 'in the second half of the sixteenth century ... the cash nexus increasingly determined economic activity; familial service began to give way to contractual service' (Evett, 2007, p. 415). The late-sixteenth-century writer I. M., for example, attacked the extent to which 'reward only with bare wages' had replaced 'kind usage and friendly familiarity', and noted that for most servants money had become 'the marke whereat they all shoote, the Maister whom they all obey ... and the Man to whom they all do reuerence' (I. M., 1598, p. 46). As Neill notes, I. M.'s fears represent the conservative equivalent to Marx's claim that the bourgeoisie has 'pitilessly torn asunder the motley feudal ties that bound man to his *natural superiors*, and has left remaining no other nexus between man and man than naked self-interest, than callous *cash-payment*' (Marx and Engels, 1975–2004, VI, pp. 486–7). But in the absence of this theoretical model, it is through the representation of appetite that the theatre conceptualises a society in flux. To an extent, the servant's obsessive concern with material gain serves to distance onstage ruling-class characters from these practices. The association of the profit motive with the servant's appetite serves to identify it as a characteristic of the lower classes, insulating the continuance of an idealised ruling-class form of service. But at the same time, the universality of the hunger drive creates the conditions of possibility for a more wide-ranging critique, attacking the self-interest not simply of the lower classes, but of characters at every level of society.

Often, these tensions are manifested in the early modern theatre through an emphasis on the unscrupulous nature of the service which such servants are prepared to carry out. In Robert Greene's *The Scottish History of James IV* (1594; Greene, 1973), for instance, the servingman Slipper declares that he 'cannot abide a full cup unkissed, a fat capon uncarved, a full purse unpicked, nor a fool to prove a justice as you do' (I.ii.21–3). Slipper is portrayed as an easy prey to the influence of corrupt courtier Ateukin, and it soon becomes evident that his reliance on Ateukin for sustenance is the source of his continuing corruption. He remarks, 'it were a hard matter for me to get my dinner that day wherein my master had not sold a dozen of devices' (II.i.100–2). Yet just as Slipper's hunger prompts him to immorality, so too does it lead him to betray his corrupt master. In Act III, Sir Bartram, anxious to obtain the lease of a manor from Ateukin, is able to bribe Slipper with offers of 'money and reward' (III.i.38). The result is the inadvertent discovery of the King's plot to murder his Queen, ensuring that the play moves towards its conclusion. The hungry servant in this instance seems not so much immoral, as amoral. His hunger leaves him worryingly open to manipulation from any side. Duty and service are reduced to the simple need to fill one's belly and the result is that the servant's appetite begins to embody wider tensions prompted by the decline of service. Appetite embodies an element of 'naked self-interest', and as such it stands for forces working to disrupt the ordered hierarchy of early modern England. It is no longer simply an inevitable characteristic of service, but has become a force which threatens the institution as a whole.

Indeed, it is striking that although servants who are loyal to their masters may be portrayed as hungry, they are rarely associated with appetite. In Shakespeare's *As You Like It*, for example, the loyal servant Adam protests that he can 'go no further' and declares 'I die for food' (II.vi.1). His declaration of hunger is not a demand for sustenance, but rather couched as a desire for death, a resolution to 'measure out [his] grave' (II.vi.2). His hunger is characterised as one of 'two weak evils, age and hunger' which have oppressed him; and the implication is that his hunger, like his age, is something inevitable, rather than a consequence of his master's actions. The result is to detach his hunger from appetite and to transfer the anxious search for food onto his master. The resulting scene in which Orlando, Adam's master, breaks in upon a group of outlawed nobles and declares 'He dies that touches any of this fruit / Till I and my affairs are answered' (II.vii.98–9) channels discordant energies around the potential consequences of hunger unsatisfied. But the overt lack of agency which Adam displays undermines any radicalism in the encounter. Orlando acts with violence not on his own behalf, but in order to relieve his servant and carry out his obligations as a master. The obligation to feed one's servant was, as Beier has emphasised, a key part of the standard contract of service and comprised a notable source of conflict which frequently spilled over into the period's courts. Here, Orlando's commitment to supporting his servant is such that, far from being a source of conflict between them, it prompts him to seek out food for Adam, sword in hand. By eliminating appetite, Shakespeare focusses attention not on the desires of the servant but on the duties of the master. The result is that the image of the hungry servant appears to embody the ideal, rather than the failure, of service. Hunger can be inscribed within the text as a legitimation of service, but appetite is almost invariably opposed to it.

It might be argued that for a ruling-class member of the audience, the emphasis upon the servingman's appetite provides a means to explore the growing emphasis upon material gain, without placing explicit strain on the system of hierarchy. In John Fletcher and Philip Massinger's *Love's Cure* (*c.* 1612–15), the hungry servant Lazarillo is lured into the corrupt Sergeant Alguazir's schemes with the promise first of 'supper' and then with the offer of 'a project to employ you in shall make you drink, and eat merrily this moneth' (II.i.207–8). They soon engage in a series of robberies, utilising their ostensible position as members of the city watch in order to steal with impunity. It is precisely his ravenous desire for food which prompts Lazarillo to join Alguazir's criminal gang. Lazarillo declares his loyalty to Alguazir by saying 'If there be meat / Or any banquet stirring, you shall see / How ile bestow my selfe' (IV.ii.129–31). The Lazarillo of Fletcher's *Love's Cure* declares in his very name his indebtedness to the notorious picaresque anti-hero.[9] But by contrast with both the servants of

[9] The Spanish picaresque text *Lazarillo de Tormes* had been translated into English in 1586. The tale recounts the adventures of the young rogue Lazarillo, who serves a series of masters of increasing social status. The narrative is told from the perspective of the older, if not necessarily wiser, Lazarillo, who has risen to the position of servant to an Archpriest. As a consequence, Theresa Ann Sears has argued, 'hidden within the poor child Lazarillo's pathetic search for food is Lázaro's quest for status'

earlier plays such as *Campaspe* and his Spanish namesake, Fletcher's Lazarillo is defined by the total, rather than the partial, effacement of the connections between hunger and appetite. Despite the band's initial success, he continues to declare 'Yet still / I am monstrous hungry' (IV.iii.2–3); he claims to have 'A legion in my stomach that have kept / Perpetuall fast these ten years' (IV.iii.7–8). His appetite is presented not only as the motivating force which drives him towards crime, but as a constant, which has little to do with the amount of food he has consumed. Even as he attempts to move beyond his origins and better his position, he remains constrained by his appetite. For the elite of the audience, at least, the wider metaphorical association of appetite with desire is potentially troubling, threatening the overturn of social institutions. But the essentialism inherent in the consistent reduction of that desire to an appetite for food defuses that tension. For all his mobility, the hungry servant remains just a servant. Appetite retains its inscription within a Hobbesian dynamic of laughter as ridicule.

Yet there remains a repeated tendency for the servants' appetite to appear dangerously similar to that of their masters. At times, these parallels have the potential to emerge as an extended critique of early modern society. A key example is Philip Massinger's *The Bashful Lover*.[10] In many ways a text which reprises the themes of Shakespeare's *As You Like It*, the play deploys the well-worn stereotype of the hungry servant to convey an ironic commentary on its apparent endorsement of conventional idealism. The primary plot depicts a series of suitors, competing for the attentions of Matilda, Princess of Mantua. Galeazzo, the eponymous lover, claims to be unworthy of her attentions, but requests the opportunity to serve her, without hope of reward. Others, however, are less moderate in their advances, and in the opening act the tyrannous Duke of Florence threatens invasion if his offer of marriage is refused. Faced with the prospect of war, Galeazzo asserts the power of a romanticised ideal of service and duty to repel the invading forces, declaring:

(Sears, 2010, pp. 100–1). The character exerted a significant influence on the contemporary theatre. A number of other plays in the early seventeenth century include a 'Lazarillo' character. *Blurt, The Master Constable* (1602) depicts a Lazarillo who is described as a cousin to the Spanish original. The subplot of Beaumont and Fletcher's *The Woman-Hater* (1607) is centred on an aspirational Lazarillo, who has risen to the position of courtier, but whose enduring appetites reveal his more humble origins, as part of the play's satirical attack upon the sale of honours.

10 The title page of the 1655 edition announces that it was performed at the second Blackfriars theatre, although performance at the Globe is also probable. By contrast with much of the King's Men's work, it appears not to have received a court performance.

In a cause like this,
The Husbandman would change his ploughing-irons
To weapons of defence, and leave the earth
Untill'd, although a general dearth should follow:
The Student would forswear his book; the Lawyer
Put off his thriving gown, and without pay
Conclude this case is to be fought, not pleaded:
The women will turn *Amazons*, as their sex
In her were wrong'd; and boys write down their names
I' th' muster-book for soldiers. (I.ii.81–90)

There are clear parallels here with the contemporary ideal of service, identified by critics such as Evett and Schalkwyk, as a principle which exists detached from or in opposition to material interest. Yet it is significant that in applying that concept to society as a whole, Galeazzo lapses into a series of carnivalesque images which are markedly reminiscent of early modern paranoia regarding disorder. Galeazzo here constitutes the traditional ideal of service not merely as a fantasy, but one which, with its images of 'general dearth', threatens to imperil rather than sustain the social order. Indeed, as Martin Butler has noted, the idealised nature of these images is swiftly undercut by 'the abject failure of these noble lovers on the battlefield' (Butler, 1984, p. 51). Certainly, Galeazzo performs a range of exploits, claiming that 'What I did, she gave me / The strength to do' (II.v.67–8). But the fact remains that Lorenzo's troops cannot be beaten, and the defenders are forced to acknowledge that 'valour cannot save us' (II.v.1). Throughout Acts II and III, the model of service founded on love is situated in overt opposition to the mercenary loyalty of an army motivated by profit and plunder. It is the latter which emerges victorious.

Similar tensions define the play's secondary plot, which depicts the actions of Maria, a young woman who has been abandoned by her lover, and who has adopted male disguise as the page Ascanio. She rapidly falls into the service of the play's eponymous lover, Galeazzo, claiming to 'bring a will that shall / Survive my want of power' (II.ii.12–14). But following their defeat at the hands of the invading army, Galeazzo and the disguised Maria find themselves lost in the wilderness, where she rapidly succumbs to the force of hunger. Like Orlando in *As You Like It*, Galeazzo attempts to demand sustenance for her, sword in hand. When none is forthcoming, he resolves to 'open / A vein, and pour my blood . . . Into his famish'd mouth' (III.i.57–60). Galeazzo's actions evoke the pelican, which was popularly believed to feed its children with its own blood. He consequently assumes a paternal position with regard to the starving Maria. But the pelican was also a religious symbol, associated with Christ's bleeding wounds on the Cross.[11] The passage therefore participates in the broader tendency which David Evett has identified, for contemporary texts to justify the practice of service through the evocation of Christ's self-sacrifice for humanity (Evett, 2005, p. 5). The image of the master feeding the servant is elevated to a symbol of service as a religious ideal, rooted not in obligation or fear, but in love.

However, this image of self-sacrifice and reciprocal service appears only moments after the first appearance of Gothrio, a hungry servant who displays an overt predilection for vice. Galeazzo's selfless attempts to sustain his page with his own blood are followed almost immediately by a pantomime routine in which Gothrio attempts to secure a bottle belonging to his master, who responds with the claim that 'A tough cudgel / Will take this gentle itch off' (III.i.83–4). Gothrio's unbounded appetite embodies a greed which can be kept in check only by the violent actions of his master. His presence calls into question the typicality of both Galeazzo's beneficence and Ascanio's loyalty, at the very moment when the ideal of service appears to receive its most profound expression. The comic business of the pursuit of the bottle embodies low-level struggles around the provision of food and drink which would have been familiar to both servants and masters in early modern England. This non-vocal stage-play may have threatened to dominate the scene. At one level, this emphasises the fundamental difference between upper- and ruling-class service. Where Ascanio and Galeazzo engage in a reciprocal relationship rooted in love, Gothrio seeks only to fill his belly. But at the same time, Gothrio's actions also demonstrate the fantastic nature of Ascanio's restraint. The mirth produced by Gothrio's antics is directed as much at the concept of hunger without appetite as it is towards his own subjection to bodily impulses. And this effect is accentuated by the fact that the page in question is a disguised gentlewoman, rather than a real servant. A ruling-class performance of service is juxtaposed with the grim reality of Gothrio's appetite.

Furthermore, by contrast with many incarnations of the type, Gothrio's appetite is also figured as comparable to, or even lesser than, that of his ruling-class counterparts. This is clearest in his preference for alcohol, which is presented not simply in terms of a lower-class inability to control bodily urges, but also as a satiric portrayal of his upwardly mobile attempt to acquire specifically ruling-class vices. He declares:

[11] See V. E. Graham, 'The Pelican as Image and Symbol' (1962).

How? Drunkard, sir!
I am a poor man, you mistake me, sir,
Drunkard's a title for the rich, my betters;
A calling in repute: some sell their lands for't,
And rore, Wines better than mony. Our poor beveridge
Of buttermilk or whey allaid with water,
Ne'r raise our thoughts so high. Drunk, I had never
The credit to be so yet. (III.i.40–7)

The references to the selling of land, to drunkard as a 'title for the rich' and the punning allusion to 'credit' associate Gothrio's thirst with ruling-class vices which were widely condemned in Caroline England (III.i.47). Linda Woodbridge has described early modern England as a culture 'preoccupied with repayment, enmeshed in webs of credit, worried about foreclosures, defaults and inflation', in which 'a language of owing pervaded life' (Woodbridge, 2010, p. 105). John Brewer notes that 'the first two Stuarts raised at least £620,000 through the sale of honours between 1603 and 1629', much to the distaste of the traditional aristocracy (Brewer, 1990, p. 14). Whereas Galeazzo's ideal of service has been presented as a fantasy, the use of these contemporary references ensures that its corruption is rooted in the present. Gothrio's portrayal of ruling-class excess bears a striking resemblance to Walter Cohen's assessment of the decline of the nobility, whereby 'Rising expenses on consumption, court and borrowing combined with declining revenues from estates to produce a fall in real income that coincided with a general deterioration of the titled nobility's position within the ruling class and in society as a whole' (Cohen, 1985, p. 143). While Cohen reads this decline as the product of material changes at the base of society, in Massinger's text it is visible as a crisis of morality. Once again, appetite becomes a tool to conceptualise the fluidity of the capitalist system. Where *Love's Cure* associated that appetite with the servingman, *The Bashful Lover* implies that it is pervasive.

The tensions surrounding the apparent failure of the ideal of service are ostensibly dispelled by the play's resolution, in which the beauty of Princess Mathilda is such that the tyrannous Lorenzo is transformed to a doting lover. Yet this ostensible justification of a model of service built on love is almost immediately destabilised by the play's insistence on Gothrio's enduring appetites. Having been returned to his position of power, Gothrio's master Octavio initially tells his servant that 'such foul pollution is / To be whipt from court; I have now no more use of you; / Return to your trough' (V.i.41–3), constructing his servant as little more than a beast and implying a concession to a model of service based on animal urges. But, like Prospero at the conclusion of

Shakespeare's *The Tempest*, he soon recognises that the bond between master and servant cannot be so readily discharged.[12] He resolves:

> I'll reward
> Your service; live in your own element,
> Like an honest man; all that is mine in the cottage,
> I freely give you. (V.i.44–7)

Gothrio receives the reward of a faithful servant. Octavio's generosity clearly stands at odds with the behaviour which both master and servant have demonstrated throughout the play. Yet perhaps more significant is the nature of Gothrio's reaction. Rather than gratitude, he continues to deploy the notion of thirst in the service of social critique, stating:

> O sir!
> 'Twas well for me that you did reward my service
> Before you enter'd the court; for 'tis reported
> There is a drink of forgetfulness, which once tasted,
> Few masters think of their servants, who, grown old,
> Are turn'd off, like lame hounds and hunting horses,
> To starve on the commons. (V.i.50–6)

The text fluctuates between images of exclusion and reward, with Octavio's own reference to Gothrio's 'trough' mirrored in the association between discharged servants and 'lame hounds and hunting horses' (V.i.55). In both cases animal appetites are a product of ruling-class indifference. Likewise, Gothrio's reference to servants starving on commons is counterpointed by allusion to Lethe, the 'mythical river of forgetting' (Weinrich, 2004, p. 4). The unpleasant reality of ruling-class indifference is recast in classical imagery, introducing a satirical counterpoint to the glorified concepts of service propagated by Galeazzo. The result is that the audience's attention is drawn not to the generosity of the master, but rather to the atypical nature of his behaviour, enabling Massinger's text to make an explicit association between the failings of the ruling classes and the decay of service. Gothrio's reward, like the romantic conclusion as a whole, is clearly represented as the exception, in a period when Galeazzo's ideal of reciprocal service is in disarray. The audience is encouraged to reflect upon the extent to which, outside the theatre, elite indifference is allowing hunger and appetite to spread without restraint.

Furthermore, that air of discord is accentuated by the response of the upstage upper class, for although apparently innocuous, it is fraught with

[12] The relationship between Prospero and Caliban is productively explored in Paul Brown's essay 'This thing of darkness I acknowledge mine' (1994).

tension. Alonzo remarks that 'there's craft / I' the clouted shoo' (V.i.56–7) and swiftly changes the subject. Technically a form of peasant footwear tipped with iron and secured with iron nails, the term 'clouted shoon' was almost as loaded with meaning as the concept of hunger itself. Often, it was a form of abuse. Nashe, for example, attacks the unrestrained appetites of 'clowns and clouted shoes, and the rubbish meniality' (Nashe, 1972, p. 411). Yet it also embodied a manner of thinking that contained the seeds of a clearly defined class-consciousness. During Kett's Rebellion, the peasants derived confidence and identity from a prophecy which claimed that:

> The country gnoofes, Hob, Dick and Hick,
> With clubbes and clouted shoone,
> Shall fill vp Dussyn dale:
> With slautered bodies soon. (Neville, 1615, sig. K1v)

And most memorably, Shakespeare's Jack Cade resolves to 'Spare none but such as go in clouted shoon' (IV.ii.175). The apparently comic and trivialising nature of Alonzo's response to Gothrio's ingratitude masks a moment of tension, an awareness that the failure of service may prompt something far more dangerous than simply theft and complaint. Yet the text has produced an insoluble ambiguity. Service is presented as both fundamentally untenable and absolutely necessary. The actions of the ruling class are subject to an explicit critique; but the depiction of the idealised model of service which they have notionally betrayed is hugely ambiguous. The most significant expression of this central tension is the portrayal of the hungry servant. Gothrio, simultaneously ludicrous and unsettling, stands for the impulses of a market-dominated society in which the old loyalties have failed, but which in the absence of capitalist hegemony lacks any means of conceptualising a real alternative. The New World is conceivable only in this image of insatiable appetite. But it is an appetite which the ruling classes themselves may well have created.

In these plays, appetite emerges as the surrogate for a more general drive towards material gain. As a consequence, the association of appetite with the servingman functions most obviously as a means of alleviating a pervasive anxiety regarding the increasing dominance of profit, acquisition and wage labour within early modern society. By reducing the desire for wages or profit to the level of appetite, these texts associate it with the lower classes. But at the same time, the sheer dominance of service as a governing ideological structure means that the extent to which this drive can be confined to the domestic servant is invariably limited. The servant's appetite has the potential to function as the embodiment of, rather than the exception to, the dominant principles of society. Perhaps the most striking instance of this tendency occurs in *The Bashful Lover*. The play not only draws parallels between the actions of the elite and their servants; it also depicts the ideals of service themselves as both illusory and ineffective. In *Campaspe*, the parallels between the upper class and their servants are deployed as a means to inculcate particular virtues. In *The Bashful Lover*, by contrast, those parallels situate the unbridled appetites of the lower class as a product of elite indifference and indulgence. Gothrio undoubtedly embodies many of the servant stereotype's more general characteristics. His appetite can only be obliquely connected with hunger, and is associated with a tendency towards vice which places it in opposition to the settled hierarchies lauded by the dominant forces of early modern England. The tensions raised by the restless appetites of the poor can no longer be dismissed as instances of vice. The lower classes of England are no longer an Other which functions to legitimate the status quo, but, on the contrary, have become the very reason for which change is necessary. The appetite of the servingman has shifted from a form of legitimation to a means of critique.

## Husbands, Wives and Servants

The ambiguous distinction between the appetites of masters and their servingmen is of particular interest in those plays which draw parallels between husbands, wives and servants. Recent critical work has outlined the preponderance of female servants in the early modern theatre.[13] But these characters are associated only infrequently with hunger and appetite. At times, they are associated with the metaphorical consumption of food, often with a sexual emphasis. In Middleton's *The Honest Whore* (1604), for instance, Bellafront refers to her 'pretty servant [who] sees three court dishes before her, and not one good bit in them' (vi.149–50). On other occasions, female servants can be presented as producers of food, such as in Massinger's *A New Way to Pay Old Debts* (1625), in which Allworth is offered 'few quince-cakes into your pocket . . . of mine own preserving' (II.ii.8–9), by an amorous lady's maid. Even in this case, however, the masculine emphasis is more normal, for cooks on the early modern stage are generally male professionals. Female servants are almost invariably detached from the emphasis on hunger and appetite that defines most of their male equivalents.[14]

[13] See Wall (2002); Sanchez (2008); Dowd (2009).

[14] The most significant exception to this tendency, the serving woman Ero who joins her mistress in an act of food refusal in *The Widow's Tears*, is discussed in Chapter 5.

However, if female servants are rarely associated with appetite, the connections between hungry servants and their female masters are the object of repeated scrutiny. In large part, this can be situated as a product of the ambiguous position which women occupied within the early modern household. Although ostensibly placed in a subordinate relationship to their husbands, they also exerted varying degrees of power over the household staff. Indeed, as Wendy Wall has noted, while the husband was notionally 'sovereign over the household' he could also find himself 'in the uncomfortable position of submitting to his wife's and servant's medical ministrations' (Wall, 2002, p. 7). The result was the establishment of 'competing lines of allegiance and dependency', which are of fundamental importance for understanding the representation of the male domestic servant (Wall, 2002, p. 7). In some contemporary texts, the representation of hunger is deployed to explore the complex relationships between husbands, wives and their servants. In Shakespeare's *The Taming of the Shrew* (1592), Petruchio starves his wife as a means of establishing her position within a broader hierarchy of service in his household. In Fletcher's *Women Pleased* (*c.* 1619–23), the wife and servant of a miser are placed in parallel positions of want. And in Massinger's *The Picture* (1629), it is the wife, Sophia, who uses hunger to tame first her servant, then two lustful courtiers and finally her own husband. In all three examples, the intersection of hunger and service disrupts the mystification of household hierarchies and invites the audience to explore the parallel positions of wives and servants.

In *The Taming of the Shrew*, hunger provides a means to enforce a conventional domestic hierarchy. Faced with a rebellious wife, Petruchio adopts a strategy which mirrors training techniques derived from falconry. He declares:

> My falcon now is sharp and passing empty,
> And till she stoop she must not be full-gorged,
> For then she never looks upon her lure.
> Another way I have to man my haggard,
> To make her come and know her keeper's call:
> That is, to watch her, as we watch these kites
> That bate and beat and will not be obedient.
> She ate no meat today, nor none shall eat . . . (IV.i.179–86)

As critics such as Kathleen M. Davies and Lorna Hutson have demonstrated, Shakespeare's deployment of the imagery of falconry constitutes a variation on a more general tendency to equate the taming of a wife with the taming of an animal (Davies, 1977; Hutson, 1994). The parallels serve most obviously to dehumanise Katherina, situating her rejection of Petruchio's authority as brute, animal disobedience. Yet the consequent emphasis on the role of hunger and food in the taming relationship immediately invites parallels with the service relationship. The centrality of hunger to Petruchio's attempts to ensure that she will 'know her keeper's call' embodies a model of service which closely parallels figures such as the serving boys of *Campaspe*. In exercising the right to deprive her of food, Petruchio establishes their relationship as one of dependency. He is her 'keeper' who, like the conventional model of the good early modern master, rewards obedience with sustenance and rebellion with hunger. The result is an implicit drop in status. Katharina is presented as no different from any other servant in Petruchio's household, forced into obedience not by a sense of duty, but rather by the 'iron chaynes' of hunger (Guazzo, 1581, p. 47).

At the same time, the strategy entails Petruchio adopting many tasks conventionally gendered as female. As Marion D. Perret has noted, 'In his carefully calculated denial of food Petruchio encroaches upon his wife's authority' (Perret, 1983, p. 226). The deployment of hunger as a means to ensure Katherina's submission is consequently reliant not only upon an act of subjugation, but also upon the implicit recognition of the domestic power inherent in the role of the wife. Indeed, Katherina's hunger is justified by means of a recourse to humoral theory, which comically affirms good household governance as a more appropriate means by which Katherina might regulate her husband's behaviour. Petruchio declares:

> I tell thee, Kate, 'twas burnt and dried away,
> And I expressly am forbid to touch it;
> For it engenders choler, planteth anger,
> And better 'twere that both of us did fast,
> Since, of ourselves, ourselves are choleric,
> Than feed it with such over-roasted flesh.
> Be patient, tomorrow't shall be mended,
> And, for this night, we'll fast for company. (IV.i.159–66)

Petruchio here, ostensibly at least, purports to be regulating not only Katherina's behaviour, but also his own. In part, as with his strategies more generally, this serves to establish a thinly veiled threat of violence. But it is also the case that Petruchio's comments on the dangers of the choleric properties of certain foods reflect widely accepted medical practice. As Albala notes, the interaction between predisposition and sustenance 'was one of the central concerns of dietetics' (Albala, 2002, p. 5). Thomas Elyot, for instance, explains that men and women of a choleric 'complexion' are 'hote and drie, in whom the fyre hath preeminence' (Elyot, 1539, p. 3), and advises those who are distempered to avoid the consumption of 'meates beynge very salte or sowre, olde, burned' (Elyot, 1539, p. 69). In emphasising the capacity of certain foods to influence behaviour, Petruchio implicitly acknowledges his own vulnerability with regard to the household labour of both wives and servants. Even as he places Katherina in a subordinate position, Petruchio emphasises the potential power of roles considered the province of the wife. Good service emerges as a more effective means of control than disobedience.

Furthermore, central to Petruchio's strategy is an emphasis upon relationships not merely between himself and his wife, but also with the wider hierarchy of household servants. In order to satisfy her hunger, Katherina is forced to beg not simply from Petruchio, but also from the servingman, Grummio. In her efforts to persuade the recalcitrant servant to provide her with sustenance, she declares:

> Beggars, that come unto my father's door,
> Upon entreaty have a present alms;
> If not, elsewhere they meet with charity.
> But I, who never knew how to entreat,
> Nor never needed that I should entreat,
> Am starved for meat, giddy for lack of sleep,
> With oaths kept waking and with brawling fed[.] (IV.iii.4–10)

Katherina moves from a position of command, to one of entreaty. In rejecting her duties of service to her husband, she finds herself in a position outside the hierarchical structures of the household in its entirety. Katherina's behaviour leads to her adopting a position that is both physically and metaphorically akin to that of a masterless vagabond. Once again, however, Petruchio's strategy is reliant upon intruding into areas of household management which were often primarily the office of the wife. He demonstrates not only the consequences of her disobedience, but also the power which she might gain by submitting to him. In obeying Petruchio, she earns the right not only to serve, but also to command. The potential parallels between wife and servant are deployed not to assert their similitude, but rather as a strategy ensuring that Katherina accepts her position within the household hierarchy.

Elsewhere, however, hunger provides a means not to enforce the domestic hierarchy, but to disrupt it. In John Fletcher's *Women Pleased* (*c.* 1619–23), the miser Lopez deprives both his wife Isabella and his servant, Penurio, of sufficient food. As such, the text differs from many examples of the hungry servant type, in that the appetites of Penurio are unambiguously associated with his material conditions. Lopez may decry Penurio for being a 'ravening fellow' (I.ii.83), but his claim that his servant's consumption of 'two apples' is 'monstrous' (I.ii.83), establishes the object of the humour as, in the first instance, the master's miserly attitude, rather than the servant's greed. Indeed, in the case of Isabella, hunger is heavily associated with sexual as well as culinary want. Lopez justifies her scant diet on the grounds that 'Surfits destroy more than the sword' (I.ii.68), and the implication of the phallic imagery is further developed when Penurio declares that she would be 'Getting a good stomack Sir, and she knew where to get meat to it' (I.ii.22). Lopez emerges as both miserly and impotent, with the hunger of the servant existing in parallel with the sexualised hunger of the wife. In large part, this characterisation is associated with Lopez's ambiguous ethnic identity. Celia Caputi argues that 'his surname and characterization betray a vestige of . . . Hispanophobia' (Caputi, 2017, p. 9). It is also possible, however, that the name alludes to Roderigo Lopez, a Portuguese convert to Catholicism, of Jewish ancestry, who was executed in 1594, following accusations that he had attempted to poison Queen Elizabeth. Whether Hispanophobic or anti-Semitic, the text constructs the master as an Other whose treatment of both his servant and his wife situates them in positions of deprivation.

The twin hungers of servant and wife rapidly prompt the awakening of parallel appetites. Penurio emerges as pander to Isabella, providing access to her in exchange for sustenance. Once again, the play deploys the punning conjunction of pregnancy and obesity, with the two characters conceived of as expanding their bellies in tandem. Isabella is described swallowing the messages which Penurio passes to her 'as greedily, / As great-bellyed women do Cherries, stones and all Sir' (II.iv.27–8). The message of her lover is conceived as sustenance, the object of pregnancy cravings, while the sexual intercourse it precedes threatens to prompt her own belly to swell. Penurio, meanwhile, is enjoined by her potential lover Claudio to 'Be fat, be fat' (II.iv.38), and told that he will be fed until he 'crack'st at both ends' (II.iv.44). The parallel mistreatment of servant and wife threatens to produce the inversion of the domestic hierarchy, and establishes the possibility of culinary and sexual rebellion, embodied in their twin swelling bellies. Whereas in *The Taming of the Shrew*, the act of reducing a wife to the status of a servant served to restore the domestic hierarchy, here it threatens to topple it. But at the same time, the play's emphasis upon the culpability of Lopez for the situation of both serves to identify his failings as the cause of these subversive appetites. Like *The*

*Merchant of Venice*, in which the famished Lorenzo finds common cause with his master's daughter, the parallels between servant and wife serve as a means of critiquing a particular, implicitly Othered, form of mastery.

Women, however, are also depicted commanding servants. A significant example is Massinger's *The Picture*, originally performed by the King's Men at both the Globe and the Blackfriars. The plot concerns Mathias, a Bohemian knight who leaves his wife Sophia in sole charge of the family home, to fight for the Kingdom of Hungary in the hope of receiving an extensive reward. The first half of the play features the chastisement of Hilario, a servant and allowed fool whose humour oversteps the mark. Seeking to distract his lady Sophia from her sorrow at her husband's absence in the wars, Hilario resolves 'if I put her not out of her dumps with laughter, / Ile make her howle for anger' (II.i.5–6). The resulting, farcical performance purports to be a report on the progress of the wars, but quickly descends into joking references to her husband's supposed death and accounts of Hilario's own exploits on the field. The response of Sophia is telling. She askes 'am I growne / Contemptible to those I feed?' (II.i.137–8) and declares 'Till his returne, or certainty of his safety, / My doores are shut against thee' (II.i.149–50). By the third act Hilario claims to be 'dieted / Like one set to watch hawkes, and to keepe me waking / My croaking guts make a perpetuall larum' (III.i.1–3). As with Katherina in *The Shrew*, the alternative to good service is a temporary experience of the absolute hunger of vagabondage. However, central to the success of the scheme is the fact that Sophia is prepared not only to punish Hilario's insolence, but also to reward his loyalty. When he is finally able to produce news of her husband's well-being, and is therefore forgiven, the overjoyed servant declares:

> O comfortable wordes; eate I forgiue thee
> And if in this I doe not soone obey you
> And ramne in to the purpose billet me againe
> I' the high way, butler and Cooke be ready
> For I enter like a tyrant. (III.ii.14–19)

The episode establishes Sophia as a woman who is capable of controlling her servants in her husband's absence. And the means by which she achieves this are rooted in her ability to distribute food within the household.

Furthermore, Hilario is not the only character against whom Sophia deploys this strategy. When the absent Mathias attracts the attention of the Hungarian Queen, she dispatches two corrupt courtiers to seduce his wife. Sophia responds by imprisoning the courtiers, depriving them of food and insisting they labour, dressed as women, until they learn to control their desires. She declares that they have 'forgot all hospitable duties' and advises a course of 'labour, and spare diet', insisting that, if they refuse, they will 'perish for hunger' (IV.ii.162; IV.ii.179–80). As with both *Women Pleased* and *The Taming of the Shrew*, the means she adopts are ostensibly justified in medical terms; she asserts 'Ease and excesse in feeding made you wanton; / A plurisie of ill blood you must let out' (IV.ii.176–7). Fasting was specifically prescribed by many humanist educators to control sexual desire, so that Joannes Vives, for example, claimed that 'moche fastynge shall be good, whiche dothe nat feble the bodye but brydell it, and presse it downe, and quenche the heate of youthe' (Vives, 1541, sig. f2$^{v}$). The connections between appetites and desire are thus ostensibly held up as causal, with a basis in the physical bodies of the courtiers. Sophia's solution to the courtiers' uncontrolled appetites implies their resemblance to the grotesque, lower-class body. Having dressed them as female servants and presented them to the Queen and her husband, Sophia declares:

> they have learnd
> Their severall trades to live by, and payd nothing
> But cold, and hunger for 'em, and may now
> Set vp for them selves for heere I give 'em over[.] (V.iii.151–4)

The language is of service and apprenticeship. The speech places Sophia in a position of mastery over the courtiers, while ironically asserting a degree of progression on their part, claiming that under her tutelage they have achieved the status of journeymen who have 'learnd / Their severall trades'. The implication of the class and gender roles into which the courtiers have been forced is that their inability to control their appetites has led them to forfeit their ruling-class identity. They have 'forfeited' the 'usage of men', and can only hope to 'suffer / Like the most slavish women' (IV.ii.73–5). Sophia can assert that they are 'slaves to [their] lust, not me' (IV.ii.192), specifically linking their present subjugation to their former actions. At the same time, she locates them within a model of household labour which is implicitly opposed to the excesses of the court. Indeed, there are parallels here with the position of Katherina in *The Shrew*, for the humiliation of the courtiers is in large part engineered through the deployment of Hilario's play-acting. Once the two men have been stripped, Sophia dresses Hilario in Ricardo's suit. He then tells the courtier 'thinke of thy taske. / Forget such vanities; my livery there, / Will serve thee to worke in' (IV.ii.195–7). Hilario becomes the self-proclaimed 'governor' of the two courtiers and engages in a parodic performance of elite status.

It is not only against the courtiers that Sophia deploys her control of food. By the end of the play, her husband too has been situated as a servant. In the final act, he returns home believing that she has committed adultery in his absence. Her response is to punish him for his lack of trust in her, placing him in a position of vulnerability parallel to that of both the servant Hilario and the chastised courtiers. He arrives to find an absence of any hospitable welcome, asking 'is my house turnd / To a wildernesse?' Not only does she withhold food, but also the possibility of sexual intercourse, for having presented Mathias and the Queen with the courtiers, she declares that she intends to enter a nunnery. Mathias can safeguard his marriage only by asserting his wife's right to retain control of the distribution of food and, by implication, her own sexuality, declaring that she may 'Feast, revele, banquet, and make choise with whom' (V.iii.212). Sophia's neglect of household duty is explicitly justified by her husband's servile inability to master his jealousy; as he himself acknowledges, 'Tis not in me to master so my passions' (I.i.136). On the return of Mathias, she disciplines him for his lack of trust in her fidelity. Through his susceptibility to jealousy and his hypocrisy in only narrowly avoiding the seductive designs of the Queen, Mathias has forfeited his rights as a husband, just as the two courtiers forfeited the privilege of rank. Acting according to instinct, they have reduced themselves to the level of servants. Yet by contrast with texts such as *Campaspe* or *The Bashful Lover*, the play explicitly holds up hunger and service as remedies for their base indulgence of appetite.

Women occupied an ambiguous position within the early modern household. They were defined by duties of both service and command, and their service was implicated within the basic production of food. That ambiguity introduces an additional level of complexity to the representation of the hungry servant. In *The Taming of the Shrew*, the spectre of the servant's hunger is deployed as a means of asserting the relative privilege experienced by those wives who acknowledge their place in the social hierarchy. In *Women Pleased*, by contrast, a shared experience of hunger becomes the basis of a troubling solidarity. Perhaps most significantly, however, the inevitable centrality of food in these depictions of service raises the possibility of a particular form of domestic power. In the case of *The Shrew*, that power is endorsed, precisely as it is appropriated, by Petruchio's attempts to inculcate submission in his wife. But in *The Picture* the troubling spectre of parallel appetites places both servant and master in positions of subjugation. Indeed, the episode also highlights the position of power which Sophia holds within the household. For all that the play notionally endorses moderation, an air of profound discord is introduced, through the necessity 'Neither to dote too much nor doubt a wife' (V.iii.225), through the images of subjection with which the play ends, and through the absolute freedom which Sophia is promised. If to control food is to command obedience, then women assume a potentially troubling position of power for the contemporary audience.

## Conclusion

The servant's appetite is ostensibly reduced to a purely comic trope. Detached from the material conditions of hunger, it is reconstituted as an inherent characteristic of the lower-class servingman. The servingman's desire for food is consistently used as an Other against which to define an onstage elite. In *Campaspe*, this opposition is presented as one of body to mind and excess to restraint which, while it emerges from pressure at the base of society, disavows these material factors, presenting the servant's appetite as an historical constant. The representation of the servant serves to detach appetite from hunger, justifying ruling-class superiority and binding an elite together in disdain. Once detached from the literal referent of hunger, however, the servant's appetite increasingly accrues metaphorical connotations, becoming inscribed within the context of an emergent capitalist economy as a mechanism to comprehend disruptive processes of acquisition and social mobility. It provides the elite with a way of conceptualising, but simultaneously distancing themselves from, forces threatening their society. At a time when major economic changes were subverting the ordered system of rank around which early modern society was structured, the restless, material character of the servant's appetite embodied those forces at the base of society which threatened to overturn its ideological superstructure. By associating these forces with the resolutely lower-class appetites of the male domestic servant, the theatre distances them from the upper classes.

Yet that process of mystification is only ever partial. Precisely because hunger constitutes an inherent constituent of human experience in the period, the servant has the capacity to become the embodiment of, rather than the exception to, the dominant social principle. Indeed, attention to the servingman's appetite reveals not only the existence of a profound crisis in service, but also the extent to which that crisis is perceived as threatening the entire social order. It is easy, of course, to dismiss these fears as paranoia. As Schalkwyk has noted, 'Master-servant relations were . . . not displaced by capitalism; rather their worst aspects were mobilised as an instrument of complete exploitation of workers' (Schalkwyk, 2008, p. 30). While this is at least partially true, it is unwise to overemphasise the degree of continuity which it entails. The extraction of surplus value is a characteristic of every class society. But the specific form which that extraction takes exerts a profound, determining influence on that society. Attention to the representation of the servant's appetite reveals a society which is not only changing, but actually thinking about that process of change. Critics such as Neill have tended to emphasise the role played by ideas in the texts of the period, arguing that 'In some ways it may actually be more important to understand what people *thought* was happening to their world than to gauge the accuracy of these beliefs, since what people believe to be true is typically what determines the way they act' (Neill, 2000, p. 4). But attention to the servingman's appetite demonstrates that the way people think is in turn dependent on the material reality which they encounter. Representation of the common servingman is bound up with the ways in which the theatre thought about, and in its own way attempted to theorise, the alarming changes within service and society. Their appetites embody a wider tendency to consume, prompted by the rise of capitalism.

It is therefore significant that representations of the intersection of service and gender are frequently defined by the reinsertion of hunger. In *The Shrew*, hunger is deployed as a means to lower Katherina to a position below that of the servants within the domestic hierarchy. In *Women Pleased*, a shared experience of hunger provides the basis of an aspirant solidarity between servant and wife. And in *The Picture*, hunger is a tool deployed by Sophia to ensure obedience on the part not only of her servant and the corrupt courtiers who attempt to seduce her, but also her own husband. Indeed, it is notable that here hunger functions not as the basis of appetite, but rather as its antithesis. In a world dominated by expansive proto-capitalist appetites, it is hunger and labour which emerge as necessary barriers to desire. Nevertheless, even here there are profound tensions. For depictions of the intersection of gender and service also inescapably foreground a particular form of domestic power. In Greene's *The Scottish History*, the appetite of the servant Slipper leaves him dangerously open to external influences. In a similar manner, representations of husbands, wives and their servants raise the possibility that it is women, rather than men, who may acquire ultimate control over servants. In a world where the ability to instil loyalty is dependent upon the ability to fill bellies, women's dominant position in relation to the production of food in the household becomes a source of profound concern.

CHAPTER 3

# *The Food Gift*

The representation of food gifts is crucial for understanding the role played by hunger and appetite in the Renaissance theatre, because the gifts tend to highlight that these drives could be transitory, produced by material circumstances. While the appetite of the hungry servant is primarily visible as a definitive characteristic, food gifts raise the possibility that hunger might be alleviated. The texts in which they appear are replete with sudden shifts from hunger to satiety, or depict those who gorge to excess only to find themselves suddenly hungry and in need of aid. In doing so, these texts reflect the importance of food gifts within the material practice of early modern life. Residual traditions of patronage were rooted in the mutual exchange of food gifts. In the absence of an established welfare state, charitable distributions of food played a critical role in alleviating the distress and discontent of the poor. But these texts also respond to perceptions of a crisis within these traditions. A huge body of popular literature decried the decline of hospitality. And as Felicity Heal has noted, although it is true that these texts draw upon well-established tropes of a lost golden age, there is nevertheless a 'proliferation of comment and advice in the half-century between the 1580s and the 1630s' (Heal, 1984, p. 68). Attention to the representation of the food gift provides a means to explore how the early modern theatre conceptualised both the causes and consequences of these broader material and ideological shifts, and reveals one of the most significant means through which the drama engaged with issues of plenty and want at a time of pronounced socio-economic change.

Existing critical material on contemporary hospitable practice provides an invaluable resource for understanding these transactions, highlighting the degree to which the distribution of food gifts serves to announce socio-economic identity.[1] The utility of this work for an analysis of hunger and

[1] Key work in this respect has been carried out by Daryl Palmer, Kari Boyd McBride and Lisa Celovsky. The most wide-ranging approach is that of Palmer, which emphasises the plurality of hospitality in this period, highlighting '*moments when a representation of hospitality becomes useful, strategically and tactically, for a narrowly defined class interest which either succeeds or fails at turning*

appetite is, however, hampered by terminological confusion. Critics invariably distinguish between charity and hospitality, but while these words appear to reflect the language used by contemporaries, they imply the existence of clear-cut distinctions between different practices of giving which did not exist in the early modern period. As Heal notes, although many texts distinguished between 'the sort of feasting that promoted love and amity, and alms-giving, which could take various forms, but was not closely related to hospitality', these distinctions were still fragile and ambiguous (Heal, 1990, p. 16). Ballads such as 'Times Alteration' treat the two forms of gift giving as essentially synonymous, recalling a point at which hospitality was 'cherisht . . . of many' and condemning a contemporary society in which 'Charitie waxeth cold' (Parker, 1629). And the English defended themselves against charges of gluttony by declaring that their tables were 'not furnished with many dishes, all for one man's diet, but severally for many mens appetite, and not only prepared for the family, but for strangers and relief of the poor' (Moryson, 1617, p. 150). Failure to acknowledge these ambiguities has prompted a tendency to detach analysis of the food gift from wider critical approaches to poverty.[2] Thus, issues of order and need have frequently been detached from those of power and status. Only by understanding the boundaries between charity and hospitality as fundamentally ambiguous and contested is it possible to comprehend the significance of the food gift for the representation of hunger and appetite on the early modern stage.

The period's diverse and interlinking traditions of charity and hospitality can therefore be usefully interpreted through theories of gift exchange, which provide a framework for the exploration of the degree to which hunger and appetite are constructed as the material motivation for the exchange of onstage food gifts. Since the work of Marcel Mauss and

*(appropriating) that representation for its own needs*' (Palmer, 1992, p. 26 [Palmer's italics]). Palmer's analysis is reminiscent of a Gramscian notion of hegemony, whereby 'the development and expansion of [one] particular group are conceived of, and presented, as being the motor force of a universal expansion' (Gramsci, 1971, p. 181). It provides an invaluable tool for highlighting the degree to which the representation of hospitality served specific class interests, while functioning as a 'total mystification of the culture's patterns of dominance' (Palmer, 1992, p. 28).

2 Since the 1980s, critics have displayed a pronounced interest in the issue of poverty, with work focussing primarily on the image of the masterless rogue. Key texts include the work of Stephen Greenblatt, Paul Brown, Steve Carroll and Linda Woodbridge. But attention to these marginal figures, and a consequent propensity to ignore the role of gift giving outside the immediate context of charity, has tended to underestimate the role played by material change and the shifting nature of hunger and need in this period. Likewise, the work of Palmer, McBride and Celovsky has been hampered by overestimates of the degree of differentiation between various forms of gift giving, which has led critics to identify the gift as primarily a status-building tool, without interrogating the material basis of the power which it lends to the various hosts which appear in early modern literature.

Bronisław Malinowski, theorists have tended to situate different forms of gift giving on a spectrum. On one side lies the commodity proper, motivated purely by the force of exchange and, on the other, the arguably impossible 'pure' gift, in which notions of reciprocity or personal gain are entirely absent.[3] The distribution of food to the hungry may appear to entail the latter approach, but gift theory highlights the implication of these transactions in the exertion of power and the acquisition of status. Particularly significant, however, for a Marxist perspective, is the degree to which this opposition enables critics to situate these transactions within a more general transition from feudal to capitalist modes of production in the early modern period. Analyses of the gift have consistently associated the exchange of gifts with anti-capitalist forces, and in particular with pre-capitalist society, while identifying capitalist society with the circulation of commodities.[4] In this sense, the early modern period can be read as a time when these two forms interact and conflict with each other, and the representation of the gift takes on a particular significance as a means of conceptualising or dispelling the tensions consequent on this confrontation. In the final instance, therefore, gift theory provides a framework to highlight the role of hunger and appetite in articulating this overall process of transition.

The impact of these insights has, however, been weakened by an emphasis upon the process of exchange. Despite their predominantly anti-capitalist slant, gift theorists, with the notable exception of Chris Gregory, have tended to eschew the analytical resources offered by Marxist tradition. More recently, however, significant work in this vein has been carried out by Costas Lapavitsas, whose primary focus is on use value. Lapavitsas argues that the most significant aspect of the role played by use value in the gift is its contingency. He notes that a gift 'might or might not be useful to its giver', whereas in the case of the commodity 'if the buyer perceived that use value did not exist, the transaction would not take place at all'

[3] Mauss, for example, argues that primitive systems of gift exchange are defined by the fact that although 'in theory [gifts] are voluntary, in reality they are given and reciprocated obligatorily' (Mauss, 2002, p. 3). But for Derrida, by contrast, the true gift is that which 'in suspending economic calculation, no longer gives rise to exchange' (Derrida, 1992, p. 7).

[4] Gregory argues that 'Marx was able to develop a very important proposition: that commodity exchange is an exchange of alienable things between transactors who are in a state of reciprocal independence . . . The corollary of this is that non-commodity (gift) exchange is an exchange of inalienable things between transactors who are in a state of reciprocal dependence. This proposition is only implicit in Marx's analysis but it is . . . a precise definition of gift exchange' (Gregory, 1982, p. 12). Likewise, within the field of literary criticism, Eagleton frames this opposition within the context of contending classes, noting that 'an obsession with strict exchanges is typical of middle-class utilitarianism; the aristocracy are traditionally more spendthrift' (Eagleton, 1992, p. 395).

(Lapavitsas, 2003, p. 40). It is this unique relationship with use value, and therefore with need, which distinguishes the gift from other types of exchange. It is only through an understanding of this relationship that it becomes possible truly to understand the relationship between hunger, appetite and the food gift. A focus on the presence or absence of use value within gift exchange provides a means to root early modern depictions of the distribution of food within the context of an underlying awareness of the interrelation of plenty and want. In doing so, it becomes possible to move beyond an analysis which privileges the perceived benefits to the donor, in favour of an approach which acknowledges the significance of the recipient.

I will begin my analysis with *Pericles* (1607), a play in which a nostalgic image of hunger alleviated by the gift emphasises the degree to which the power associated with the position of host was reliant upon the existence of scarcity and want in early modern society. Through attention to *Timon of Athens*, I will explore the failure of these bonds of necessity on the advent of the excessive distribution of gifts made possible by the rise of a credit-based economy, and will highlight the consequent marginalisation of use value in the representation of these exchanges. With reference to Massinger's *The Unnatural Combat* (*c.* 1626), I consider how early modern texts associate the development of expansive appetites with the decline of charity and the exclusion of the poor from the space of gift giving. By drawing upon these three texts, I will assess how notions of a crisis in charity and hospitality are used to articulate specific attitudes towards hunger and appetite, with particular emphasis on the degree to which representation of these drives provides the theatre with a means to evaluate wider changes within early modern society.

## Hunger, Nostalgia and the Gift

In early modern England, an abundance of biblical precedent insisted upon the importance of distributing food to the poor. The Book of Job declared 'If I have withheld the poor from their desire, or have caused the eyes of the widow to fail; Or have eaten my morsel myself alone, and the fatherless hath not eaten thereof ... Then let mine arm fall from my shoulder blade, and mine arm be broken from the bone' (Job 31:16–22). Isaiah asserted that 'if thou draw out thy soul to the hungry, and satisfy the afflicted soul; then shall thy light rise in obscurity, and thy darkness be as the noon day' (Isaiah 58:10). In Luke, Christ explains that obedience to the Ten Commandments is not enough to ensure salvation, and enjoins his followers 'sell all that thou hast, and distribute unto the poor, and thou shalt have treasure in heaven' (Luke 18:22). This was also a period, of course, in which commentators were increasingly desirous to identify who, precisely, was in need of such assistance. Beier notes the rise of 'a more critical opinion of idleness, rising numbers of itinerant poor, and state intervention to separate the deserving from the reprobate' (Beier, 1985, p. 122). Yet in order to understand that process of exclusion, it is first necessary to take charitable distribution seriously. In late Elizabethan and early Jacobean England, even the most radical reformers acknowledged the need to distribute food to the deserving poor, and this emphasis must be understood not solely as an instance of hypocrisy or legitimation. For a broad range of social, religious and political reasons, the distribution of food to the hungry played an integral role within early modern society.

Indeed, in the case of hunger, the food gift has the potential to alleviate one of the most basic human drives, and that element of usefulness therefore acquires a degree of importance which has the potential to take priority over exchange. It is this emphasis on use value which recurs most frequently in contemporary texts lamenting the decline of charity and hospitality. Thomas Cooper demands of his readers in *The Art of Giving*:

> Hath not the abundance of selfe-loue eaten out all hearty and true affection to each other, while euery one seekes his owne, and not that which may concerne the common good: nay, with the generall wracke of the publike weale? (Cooper, 1615, p. vii).

The *Christmas Lamentation* declares that 'Places where Christmas Reuells did keepe, / Is now become habitations for shéepe' (*Christmas Lamentation*, 1635). Contemporary complaints at the demise of charity and hospitality consistently emphasise the degree to which the decline of the food gift entails the triumph of exchange value over use value. For this reason, in exploring the relationship between use value and the gift it seems unwise wholly to disregard Derrida's claim that the gift is 'that which interrupts economy', and which 'in suspending economic calculation, no longer gives rise to exchange' (Derrida, 1992, p. 7). The unique characteristic of the gift is not only that use value is contingent, but also that in certain circumstances it may be placed in a position of priority over and above the impersonal logic of exchange. The existence of this possibility means that hunger has a significant role in defining the precise nature of gift exchange. Through the medium of the gift, early modern writers are able to deploy hunger to challenge the logic of the market and assert the overriding significance of use value and need.

In deploying the food gift in this manner, the early modern literature of hospitality prefigures the tendency within theoretical accounts of the gift to associate its decline with the rise of the commodity and the shift to a capitalist mode of production. Although the binary nature of these accounts has been criticised by Lapavitsas, it can scarcely be denied that in the texts of the early modern period, the gift constitutes a key symbol of residual practices and of class subjects opposed to emergent capitalist forms of exchange.[5] As such, it is instructive to turn to the play *Pericles* (1607), by George Wilkins and William Shakespeare. A product of dual authorship and multiple sources, its fragmented text is rooted in an imagined past, but one which is repeatedly threatened by references to emergent forms of exchange and exploitation. The narrator, 'ancient Gower', would have been a familiar figure for an early modern audience, but one who, above all, was associated with a past that had been lost (I.0.2). The story has its origins in a fourteenth-century text by John Gower himself, and as such the 'song that old was sung' is defined by its openly acknowledged relation to antiquity (I.0.1). Yet it seems clear that this association with the past is only ever partial. References to vagrancy legislation, to engrossers who 'never leave gaping till they swallowed the whole parish' (II.i.33–34), and to the commodification of the female body in the context of the brothel, ensure that the contemporary experience of commodity exchange constantly threatens to break through. If one accepts John Jowett's claim that 'it is precisely the interaction or, in Masten's term, "intercourse" of the agents that defines the particular sociality of a given text', then it is possible to read the diverse sources and collaborative authorship of the text as accentuating this underlying conflict between modes of production (Jowett, 2003, p. 220). Through particular attention to those scenes written by Shakespeare's collaborator, defined as they are by episodes of famine and hardship, it is possible to discern the extent to which the depiction of hunger is implicated within a contested periodisation, both acknowledging emergent capitalist elements and, through the representation of the gift, seeking to efface them.

As with laments at the decline of hospitality, *Pericles* is a play which places great stress on the hunger of those who receive food gifts, and a consequent emphasis on the significance of use value in the exchange. The play is episodic in structure, depicting the travels of the eponymous

[5] Lapavitsas claims that 'the binary opposition between commodity and gift cannot adequately serve Gregory's purposes because it is exclusively based on the property of exchangeability' (Lapavitsas, 2003, p. 34). Instead, he notes that in reality 'the capitalist mode of production leads to emergence of a multitude of non-market relations that are stamped by capital' (Lapavitsas, 2003, p. 33).

Prince through the Mediterranean, where he encounters a wide range of different societies, ruled by monarchs who range from benevolent kings to incestuous tyrants. At the end of the first act, Pericles arrives at the city of Tarsus to discover that the population has reached such extremes of hunger that they have been forced to eat each other. Although his fleet is initially mistaken for an invading army, the Prince tells the citizens that his ships are instead 'stored with corn to make your needy bread' (I.iv.93). Bread was often a central component of charitable gifts, and by implication the foodstuff marks the recipient as one defined by hunger and need, rather than desire and appetite.[6] But more significantly, the state of hunger is one that the gift will end. Pericles declares that his gift will 'give them life whom hunger starved half dead' (I.iv.94). The poor of Tarsus are capable of being relieved by Pericles's generosity. It can therefore be argued that the interrelation of hunger and the food gift in this text highlights the temporality of the former condition. Where the ambiguous distinction between hunger and appetite found in the representation of the servingman in the period's theatre derives from the permanent nature of the lower-class character's need for food, the distribution of food to the hungry demonstrates the extent to which hunger is a state that can be ended through the action of others.

Indeed, even the representation of these gifts seems to emphasise their relationship to need, and to undermine the significance of exchange. The early modern theatre is notable for the frequency with which it depicts the act of feasting. But the simple act of distributing bread to the hungry takes place offstage, removing that element of vicarious enjoyment which Nunn has outlined as central to the staging of food. In similar fashion, when Pericles is shipwrecked and offered aid by a group of fishermen, the foods which they offer him are never displayed, but are simply described in dialogue. The master of the fishermen declares that he shall 'have flesh for holidays, fish for fasting-days, and moreo'er puddings and flap-jacks' (II.i.79–80). By concealing the act of giving and the act of consumption, the play eliminates the sensuous dimension of the eating of food and

[6] In Callowdon, Warwickshire, Henry Lord Berkeley distributed 'pottage, beef, mutton, bread, and beer three days a week' (Greaves, 1981, p. 580). William Oglander regularly left bread for the poor on his father's tomb (Greaves, 1981, p. 581). More generally, Andrew Appleby remarks that 'wheaten bread loaves' constituted 'the poor man's single most important expense' in sixteenth- and seventeenth-century London (Appleby, 1978, p. 5). By contrast, Felicity Heal has noted that food gifts intended for the maintenance of patronage relationships are notable for the infrequency with which they involve bread, for there is 'hardly a mention of grain or its products' in those account books of the period which detail the distribution of food gifts to those of equal or higher social standing (Heal, 2014, p. 38).

reduces it to the simple condition of ending hunger. This in turn highlights the role of need in the exchange. What is important for the people of Tyre is not the nature of the food which they consume, but simply that they have food to eat. The status-building activities which accompany the act of gift exchange are relegated to a position of secondary importance precisely because the gifts in question are directed towards the satisfaction of a fundamental need.

Furthermore, this emphasis on use value is accentuated by the overtly intertextual nature of the play. Through its relation to the various incarnations of the Pericles story, the text constantly opens the possibility of actions which do not consist of the Prince's free distribution of gifts. In Laurence Twine's prose text, *The Patterne of Painefull Adventures* (1576), for example, the Prince initially takes payment for the corn, but later 'doubting lest by this deede, he should seem to put off the dignitie of a prince, and put on the countenance of a merchant rather than a giver, when he had received the price of the wheate, he restored it back againe' (Twine, 1966, VI, p. 433). In the play, by contrast, Pericles declares that he looks not 'for reverence but for love, / And harbourage for ourself, our ships, and men' (I.iv.97–98), appearing consciously to distance himself from the initial element of exchange which characterises the earlier text. For Stephen Mullaney, the substitution constitutes part of Shakespeare and Wilkins's more general project within the play to reconstitute drama as a 'purely aesthetic phenomenon, free from history and from historical determination' (Mullaney, 2013, p. 101). Yet attention to the significance of hunger makes evident the degree to which the change emphasises specific characteristics of gift exchange, in a manner which hardly accords with a notion of the play as intentionally ahistorical. By removing the element of trade, the play foregrounds the selfless nature of the gift. But at the same time, in effacing the consideration of rank, the dominant factor in his predecessor's change of heart, the play constructs Pericles's gift as motivated not simply by a desire to act in a manner befitting his status as a Prince, but also by the element of need which necessitates the gift. In this sense, hunger alone is ostensibly constituted as a force capable of challenging an emergent economic logic. It is precisely the exception to the usual rules of impersonal exchange, in which use value can be asserted as more significant than exchange value.

Nevertheless, in *Pericles* the representation of the food gift is far from being entirely free from this element of exchange, since the distribution of food to the hungry places the Prince in a position of control. Forced to leave his daughter in Cleon's care, Pericles is told by the monarch:

> Fear not, my lord, but think
> Your grace that fed my country with your corn
> For which the people's prayers still fall upon you,
> Must in your child be thought on. (III.iii.18–21)

Immediately evident is the extent to which the speech makes clear the reciprocal nature of gift exchange. The child stands for the Prince, who is 'thought on' in her. But the complex syntax of the speech means that the substitution of child for father is divided by two clauses addressing the corn which Pericles has distributed. It is not their love for him which is most important, but rather the act of distributing corn to the hungry. The play therefore seems to endorse a conception of the gift which coincides with those theoretical texts which emphasise its reciprocal nature. To understand this element of redress or reciprocity, it is necessary to acknowledge its temporal character. As theorists such as Slavoj Žižek and Pierre Bourdieu have argued, gift exchange must be understood diachronically. Indeed, for Žižek, it is this temporal dimension which defines the unique character of the gift. He argues that 'the time elapsed between me giving a gift and the other side returning it to me creates a social link which lasts (for a time, at least): we are all linked together with bonds of debt' (Žižek, 2008, p. 7). It is this social and intrapersonal dimension that distinguishes the gift from commodity exchange, which 'enables us to have contacts with others without entering into proper relations with them' (Žižek, 2008, p. 7). The food gift has the potential not only to exist in opposition to the dominance of exchange in the commodity, but also to offset the impersonal dimension to the market.

Moreover, in *Pericles*, this temporal dimension is related to the role played by hunger. For as the pre-emptive nature of Cleon's speech makes clear, in and of themselves the bonds formed by gift exchange are fragile. He declares that: 'If neglection / Should therein make me vile, the common body, / By you relieved, would force me to my duty' (III.iii.21–3). Cleon acknowledges the possibility of 'neglection', in a manner which anticipates his later betrayal. The very fact that Pericles has no power to enforce the good treatment of his daughter highlights the element of trust inherent in the exchange of gifts. The play accords with Bourdieu's emphasis on the propensity of the gift to be deferred, forgotten or rejected. But at the same time, the speech also prepares the audience for Cleon's eventual fate, destroyed by his own people as punishment for his betrayal of Pericles. In his speech, the body politic is figured as precisely a body. Cleon, the head, has been in many ways made irrelevant. Pericles has fulfilled his commitment to feed the people of the country and Cleon has been placed in a vulnerable position by the supposedly free gift which Pericles has distributed. It is Pericles who has relieved the 'common body', resulting in the loss of Cleon's authority over them. They are prepared to 'force' him to his duty. The speech emphasises the power of the gift to forge bonds between men, but the extent to which the gift works upon the 'common body' rather than Cleon makes clear the vital importance of hunger in the maintenance of these bonds. The fragility of its reciprocal component is the foundation upon which its specifically intrapersonal character rests.

The undercurrent of lower-class violence present in Cleon's speech has particular significance in the context of the text's earlier description of famine, for the hunger which scarcity creates is figured as the source of the upheaval within the hierarchical structures of Tarsus. Cleon describes how:

> Those mothers, who to nuzzle up their babes
> Thought nought too curious, are ready now
> To eat those little darlings whom they loved.
> So sharp are hunger's teeth, that man and wife
> Draw lots who first shall die to lengthen life . . . (I.iv.42–6)

The text offsets the acquired appetites of plenty against the all-encompassing need for food which characterises the extreme hunger produced by famine. Hunger is presented as the source of perverted appetites, threatening the natural order of mothers and children, husbands and wives. The emphasis on both a sudden reversion in culinary fortune, and the cannibalism that might consequently be unleashed, reflects common tropes of the period. Thomas Dekker, for instance, provides a lengthy description of a mother during the siege of Jerusalem, who 'with hunger is constrayned to kill her best beloued and onely Sonne, and eate him' (Dekker, 1618, sig. E1$^{r}$). George Wither compares 'Those dainty pallats which could relish nought / But what was set farre off, and dearly bought', with the desperation of famine, which drives the populace to feed 'on mouldy scraps; and beg them too for need' (Wither, 1628, p. 21). In *Pericles*, however, these images of reversion and disorder acquire additional resonance from the social upheavals which preceded the play's probable date of performance. The lower classes of the Midlands area rose against local landowners between May and June 1607. The uprising was characterised by anti-gentry violence and fuelled by hopes of uniting with rioting apprentices in London, with lower-class hunger emerging as a powerful threat to social order (Manning, 1988, pp. 229–46). In *Pericles*, by contrast, images of cannibalism and disorder are raised only to be dispelled by the gifts which Pericles distributes. It is the absence of the gift which produces cannibalism, and in this manner the text embodies similar concerns to *The Art of Giving*, which declares 'if wee thus bite and teare one another, shall we not be deuoured of each other?' (Cooper, 1615, p. vi). In the Midlands, perceptions of ruling-class indifference prompted lower-class violence; in *Pericles*, the social consequences of hunger are arrested by the distribution of gifts. The text implies that it is necessary to arrest the dominance of the market, because the alternative is a far greater departure from the status quo. Hunger emerges as a force capable of restricting capitalist exchange, but by implication its power to do so springs in the final instance from the violent energies of the lower classes.

Crucially, when considered in tandem with the play's emphasis upon the strength of the bonds which gift giving might form between the hungry populace and elite figures such as Pericles, it becomes possible to read the text in the context of that form of contemporary political discourse which James Holstun has termed monarcho-populism. Through this mutually beneficial ideology, 'monarchists legitimated themselves through paternalistic resistance to capitalist encroachments on small producers, while small producers legitimated themselves by invoking loyalty to a reigning monarch or Protector against some menacing middle man or interloper' (Holstun, 2004, p. 57). The discourse emerges with particular clarity in the case of monarchical pronouncements on the decline of gift giving.[7] But it also informs wider discussions in the period regarding the Corn Laws and the precise manner in which the ruling classes should respond to outbreaks of famine and dearth.[8] Where one section of the ruling class sought to

[7] In a series of proclamations, King James lamented 'The decay of Hospitalitie in all the parts of this Our Kingdome' (Larkin and Hughes, 1973, I, p. 356), attacking those amongst the gentry and nobility who preferred to spend their time in the capital rather than the countryside, and warning that soon 'England will onely be London' (James I, 2002, p. 343). It is particularly notable that such pronouncements recurred in times of famine and dearth. Heal notes that 'proclamations in 1596, 1608, 1621, and 1622 were all issued in years of harvest failure, and the crown's enthusiasm for the enforcement of these acts seems to have owed much to anxieties about supply and the dangers of disorder' (Heal, 1990, p. 118).

[8] The records of the Privy Council are notable for the frequency with which they are forced to reissue their edicts banning the staying or engrossing of corn. In 1596, they denounced those Justices of the Peace who were themselves 'corne-masters' and who consequently, it was claimed, tended to 'neglect th'execution of suche good orders as have bin devised for the due serving of the markettes and avoidinge those abuses that are practised by covetous persons to inhaunce the prices of corne' (Dasent, 1902, pp. 94–5). Such official hypocrisy was identified as a clear risk to the social order, with one report declaring 'in some places the meaner persons complaine that they are compelled to serve the markettes where some of them being Justices of the Peace are them selves and other theire tenauntes, servantes and dependauntes for the most part spared and forborne' (Dasent, 1902, p. 82). The subjection of use value to exchange value is for some sections of the ruling class perceived as a source of profit, but for others the potential root of dangerous social upheavals.

strengthen the power of the market and exchange, others hoped to restrain it. In *Pericles*, the representation of food gifts foregrounds the power of hunger to arrest the logic of the market, while also revealing the degree to which the politics of hunger has the potential to remain constrained within residual feudal formations. It situates both giver and recipient in an intrapersonal, hierarchical relationship characteristic of a feudal ideology. Lower-class hunger works against an emergent capitalist mode of production, but through the food gift it legitimates residual upper-class forms of control.

Furthermore, the ideological meaning of the text must be seen in the context of the play's performance history. *Pericles* became a byword for popularity. It was originally performed by the King's Men at the Globe, but there were multiple revivals both by that company and by Sir Richard Cholmley's Men, including one in 1631 for the reopening of the Globe.[9] As Suzanne Gossett has noted 'the King's Men would certainly have chosen a guaranteed success to announce their reappearance and to maximise their takings' (Gossett, 2014, p. 3). Yet, as Pierre Bourdieu argues, 'position-taking changes, even when the position remains identical, whenever there is a change in the universe of options that are simultaneously offered for producers and consumers to choose from' (Bourdieu, 1993, p. 30). The significance of *Pericles* at its first performance is, of necessity, very different from that which inheres in a revival twenty-four years later. Ben Jonson, in his poem 'Ode to Himself' (1629), condemned those audiences who preferred the play to his own work, declaring:

> Some mouldy tale,
> Like *Pericles*, and stale
> As the shrieve's crusts, and nasty as his fish-
> Scraps, out of every dish
> Thrown forth and raked into the common tub,
> May keep up the play-club;
> There sweepings do as well
> As the best ordered meal. (l.21–28)

Jonson's culinary imagery figures the play itself as a food gift, the leftovers of the Sheriff's feast, designed to ease the hunger of the many, rather than the refined appetites of the few. The terms 'mouldy' and 'stale', meanwhile, attempt to rework the play's persistent presence on the stage as a mark not

9 Pericles was amongst the repertoire of Sir Richard Cholmley's Men when they performed at the household of Sir John Yorke in Yorkshire at Christmastide, 1609–10 (Greenfield, 2009, pp. 299–300).

of its classic status, but rather of its irrelevance. Yet *Pericles* is a play which from the very beginning was designed to be old. Its investment in the representation of a threatened antiquity may, arguably, have constituted a significant factor in its enduring capacity to attract large audiences. The practice of reviving *Pericles* asserts, simultaneously, the significance not only of the play itself, but also of the practice of gift giving. At the same time, the association of the play with age seems likely to have reworked the delicate balance of antiquity and modernity which defines the text. The very fact that those watching the play are aware of its relative age as a cultural product makes possible a reading which assumes not the threatened nature of gift giving, but rather its complete erasure.

## Appetite and the Crisis of Plenty

On the early modern stage food gifts are not distributed simply to those who are hungry, but also to the elite, so it is necessary to consider the gift as it relates to the representation of appetites which are detached from hunger. This was a period when traditions of hospitality were increasingly distinct from charitable giving, as hospitality became associated with a select group or elite. Processes of urbanisation and an accompanying rise in the discourse of civility prompted separation from the land and a tendency to restrict hospitality to an immediate social circle. The moralist Philip Stubbes, for instance, declared 'such is their hospitality, that the poor have the least part of it: you shall have 20, 40, 60, yea a C. li. spent in some one house in banqueting and festing, yet the poor shall have little or nothing' (Stubbes, 1583, sig. $J3^{r}$). Caleb Dalechamp distinguished true hospitality from hospitality 'falsely so-called', identifying the latter as 'the keeping of a good table; at which seldome or never any other are entertained then kinsfolks, friends, and able neighbours, merry companions, parasites, jesters, and tellers of news' (Dalechamp, 1632, pp. 6–7). This process was a source of anxiety not only because it risked excluding the needy, but because it implied potentially ruinous expenditure and the distribution of food to those who were not hungry. Stubbes cautions that 'if hospitalitie flowe over into superfluitie and riotous excesse, it is not tollerable', and expresses his fear that such excess has continued 'so long and so greevously', that it will see 'many of his Maisters out of dores before it be long' (Stubbes, 1583, sig. $J1^{r}$; sig. $J3^{r}$). Likewise, John Downame condemns those who, rather than give to the poor, 'spend like prodigals ... in feasting and banquetting, in building and brauerie, in gaming and reuelling, and all other excesse and riot' (Downame, 1616, p. 14). With the exclusion of the poor, the food gift emerges not as a means of alleviating hunger, but rather as a practice generating dangerous levels of consumption.

One text which embodies the tensions emerging from this widespread distribution of gifts is *Timon of Athens*, by Shakespeare and Middleton. By contrast with *Pericles*, there is a complete absence of evidence regarding its contemporary performance, and as Anthony Dawson and Gretchen Minton have noted, it is 'distinctly possible' that it was never staged at all during the Renaissance (Dawson and Minton, 2008, p. 109). The play depicts the downfall of a wealthy Athenian whose profligacy leads him to be surrounded by flatterers. They feast at his expense and receive extravagant gifts, which eventually, and predictably, lead to his bankruptcy. Coppélia Kahn reads *Timon* as embodying the excesses of the Jacobean court, arguing that it deploys the gift to comment on wider practices of patronage. Bevington and Smith likewise situate the text in the context of James's extravagance, although stressing that they read it not as a conscious reworking of Jacobean decadence, but rather 'to ask what sort of contemporary resonance an English audience might have seen in this play' (Bevington and Smith, 1999, p. 80). Critics have tended to emphasise either the basic material changes taking place in early modern society or the specific agency of Timon or the King.[10] But most have acknowledged the significance of a culture of borrowing, of the honours scandal and the rising cash nexus. However, in exploring the relationship between these systemic and individual aspects to the crisis of gift giving in *Timon*, few critics have acknowledged the degree to which these gifts are portrayed through the depiction of appetite.[11] Despite the fact that the actual gifts which he distributes involve a vast variety of goods, including jewels, horses and gold, the language with which Timon's bounty is described is repeatedly that of 'meat' and feasting. His gifts are bound up with the depiction of an ambiguous line between literal and metaphorical appetites, and this necessarily prompts consideration of what it is about appetite that prompts

10 Pettet, for example, claims that the play constitutes 'a portrait of the ideal feudal lord living up to the full obligation of bounty and housekeeping', and that the origin of his tragedy lies not in his own actions but in the declining power of the nobility as a whole (Pettet, 1947, p. 324). In a similar vein, Bevington and Smith declare that 'the system itself requires him to be lavish as a way of showing his power of patronage' (Bevington and Smith, 1999, pp. 76–7). But Kahn differs from these approaches by tending to emphasise the specific failings of Timon as a character, and reading these failings as implicit criticism of the court. She declares that 'Both the king and Timon make gift-giving serve their emotional need', and situates that emotional need as the cause not only of Timon's downfall but also of the imbalance in the King's finances (Kahn, 1987, p. 43).

11 One key exception is Joan Fitzpatrick, who has noted that 'Throughout the play, feeding metaphors are used to denounce the greed and hypocrisy of humanity with profane feeding described in cannibalistic terms' (Fitzpatrick, 2007, p. 113).

the writers to deploy it as one of the primary images through which wider forms of excess are conceptualised. Recognition of its diverse connotations makes clear the degree to which Timon's gifts are divorced from need and consequently lack the power to enforce bonds between men. It is this shift which differentiates his actions from those of characters such as Pericles, whose gifts satisfy the hunger and not the appetites of their recipients.

In the first instance, appetite provides a means of envisioning the emergence of desires beyond immediate necessity. This is the process which Bloch describes as that by which man, if he 'has what is necessary' becomes afflicted by the 'enjoyment of new desires . . . which torment him differently, but no less intensely than the previous naked privation' (Bloch, 1995, I, p. 49). Thus 'luxury above all (which does appear to fulfil everything) is an insatiable driver' (Bloch, 1995, I, p. 49). The food gift is implicated in the wider contemporary tendency to associate gluttony and excess with an exponentially increasing appetite.[12] In *Pericles*, plenty is characterised as a force which drives the citizens of pre-famine Tarsus to satisfy ever more exotic appetites, in a manner which is explicitly dissociated from hunger. Cleon contrasts their desire for 'inventions to delight the taste' with the simple bread which hunger later prompts them to demand (I.iv.40). In *Timon*, the lord's plentiful gifts produce not merely delicate appetites, but unrestrained ones. The steward declares: 'How many prodigal bits have slaves and peasants / This night englutted?' (II.ii.165–166). The word 'englutted' encapsulates connotations of both consumption and satiation, but the rhetorical nature of the exclamation implies an inability to number the various foodstuffs which have been eaten. Likewise, references to the prodigal son and to the guests as 'slaves and peasants' imply a loss of status, with the insatiable appetites of the elite mirroring those of the theatre's numerous hungry servants. The citizens of Tarsus were merely relieved by Pericles's generosity, but Timon's gifts inspire an unrestrained and perpetually increasing appetite. As a consequence, the former play's emphasis on use value is supplanted by a concern with the gift as a means of exchange. The constant, but fruitless, desire to satisfy the unquenchable appetites of his guests constitutes a central factor in the construction of Timon as a character who, as Eagleton has argued, is 'superbly indifferent to different persons and use-values' (Eagleton, 1992, p. 395). The space of gift giving within the play is concerned not with the relief of hunger, but with the perpetuation of excess.

Indeed, as the play enters the second half, Timon's predicament becomes more clearly associated not simply with his tendency to prioritise

[12] See Chapter 1.

appetite over genuine hunger, but with an inability to distinguish between the two. Having left Athens for the wilderness, he encounters a group of thieves, who tell him that they are simply 'men that much do want' (IV.iii.408). Timon's response to their protestations of want is to insist on the capability of the natural world to provide for them. He insists:

> Your greatest want is, you want much of meat.
> Why should you want? Behold, the earth hath roots;
> Within this mile break forth a hundred springs;
> The oaks bear mast, the briars scarlet hips;
> The bounteous housewife, Nature, on each bush
> Lays her full mess before you. Want! Why want? (IV.iii.409–14)

The speech conjures up an image of plenty which disputes the degree to which hunger can be considered a reality and which resembles the portrayal of natural bounty found in poems such as Jonson's 'To Penshurst'.[13] Timon perceives a world in which nature provides for the alleviation of hunger, but in which man's appetites drive him to desire more. Yet Timon's own attempts to elicit sustenance from nature are markedly unsuccessful, producing only gold. As Fitzpatrick has noted, Timon's desperate foraging for roots 'would have struck an early modern audience as distinctly bestial, indeed pig-like' (Fitzpatrick, 2007, p. 118). It might therefore be argued that Timon misreads their genuine desire for food in much the same way as he does the corrupt appetites of his earlier guests. Eagleton suggests that 'the snarling misanthropy which overtakes him is merely an inverted image of his erstwhile beneficence' (Eagleton, 1992, p. 395). It is telling that the parallels between his munificence and misanthropy are primarily manifested through a continued inability to distinguish between hunger and appetite.

Nevertheless, the characteristics of the staging of hunger and appetite lend a degree of complexity to Timon's ostensibly simplistic perspective, for Timon's relationship to the three men he encounters in the wilderness

[13] In 'To Penshurst', carnivalesque imagery of feasting and plenty is mobilised in order to assert an image of hospitality emerging from a natural relationship between a noble family, their estate and the lower orders who serve them. Jonson claims that 'Fat, agèd carps . . . run into thy net' (l. 33); and 'Bright eels . . . leap on land, / Before the fisher, or into his hand' (ll. 37–8). The animals are imbued with a willingness to die in order that the feasting may continue. Critics such as Raymond Williams have noted that the deployment of this carnival imagery effaces the labour required to allow the estate to function (Williams, 1975, pp. 27–31). But while this is certainly the case, it should be acknowledged that the carnivalesque imagery of the poem effects another process of effacement. For by associating feasting with fantastic images of self-sacrificing livestock, the poem detaches its nostalgic images of country life from their situation within an economy which was increasingly the subject of a process of marketisation. If labour has been effaced, the land has not.

is defined by an ambiguity which embodies the wider complexity of appetite itself. Although the stage instructions of the first folio describe them as 'bandetti' and 'theethes' there is little in the dialogue to determine whether they are lying when they claim to be 'Soldiers, not thieves' (IV.iii.407). In performance, it is possible that either Timon or the men can be proved to be telling the truth, depending on the degree to which hunger is embodied through characterisation. No less possible is the perpetuation of the text's original ambiguity. The key consequence of these conflicting possibilities is to place the material experience of the audience in a position of interpretative priority. For those whose wealth tended to detach them from hunger, Timon's response might well have seemed a rational one, providing an invaluable judgement upon the excessive demands of the masterless poor. For others, his attitude must surely have been deemed indicative of wider failings in hospitable practices traditionally associated with the relief of genuine hunger. Above all, the ambiguity which the text presents must have embodied the wider concerns of many at the sheer unknowability of the poor in a period characterised by the decline of the intrapersonal bonds which dominate gift giving in texts such as *Pericles*. It might even be said that the theatre itself highlights this element of unknowability. For in the theatre, all hunger is performance.

This element of performance within the representation of appetite acquires a special significance when placed in the context of James's court, for it enables the text to manifest concern at the rise of flattery and favouritism within early modern culture. It is notable that while hunger is invariably linked to honesty and plain-speaking, appetite alone acquires connotations of insincerity. In *Pericles*, hunger is presented as a force which admits of no pretence. Cleon asks his wife 'Who wanteth food and will not say he wants it, / Or can conceal his hunger till he famish?' (I.iv.11–12). It is a force which is written on the body and which enforces honesty. *Timon*, by contrast, is characterised by an obsessive emphasis on the connections between appetite and insincerity. Appemantus declares of Timon's feasting that 'The fellow that sits next him, now parts bread with him, pledges the breath of him in a divided draught, is the readiest man to kill him' (I.ii.45–7). The distribution of food gifts has ceased to be the basis of bonds between men and has become the very practice upon which betrayal is based. Likewise, references to 'Mouth-friends' associate the act of flattery with the act of consumption. The degree to which the theatre acknowledges these intricate connections between the food gift and truth is attested by the extent to which those characters which attempt to detach themselves from the hierarchical structures of early modern society are defined by their propensity to reject the food gift. The Philosopher Appemantus refuses Timon's offer of meat, declaring 'I'll nothing; for if I should be bribed too, there would be none left to rail upon thee, and then thou wouldst sin the faster' (I.ii.236–8). Hunger remains a guarantor of truth, but in a world defined by the permanent carnival of Timon's liberality, it must be artificially produced. Like the definition of the epicure in John Stephens's *Satirical Essayes*, who 'will grow frends with any man, that serues his stomacke' (Stephens, 1615, p. 245), the text connects insincerity and an excessive desire for food. When the gift satisfies appetite, but not hunger, it will create bonds that are impermanent, defined by hypocrisy and insincerity.

The depiction of appetite provides an invaluable vehicle for this critique because it enables authors to highlight the tension within the distribution of gifts to those who do not need them. The sheer volume of Timon's gifts means that the element of instability inherent in the temporal nature of gift exchange is greatly magnified. The play manifests a profound anxiety about the impossibility of calling back a gift which has been given; a tension which receives its clearest expression in the text's numerous images of the degradation and corruption of food. In Act III, for example, faced with the ingratitude of Timon's former guests, the steward Flaminius declares:

> This slave
> Unto this hour has my lord's meat in him.
> Why should it thrive and turn to nutriment,
> When he is turned to poison?
> O, may diseases only work upon't! (III.i.50–4)

The ambiguity of 'lord's meat' emphasises the parasitic nature of the guest, eliding the man who feeds on the gifts which Timon provides and the man who feeds on Timon himself. The subsequent distinction between the meat, which will 'turn to nutriment', and the guest, who has 'turn'd to poison', highlights the steadfast nature of the steward's master. But perhaps the most significant aspect to the curse is precisely its inefficacy. Once a gift has been devoured there is no way of enforcing its return. For this reason, without the stronger ties prompted by the possibility of hunger, the distribution of the food gift risks becoming a relationship of exploitation.

Furthermore, the depiction of appetite enables the text to explore the material basis of this exploitation. Conventional accounts of hospitality emphasise the extent to which the distribution of food gifts relies on the produce of the lord's estate. In 'To Penshurst', for instance, Jonson declares that 'The painted partridge lies in every field, / And for thy mess is willing to be killed' (l. 29–30). In *Timon*, however, land has become a source of capital. Although Timon declares that 'To Lacedaemon did my land extend' (II.ii.146), it is evident that it has been used not as a resource, but to acquire credit. It is 'all engaged, some forfeited and gone' (II.ii.141). The unrestrained appetites of Timon's guests are indulged through the unrestrained borrowing of the host. This borrowing is constructed in a similar manner to appetite, as a process which defies restraint, so that 'Plutus, the god of gold, Is but [Timon's] steward' (I.i.281–2). Yet the use of appetite as an image simultaneously undermines this characteristic of lending, for as with many contemporary texts, the notionally boundless nature of Timon's wealth is consistently undercut by cannibal imagery.[14] Appemantus declares 'What a number of men eats Timon, and he sees 'em not! It grieves me to see so many dip their meat in one man's blood; and all the madness is, he cheers them up too' (I.ii.38–41). The 'meat' and 'blood' which his guests consume invite parallels with the Last Supper and the Eucharist. Timon, the host who invites his own destruction, is figured as a Christ-like martyr, who 'cheers' men on to devour him. But the cannibal dimension lends a pronounced element of vulnerability to that position. The literal food and drink which the guests devour become an extension of Timon's body. The image of consumption simultaneously insists on the finite nature of his resources, implicitly satirising his reliance upon credit and its ostensibly god-like power to produce unlimited funds. The result is to emphasise Timon's implication within the destructive forces of an emergent capitalism.

In *Timon*, the imagery of appetite is deployed to explore the dangerous excesses of a society in which gifts are directed at desires, rather than needs. In part, this can be read as localised critique of practices associated, in particular, with the court of James. Yet the repeated use of culinary imagery also enables this text to speak to broader concerns, regarding the apparent restriction of gift giving to a privileged, well-fed elite. The play manifests an obsession with food that figures it as both grotesquely material and

[14] In Thomas Heywood's translation of Lucian's *Timon* it is claimed of Timon's flatterers that 'When even unto the bare bones they had gnawne him / They suckt his very marrow, and then fled' (Lucian, 1903, p. 60). In Shakespeare's *Titus Andronicus*, the eponymous revenger translates traditions of hospitality into a literal act of cannibalism, serving up his enemies' sons. In *The Bloody Banquet*, courtiers become 'court wolves' and 'foule eaters', while the play's climax elides feasting and cannibalism (II.i.36–7). Hosts in early modern literature are increasingly shown to be consumed by their guests.

fundamentally insubstantial. Timon's guests engage in visceral excess, yet the steward's futile wish that such food might turn poisonous in their bellies makes evident the impermanence of bonds of obligation generated in the absence of genuine need. At the same time, the period's emphasis on the exponential nature of appetite detached from hunger provides a means to assert the untenable nature of such practices, and their worrying detachment from traditional perceptions of hospitality as rooted in the produce of one's own estate. While in *Pericles*, the distributor of gifts remains detached from the forces of exchange, Timon's desire to satisfy the appetites of his guests forces him to rely upon those practices of usury characteristic of the emergent capitalist system. In the final instance, this distinction finds its expression in the images of the host torn apart by the anthropophagous impulses of his guests.

## Identification and Exclusion

The depiction of food gifts highlights not only the problems associated with England's growing wealth, but also those resulting from its concurrent polarisation. The increasingly exclusionary nature of hospitality in the period coincided with a huge increase in the number of those living in poverty. Precise figures for the number of masterless men are hard to verify, with Elizabethan estimates ranging from 10,000 to 200,000, but they remained the object of obsessive concern throughout the early modern period (Beier, 1985, p. xix). They represented a new form of poverty, divorced from both the land and traditional structures of hospitality.[15] The significance accorded to these figures is evident in the theatre's marked concern not only with excessive appetites, but also with those who have no access to the food gift. Indeed, early modern texts are notable for the extent to which they relate the two, since the emphasis on appetite coincides with a pronounced distaste for charity. In *Pericles*, the audience learns that in pre-famine Tarsus, 'All poverty was scorned, and pride so great, / The name of help grew odious to repeat' (I.iv.30–31). The sentiment would have been familiar to an early modern audience, for it recurs in religious literature. Moderation in the consumption of food and drink, and a consequent restraint upon appetite, was considered necessary if the

[15] Beier notes that between 1560 and 1640 'the poor no longer had the security of smallholders in a manorial economy and received a severe buffeting in the marketplace' (Beier, 1985, p. 18). Greenblatt has emphasised the antipathy which these figures produced, characterising them as 'the very types of Elizabethan subversion' and 'the natural enemies of social discipline' (Greenblatt, 1994, p. 30).

hunger – whether divine or otherwise – of others were to be remembered. In a translation of a French text, the writer implores the Lord, 'let me remember thy hunger. Oh let me not forget thy thirst, that I may be sober in my diet, and temperate in my drinke, and remember to refresh poore hungry *Lazarus*, when he lieth crying and crauing at my gate' (St. Bernard, 1614, pp. 228–9). Calvin, in a gloss on the Book of Job, argues that:

> Rich men haue no compassion bycause they lyue at ease. For they know not what it is to stand in neede, they knowe not what necessitie meeneth: and therefore they are not touched therewith. Too bee shorte, when they be full, they thinke that all the world is so as well as they. (Calvin, 1577, p. 432)

To subjugate oneself to one's appetite is not simply a moral crime, but also a social one, for it precludes that basic element of identification with suffering which Calvin implies is necessary for the act of charity. Whether the identification is with the poor, or with Christ himself, it is clear a lived experience of hunger is a necessary characteristic not only of those who receive charity, but also of those who distribute it. The implied message of these diverse texts for the relationship between hunger and appetite is evident: the attempt to satisfy one's appetite entails a disregard for the hunger of others.

One of the most significant texts to engage with this interrelation of hunger and appetite is Massinger's *The Unnatural Combat*, in which the depiction of a starving captain functions as a critique of both excessive and inadequate liberality on the part of the ruling class. Deprived of his pay and pension, Captain Belgarde is forced to attend on Duke Beaufort in order to receive sustenance, and is quickly excluded from the space of hospitality. His treatment indicates wider problems in the conditions of veterans, one of the single most important groups within the wider category of masterless men. Beier notes that 'No occupational groups increased as much as sailors and soldiers among vagrants from 1560 to 1640 … In London they accounted for only 1.5 per cent before 1580, but rose to 12 per cent between 1620 and 1640' (Beier, 1985, p. 93). But the play's subplot also acquires additional resonance when placed in its immediate historical context. The precise date on which Massinger's play was originally performed has been the subject of critical debate. Claire Jowitt, Colin Gibson and Philip Edwards all situate the text in 1624–25, emphasising internal evidence and reading references to 'a forraigne Queene' as evidence of contemporary interest in the marriage of Charles and Henrietta Maria. Yet Margot Heinemann previously argued for the slightly later date of 1626, which lends the representation of the hungry soldier Belgarde a more specific relevance.[16] In the wake of a failed military expedition to Cadiz, the soldiers and sailors of the expedition were left starving and without pay, prompting a series of riots and demonstrations (Heinemann, 1993, pp. 249–50). The text, by situating the plight of a penniless captain in the context of the excessive appetites of the elite, channels these tensions and demonstrates how the depiction of food gifts can be used to explore an emerging class dynamic of rich against poor.

If Timon is characterised by an inability to distinguish between hunger and appetite, *The Unnatural Combat*'s Beaufort Senior seems consciously to exclude those who are governed by real need. In this text, the discourse of civility functions to discriminate between different types of guests: those that satisfy hunger and those that are merely seeking to relieve their appetite. He claims to 'love a table furnisht with full plentie, / And store of friends to eat it' (III.i.5–6), but nevertheless expresses a reluctance to allow his house to become 'a common Inne' (III.i.7). The class connotations are clear. Beaufort Senior wishes to remove the lower-class elements of the feast, reducing it to a collection of friends of similar status. When Belgarde arrives at the Duke's house, he is met by a servant who mockingly tells him that the Duke 'Stands most affected to you, for the freedome, / And plainnesse of your manners' noting that Belgarde will never 'Which is a master-peece, when meates before you / Forget your teeth to use your nimble tongue' (III.i.80–1). The description of Belgarde's manner of eating as a 'masterpeece' can be read as a punning reference to his newly masterless nature. The ironic praise of his manners simultaneously ridicules and highlights the bluff plainness of the soldier, while the internal rhyme asserts the comparative sophistication of the household servant. But these lines also reflect genuine changes in the practice of hospitality. Heal has noted that an increasing emphasis on manners legitimates the narrowing of the social parameters of hospitality, ensuring that 'the host was left with cultural justifications for restricting his guests to men of known "civility"' (Heal, 1984, p. 88). In *The Unnatural Combat* the class dynamics of this shift are made starkly clear. The result demonstrates the relevance of Pierre Bourdieu's emphasis on the need to ground differences in taste in underlying material differences. For Bourdieu, 'The true basis of the differences

16 Significantly, Edwards and Gibson can offer no direct evidence which limits the date of performance to 1624 or 1625, but simply argue that there are 'sufficient correspondences' between the play and contemporary events to 'strongly suggest' those years (Edwards and Gibson, 1976, p. 182). I would argue, however, that the parallels which Heinemann has noted between the situation of Belgarde and that of the English army in this period constitute a far more convincing series of correspondences. For this reason, I accept the later date.

found in the area of consumption, and far beyond it, is the opposition between the tastes of luxury (or freedom) and the tastes of necessity' (Bourdieu, 2005, p. 73). It is precisely because he is hungry that Belgarde is supposed to devour the food in a manner which sits ill with the sensibilities of the elite, and is excluded. Hospitality has become the realm of appetite alone.

Furthermore, by contrast with *Pericles*, in which the consumption of food takes place offstage, in *The Unnatural Combat* the feast is staged. Given the restrictive nature of feasting in early modern London, it seems probable that many of those in the audience would ordinarily be excluded from such spectacles. *The Unnatural Combat*, much like *Timon*, provides the audience with a privileged position of observation on a world ordinarily restricted to an elite. Indeed, this element of voyeurism is heightened by the use of the stage direction 'setting forth'. As Chris Meads has noted, the phrase is a recurrent stage notation in the period, occurring in nine plays between 1604 and 1639 and implying 'revelation, or forward movement of properties' (Meads, 2001, p. 38). The text shifts from a discussion between the page, the usher and two female servants, to the sudden appearance of the feast. The trajectory of the scene and the element of revelation implicit in the stage directions encourages the identification of the audience not with those who participate in the lives of the nobility, but with those who do not. Indeed, in the context of the playhouse as a site for the sale of food, this sense of exclusion must surely have been amplified. For if, as Nunn has argued, onstage representation of the consumption of food served in part to stimulate appetite as a means of ensuring the purchase of food within the playhouse, then for those without the funds to do so, the apparent shift from gift to commodity must have been all the more evident. Indeed, for many contemporary writers, the playhouses themselves constituted the most overt example of unrestrained satisfaction of appetite and a consequent disregard for the poor.[17] Paradoxically, the very implication of the theatre within this process of decline may have reinforced the power of its critique, predisposing large swathes of the audience to condemn practices which they could access only by means of dramatic representation.

The element of identification acquired is intensified when Belgarde returns, dressed in armour, declaring 'what court so set off / With state

[17] *The Art of Giving* asserts that stage plays constitute part of the 'eighth practise of Satan to hinder bounty . . . by enticing men to exhaust their estates in vnlawfnll recreations' (Cooper, 1615, p. 103). Contemporary texts repeatedly link the decline of rural hospitality to the moral failings of those who give up 'house-keeping at home, to take a chamber in London, where they consume their time in viewing of stageplays, in carousing of healths and (perhaps) in using of courtesans' (Vaughan, 1608, II.26).

and ceremonious pompe, but thus / Accoutred I may enter?' The opposition of simplicity to sophistication is here refigured as that between military austerity and civil extravagance. Joanne Rochester argues that the assembled nobles 'take Belgarde's long verbal attack on their ingratitude towards the army for a paid performance', and claims that in doing so they frame the events as fiction and entertainment (Rochester, 2010, p. 129). Yet this ambiguous distinction between fiction and reality acquires radical implications if one accepts Heinemann's dating of the text. For Massinger's apparent fiction seems clearly to reference the situation of Buckingham. Heinemann notes that 'the duke's chamber at Whitehall was forcibly invaded as he sat at dinner by six captains, who had served in Ireland, demanding their pay' (Heinemann, 1993, p. 250). Hunger returns as violence. Although the radicalism of that violence is covered by the veneer of upper-class approval, with the notion that Belgarde performs a 'jest', the significance of his actions emerges clearly when he comments 'Let a Souldier use no other Scribe to draw / The forme of his petition' (III.iii.125–6). Where his previous 'humble supplications' have been markedly ineffectual, the barely concealed threat of violence works with surprising ease (III.iii.127). On the one hand, the text might in this sense be expected to function as a warning to its audience. It implies that it is necessary to maintain traditions of charity and hospitality to avoid unleashing the violence of the excluded. But the degree to which the staging of the banquet encourages identification with these excluded figures raises the possibility that for certain sections of the audience violence might not simply be acknowledged as a potential danger to the state, but actively endorsed. At a time when soldiers were demonstrating in the streets, this subtext imbues the play's representation of elite hospitality with a particularly radical edge.

Yet by contrast with texts such as *Pericles*, in which the gift serves to relieve the dangerous appetites produced by extreme hunger, *The Unnatural Combat* implies not only the neglect of gift giving, but also the potentially untenable nature of traditions of charity and hospitality. As Belgarde declares, his idleness and lack of means are largely the consequence of the fact that he has not received his wages. His regular attendance at the house of the Duke is not a matter of celebration, but rather an attempt to ensure that he is paid. He tells the audience:

> I'le seek no other ordinarie then,
> But be his daily ghest, without invitement,
> And if my stomacke hould, Ile feed so heartily
> As he shall pay me suddainly to be quit of me. (I.i.112–15)

Feasting is a matter of survival for Belgarde. When, in the third act, he is refused hospitality, the play seems to unite the twin plots of *Timon of Athens*. The rejection of hospitality and the ungratefulness of the civilian population are united in the treatment of Belgarde. However, even once the courtiers have been shamed into action, and Belgarde has been paid, his position is far from improved. For as word spreads that he is 'full of crownes' (IV.ii.95), he is oppressed by 'bills of all occasions, and all sizes!' (IV.ii.29). Once again, his situation is conveyed through the imagery of hunger. His pay is 'swallow'd downe' by 'The citie cormorants, my monie-mongers' (IV.ii.44–5). The prostitutes of the city become 'she-wolves' who attempt to consume him (IV.ii.92). They justify their actions by presenting him with children, inquiring 'Will you see your issue starve?' (IV.ii.125). The result of these multiple images of consumption is to imply a world where want is general, from the lowest to the highest. Rather than offer himself up to be consumed, Belgarde prefers to return to his former state of pennilessness, demanding of the Duke 'pray you strip me / And let me be as I was' (IV.ii.141–2). Within this context, therefore, Beaufort's initial justification for the rejection of less respectable elements, who 'come rather to devoure me, / Then to present their service' (III.i.8–9), retains a certain legitimacy. In a world of generalised hunger, the distribution of food gifts is both impossible and necessary.

Particularly telling is the final solution which the text presents for Belgarde's predicament. Engaged to regain a fort seized by a corrupt general, Belgarde emphasises the extent to which the military setting has reversed the civil restrictions of peacetime society, declaring 'These are your gallants, / That at a feast take the first place . . . marry in / These foolish businesses they are content / That I shall have precedence' (V.ii.315–319). *The Unnatural Combat* frames a return to armed conflict as a means to move beyond the crisis of gift giving and excess. The military turn in part embodies wider concerns linking the decline of gift giving with the diminished military power of the aristocracy.[18] And as such it is unsurprising that the text's solution is one which recurs throughout the period. Texts advocating a return to traditions of hospitality do so in

[18] This was a period defined by 'progressive *dissociation* of the nobility from the basic military function which defined it in the medieval social order' (Anderson, 1975, p. 125). This in turn aggravated changes in the hospitality tradition. Heal has noted that 'servants of some autonomous social standing were no longer so necessary a part of the seventeenth-century world, since they were no longer the potential military supports of their lords' (Heal, 1990, p. 165). Key elements of 'the clientage system which had brought important local men to a lord's table regularly' were also in decline (Heal, 1990, p. 166). Both factors decreased the necessity of hospitality for great lords; real power increasingly lay at court.

tandem with demands that gentlemen abandon city vices in favour of sports of 'honest report . . . Such as may fit vs the better to the seruice of our country, as handling the Pike, feates of actiuity, and such as are performed laudably in the Artillery garden' (Cooper, 1615, pp. 111–12).

In earlier plays, structures of hospitality reinscribe lower-class violence in the service of the state. In *The Shoemaker's Holiday*, for instance, the festive consumption of the final feast is accompanied by a barrage of military imagery. In *The Unnatural Combat*, however, that element of militarism acquires political relevance from the context of England's failing military fortunes. As Heinemann has noted, the first printed edition of the play was dedicated to Sir Anthony St Leger, whose cousin, Sir William St Leger, was critical of the Cadiz mission's commander and intervened on behalf of the starving soldiers (Heinemann, 1993, p. 250). War becomes a way to channel the violent energies unleashed by Belgarde's experience of hunger; a means to repair a society dominated by corruption and excess. The text's opposition of hunger to appetite functions both to embody the inequality of early modern society, and to locate the source of that inequality within a culture of pacifism.

*The Unnatural Combat* raises the spectre of violence as a way to assert the perils of the exclusion of the poor from the space of hospitality. It situates the discourse of manners in the context of early modern England's increasing polarisation. And through its apparent invocation of contemporary grievances regarding the treatment of discharged soldiers, it links a localised critique of George Villiers with a broader complaint at the decline of the food gift. At the same time, this emphasis is qualified by the speed with which Belgarde is transformed from a recipient of hospitality into the object of the poor's ravenous appetites. The decline of hospitality is by implication not solely the product of neglect on the part of individual members of the elite, but rather a reflection of the insurmountable presence of inequality within early modern society. The hunger of the poor is figured as potentially insatiable, a force capable of consuming any attempts at the distribution of food gifts. In this context, the only solution which the play can conceptualise for the conflicts it has staged is a return to war.

## Conclusion

The fundamental characteristic of the food gift on the early modern stage is its capacity to foreground the power of hunger to challenge the dominance of the market. It highlights the degree to which hunger constitutes a fundamental check on the development of a system based on untrammelled exchange. It does so while framing that dynamic within a residual feudal logic of hierarchical reciprocity. Plays such as *Pericles* demonstrate how far the representation of hunger can function within a discourse of monarcho-populism, and consequently partake of the complex ambiguities which define that discourse. The distribution of food to the hungry makes clear the power of the labouring classes to exert pressure upon their ruling-class equivalents, highlighting the internal divisions which increasingly defined the period's elite. But the very nature of that gift exchange, implicated within residual models for the exertion of power, might be said to compromise the radicalism of its political stand. In order to reconcile the conflicting progressive and reactionary aspects to this politics of hunger, it is necessary to acknowledge the degree to which these fictional representations respond to the material reality of suffering within early modern society. The failure or absence of gift giving in these texts is consistently linked to the theme of lower-class violence. Attention to the food gift demonstrates the degree to which the representation of hunger and appetite is confined within an ostensibly feudal model of society, but simultaneously reveals the complex ways in which monarcho-populism responds to those lower-class energies which it attempts to co-opt.

Indeed, it should be acknowledged that hunger and appetite provide the early modern playwright with a repertoire of images which highlight the more radical components within this broader discourse. In the first instance, images of hunger and appetite draw out the universal dimension to individual examples of injustice and oppression. The depiction of hunger and appetite unites the *longue durée* of the transition from a feudal to a capitalist mode of production with the portrayal of specific conflicts emerging from that historical process. It is this implicit awareness of historical context which defines how these texts were initially conceived and received, and which is almost inevitably lost in a modern staging. Perhaps the most striking instance of this process is the way the later work by Massinger implies that the distribution of food gifts is not simply lacking, but fundamentally inadequate. Here, hunger emerges as a plea not for beneficence on the part of the elite, but more radically for social justice. Belgarde needs Beaufort's hospitality to preserve himself. When that hospitality is denied, he demands not only food, but the money to which he is entitled. When the theatre opposes hunger to appetite it threatens to castigate not just individual actions by members of the elite, but also the failings of the ruling classes in general. In these moments, ostensibly reactionary ideologies of monarcho-populism have the potential to emerge as critique of the extent to which even the monarchy is implicated within capitalist economic practices.

At its most radical, this universal dimension emerges as an implicitly class-based logic of struggle. The simple opposition of those who eat to those who starve acquires a radical resonance which has the potential to push beyond the constraints of nostalgia and feudal loyalty towards a desire for equitable redistribution and the deployment of the violence of hunger for progressive ends. Indeed, it is scarcely surprising that this dimension of the representation of hunger emerges with unusual clarity in the case of the food gift. For implicit within the representation of gift exchange is a degree of scrutiny targeted at the ruling classes. It is the action or inaction of the elite which becomes the focus of the texts, and this could explain why the decline of charity and hospitality are mainstays of populist radical literature not only in this period but throughout history. If the portrayal of the hungry servant tends towards the depiction of lower-class vice, the representation of the hunger caused by the neglect of gift giving, or the appetites prompted by unthinking hospitality, locates the source of social degeneration firmly in the realm of the elite. Indeed, of particular significance in this respect is the extent to which this class-based opposition receives affective impetus from the material conditions of the early modern playhouse. The onstage depiction of the social other mirrors the diversity of the early modern audience. For the elite, this entails observation of a troubling underclass, whose hunger stands in ambiguous relation to unsettling appetites, both literal and social. For the poorer members of the audience, especially in the public theatre, representation allows a point of access to acts of consumption from which they were increasingly excluded. It is here that authorial intention becomes submerged within the popular energies of the audience, with an upper-class fear of disorder reinscribed in performance as a lower-class desire for revolt.

CHAPTER 4

# *Sexual Desire*

Hunger and appetite recur as ways of conceptualising sexual desire on the early modern stage. In Shakespeare's *Twelfth Night* (1601), Duke Orsino identifies music as 'the food of love', on which he hopes to surfeit (I.i.1); in Beaumont's *The Woman Hater* (1607), the courtier Lazarillo develops an eroticised fixation on a fish's head; and in Middleton and Rowley's *The Changeling* (1622), the servant De Flores figures himself as a 'slovenly' dish on which his mistress may feed (II.ii.151). The frequency with which these drives are compared springs, in part, from the parallels which exist between them. Sexual desire can be defined as 'a wish, need, or drive to seek out sexual objects or to engage in sexual activities' (Regan and Atkins, 2006, p. 96). Like appetite, it can constitute a generalised craving or a desire for a specific object. Both can be figured by society as either a natural, recurring longing, or an unnatural or excessive craving. In the Renaissance, these more general parallels were accentuated by the wider tendency to assume that sexual activity and the consumption of food were related at the material level. Albala has noted that 'ideas of "diet" or "hygiene" in their original senses usually encompassed consideration of not only food and drink but also air quality, exercise, sexual activity, emotional state, and numerous other variables that were believed to affect nutrition' (Albala, 2002, p. 5). Fitzpatrick has emphasised that 'excessive consumption of alcohol and food was often aligned with sexual excess' (Fitzpatrick, 2007, p. 11). Numerous dietaries highlighted specific foods which were believed to enhance the sexual drive.[1] The production of sperm was seen as closely connected to the process of digestion.[2] And gluttony, in particular, was linked to an excessive degree

[1] A wide range of foods were believed to have this property, including chicken, veal, potatoes and wine (cf. Albala, 2002, p. 146).

[2] Albala notes that sperm 'were considered to be manufactured from a superfluity of nutrition, transformed from blood in the testes the same way milk is made in the mammary glands' (Albala, 2002, p. 76).

of sexual desire.[3] The result was the existence of what Robert Appelbaum has described as 'a metonymy of body parts, behaviours and time frames, that connected hunger and desire, the cravings of the belly and the passions of the genitalia' (Appelbaum, 2006, p. 225). The theatres of the period deployed a wide repertoire of literal and metaphorical connections between hunger, appetite and sexual desire, in a manner which rooted all three in both the body and society.

The connections between food and sex in the period have been the subject of many critical studies. Critics have argued that the elision of culinary and sexual appetite marginalises female desire in this period.[4] They have explored the role played by appetite as a means of escaping censorship.[5] And they have considered the extent to which theatre's own relationship to the sale of sex and food exerted a defining influence over the nature of these representations.[6] Perhaps the most significant theme has been how barriers between appetite and sexual desire are broken down by the representation of these parallels. Peter Stallybrass notes that it is 'striking how frequently within Renaissance discourses of the body the gradient of displacement is *from* the "sexual"/ genital *to* the digestive/excretory' (Stallybrass, 1991, p. 211). Khamphommala argues that 'the comparison between hunger and desire is so frequent in Shakespeare's comedies that it soon becomes difficult to distinguish between the two' (Khamphommala, 2008, p. 21). At the same time, it should be acknowledged that this process of elision is made possible only

3 Philip Stubbes questions, 'Dooth not the impletion and sacietie of meates and drinks prouoke lust?' (Stubbes, 1583, sig. J1r). The 'Homyly Against Gluttonie and Dronkennes' declares that 'surfetting and drunkennesse bites by the belly, and causeth continual gnawing in the stomacke, brings men to whoredome and lewdenesse of heart, with daungers vnspeakable' (Church of England, 1571, p. 208). The interrelation had a long pedigree, for as Caroline Walker Bynum notes, 'medieval people often saw gluttony as the major form of lust' (Bynum, 1987, p. 2). These long-standing parallels were accentuated by a joint emphasis upon the gaze. Hilary Nunn has noted that for many early modern writers 'The mere sight of food . . . held the power to stimulate a viewer's appetite and provoke gluttonous indulgence' (Nunn, 2013, p. 106). Sexual desire, likewise, could be kindled by sight.

4 Lennartz notes that 'seventeenth-century libertines tended to see the female sex as erotic fast food that was ravenously devoured and consequently thrown up' (Lennartz, 2012, p. 10). Khamphommala claims that women are figured as possessing a desire for food and sex, but argues that this serves the purpose of highlighting the presence of the male body of the actor.

5 Khamphommala argues that the depiction of appetite allowed playwrights to escape the restrictions of censorship, noting that 'while preserving its bodily implications, hunger would offer if not a respectable, at least an acceptable substitute to erotic desire on stage' (Khamphommala, 2008, pp. 17–18).

6 Nunn explores how the representation of food enabled the theatres to explore 'questions about the nature of hunger, temptation and human desire', with onstage food simultaneously encouraging the spectator to consume and forcing them into a position of identification with the various sexual and culinary temptations faced by the characters of a play (Nunn, 2013, p. 117).

through the reconstitution of desire and the sexual act. When the theatre insists on the literal and metaphorical connections between these drives, it presents desire as functioning according to a gustatory logic. As a result, it is repeatedly implicated within broader tensions regarding the prevalence of exchange, the coexistence of want and excess and the consequences of unrestrained consumption.

Perhaps unsurprisingly, the conjunction of appetite and desire tends to foreground the role of excess. This chapter will therefore begin by considering a range of texts in which unrestrained appetite emerges as a surrogate for or cause of an excessive desire. These moments are perhaps most visible on the early modern stage in the context of men feeding on women. But the deployment of appetite also ensures that the critique of sexual indulgence operates as part of a generalised condemnation of material excess and the abuse of power. At the same time, it is not only men who are conceived of as consuming sex and food. Indeed, numerous texts of the period are defined by a fundamental ambiguity regarding who precisely is being consumed. The next section will consequently consider the ways in which this ambiguity can be deployed to complicate or challenge the hierarchies of early modern society. It will focus on Middleton and Dekker's *The Bloody Banquet* (*c.* 1609), in which implicit parallels are drawn between the hunger of a starving population and the rebellious desires of a tyrant's wife. Lastly, the elision of sexual and culinary consumption is defined by a marked degree of vulnerability. The final section of this chapter will therefore consider Ben Jonson's *Bartholomew Fair* (1614), a play in which both sex and food emerge as commodities within the carnival marketplace. Throughout, the ambiguous nature of the elision of appetite and desire makes possible a specific process of politicisation, whereby an underlying gustatory logic foregrounds the social and political, rather than purely moral, consequences of sexual longing.

## Tyrannous Excess

Perhaps the most significant reason for which appetite is deployed as a surrogate for desire in the early modern theatre stems from the fact that it had the potential to embody both a legitimate, universal drive and a force of troubling excess. As such, it provided an invaluable conceptual resource at a time when sexual desire itself was the object of wide-ranging theological debate. As Edmund Leites has demonstrated, the rise of Protestant ideas led to the increasing valorisation in contemporary thought of marriage, rather than celibacy, as a model for the Christian life, with a consequent emphasis upon the potential legitimacy of sexual pleasure (Leites, 1982). The puritan, Daniel Rogers, for instance, declared that conjugal love entailed 'not only Christian love ... nor yet a carnall and sudden flash of affection, completely enflamed by concupiscense: (rather brutish than humane) but a sweet compounde of both, religion and nature' (Rogers, 1642, p. 150). The precise balance to be achieved between these two dimensions was, however, a matter of some ambiguity. Calvin, for example, cautioned that 'thoughe the honestie of mariage do couer the fylthienesse of incontinence, yet it oughte not fourthwyth to be a prouocation thereof', and followed Catholic teaching in asserting that a husband might become 'the adulterer of hys owne wyfe, whyche in vse of wedlocke hath no care of shamefastnesse or honestie' (Calvin, 1561, II, p. 60). The elision of culinary and sexual appetite in early modern drama is overwhelmingly associated with excessive forms of desire which exceed the bounds of moderation. It is true that, as Khamphommala has noted, Shakespearean comedy deploys 'the promise of a wedding feast that puts an end to sexual frustration while filling stomachs' (Khamphommala, 2008, p. 18). Yet it is also the case that these feasts are rarely actually staged. Repeatedly, in the early modern theatre, appetite is deployed to explore 'enflamed' desires which threaten the bounds of both chastity and social stability. Indeed, the equation of appetite and lust serves to depict not only the consequences of this dangerous excess, but also the cause. The complex relationship between hunger and appetite provided a repertoire of images and connections through which the theatre might conceptualise the origin of a shift from legitimate 'natural' desire to destabilising sexual excess.

One of the more overt instances of this tendency occurs in Shakespeare's *Measure for Measure* (1604), in which Angelo is from the very beginning associated with an unnatural resistance to both appetite and sexual desire. The Duke, resolving to test the sincerity of his apparently abstemious and incorruptible nature, remarks:

> Lord Angelo is precise,
> Stands at a guard with envy, scarce confesses
> That his blood flows, or that his appetite
> Is more to bread than stone. Hence shall we see
> If power change purpose, what our seemers be. (1.3.50–4)

Appetite emerges as a surrogate for what will rapidly be shown to be Angelo's uncontrollable sexual desires. In the first instance, the equation of the two serves to emphasise his hypocrisy. Like hunger, sexual desire implicitly appears as a natural and necessary drive. The implied universality of hunger and appetite becomes a means to express the insincerity of those who deny their desires. In part, as Fitzpatrick has noted, this stems from a broader distrust of excessive fasting in the wake of the Reformation (Fitzpatrick, 2007, p. 3). But the play also deploys a more extensive parallel between the drives of hunger and desire. It is Angelo's abstinence which prompts the awakening of an uncontrollable desire. Like hunger, sexual desire if repressed threatens to emerge as an uncontrollable appetite. Angelo's lust can consequently be read as equivalent to the unnatural or cannibalistic feasts that define contemporary depictions of famine or dearth. Moderate culinary and sexual consumption is necessary to avoid uncontrollable outbreaks of either lust or revolt.

More frequently, these twin appetites are situated as products of material indulgence. In Act II, Scene III of *The Guardian*, for instance, the cook announces the arrival of a gentlewoman to the house of the gentleman Adorio, declaring:

> I usher
> Such an unexpected dainty bit for breakfast,
> As yet I never cook'd: 'tis not Potargo,
> Fride Frogs, Potato's Marrow'd, Cavear,
> Carps tongues, the Pith of an English Chine of Beef
> Nor our Italian delicate oyl'd Mushrooms,
> And yet a drawer on too; and if you shew not
> An appetite and a strong one, I'll not say
> To eat it, but devour it, without grace too,
> For it will not stay a preface, I am shamed
> And all my past provocatives will be jeer'd at. (II.iii.22–32)

The speech invokes a series of foods notable for their association with both culinary and sexual indulgence. Chine could signify a specific joint of meat, but also meant 'open fissure or crack in a surface' which, as Jay Halio notes in his edition of Shakespeare's *Henry VIII*, probably imbued it with sexual connotations (*OED*, 'Chine', def. 1a; Shakespeare, 1999b, p. 209, n. 24). Potatoes, as Fitzpatrick has demonstrated, were 'expensive, exotic and considered an aphrodisiac' (Fitzpatrick, 2011, 340). Hall, for instance, in his *Discovery of a New World*, describes how stallions are 'dieted with Eringo's, Potatoes, Cullises, and other dishes of lusts deuising' (Hall, 1609, p. 109). The dishes which the cook is accustomed to serve are of an overtly international nature, linking this exorbitant consumption with the cosmopolitanism of urban life. Potargo, or Bottarga, was the salted roe of tuna or mullet, and was described by contemporary sources as 'an Italian meat' (Rosselli, 1598, sig. H2$^{v}$). 'Fride frogs' seem to have been associated with Spain.[7] Most obviously, the play foregrounds the cannibalistic dimension to this equation of appetite and sexual desire. Mirtilla, the gentlewoman in question, is converted into merely another luxury dish, a 'provocative' to stimulate their appetites. Yet the speech's repeated emphasis upon the decadent consumption which defines the space of Adorio's home serves to situate this cannibalistic desire as the product of pre-existing culinary appetites.

These connections become even more apparent in contemporary depictions of courtly excess. Albala has demonstrated the increasing tendency of dietary authors in the period to distance themselves from a courtly audience and argues that criticism of courtly food 'pervades' the later dietaries (Albala, 2002, p. 189). On the stage, sexual and culinary desires coalesce. Through consideration of the theatre's depiction of the physical connections between excessive appetite and sexual desire, it is possible to discern a strand linking the period's changing social and economic structure to the sexual corruption of the court. An emphasis on the material links between appetite and sexual desire grounds these dangers in an awareness of plenty, inequality and the abuse of power. A significant example can be found in Middleton's *The Revenger's Tragedy* (1606). In the opening act, Spurio, the bastard son of the Duke, describes the circumstances of his own conception, declaring:

> I was begot
> After some gluttonous dinner; some stirring dish
> Was my first father. When deep healths went round,
> And ladies' cheeks were painted red with wine,
> Their tongues as short and nimble as their heels,
> Uttering words sweet and thick, and when they rose
> Were merrily dispos'd to fall again:
> In such a whisp'ring and withdrawing hour,
> When base male-bawds kept sentinel at stair-head,
> Was I stol'n softly . . . (I.ii.178–87)

The speech partakes of a conventional association between lust and gluttony, but also emphasises the degree to which the circumstances of the banquet enable illicit sexual encounters. The speech consistently elides processes of eating, speaking and of sexual consummation. Spurio is the son of 'some stirring dish', displacing responsibility for the sexual act from

7 George Wither, for instance, claims that the 'housewife' famine first 'learn'd the Spaniards how to dresse / Their Frogs' (Wither, 1628, p. 20).

the Duke to the culinary and social conditions which made it possible. The adjective 'stirring' alludes to the sexual properties which many dishes were believed to have in the Renaissance; 'Some', meanwhile, introduces an element of interchangeability, implying the free exchange of both women, men and food. In a similar manner, the 'ladies' cheeks' are 'painted red with wine', equating the consumption of alcohol with the implications of sexual availability associated with make-up in the period. Likewise, emphasis is placed upon the 'tongues' of the ladies at the banquet, with the words they utter described as 'sweet and thick'. An active tongue was, in the period, associated not just with speech but with sexual proclivity, while the culinary image implied by sweet and thick connects both meanings to the luxurious fare which has been consumed and which triggers both speech and sex. The banquet emerges as a space where women, drink and dishes circulate, enabling the satisfaction of various illicit appetites.

Yet, in deploying the model of hunger and appetite as a means of understanding an excessive sexual desire, the contemporary theatre is representing the sexual relationship in a relatively specific way. The elision of sexual and culinary appetite serves to construct sexual activity as an act of consumption. As such, the comparison marginalises broader conceptions of sex, widespread in the period, as a reciprocal exchange of fluids from which both parties might derive pleasure.[8] As critics such as Lennartz have noted it is, unsurprisingly, often male desire which is foregrounded in this context (Lennartz, 2012, p. 10). In *Othello*, for instance, Emilia declares:

> 'Tis not a year or two shows us a man.
> They are all but stomachs, and we all but food:
> They eat us hungerly, and when they are full,
> They belch us. (III.iv.104–7)

In a text which elsewhere raises the possibility of a model of marital relations rooted in discursive communication, the deployment of culinary imagery reduces marriage to a state of cannibalistic feeding. Women, in this schema, are interchangeable. They simply constitute different varieties of food, incapable of satiating an overpowering male appetite. Marriage itself, meanwhile, implicitly reproduces the culinary cycle of glutton. Courtship and the wedding night become a period of 'hungerly' feeding, while the consequent satiation of appetite prompts the discharge of the unwanted female remnants. If desire, like appetite, is an implicitly recurrent drive, the object of

[8] Stone notes the dominance of the view, inherited from Galen, that 'the mingling of sexual fluids may not be necessary for conception, but is necessary for the production of strong and healthy children' (Stone, 1977, p. 489).

that desire is figured as a specifically finite foodstuff, destined to be consumed and discarded. The conjunction of appetite and masculine, heterosexual desire foregrounds the disruptive capacity of power and excess. Interpersonal exchange is reconstituted through the imagery of appetite as a subject–object relationship predicated on consumption.

This dimension becomes particularly apparent in the representation of sexual and political tyranny. As has been noted by a wide range of critics, early modern texts frequently construct criticism of monarchical and tyrannical politics in sexual terms.[9] Yet the deployment of appetite as a means to conceptualise this sexual tyranny foregrounds the political, as well as sexual, transition from a reciprocal relationship to one of consumption. In Fletcher and Massinger's *The Custom of the Country*, for instance, the tyrannous Clodio is a ruler who benefits from his country's eponymous custom of the *droit de seigneur*. He is repeatedly defined in terms that blur the boundaries between appetite and desire, figured as 'a Canniball, that feedes on the heads of maides, / Then flings their bones and bodies to the Devil' (I.i.155–6). His consumption of maidenheads is transformed through a punning inversion into a cannibalistic feasting on the 'heads of maids'. The visceral image of discarded bones, meanwhile, performs an inversion of Clodio's status, implying not simply the abuse of power but the reduction of the tyrant to a level of barbarism. The use of culinary imagery to explore sexual appetite emphasises the social consequences of desire's destabilising potential. The opposition of boundless appetite to finite foodstuff here emerges as a critique of Clodio's tyrannical power. Clodio's rule is figured as a parasitical consumption of his people and resources. In the context of royal excess, appetite implies wider political issues of excess, an inability to remain within conventional bounds of moderation.

Of course, this metaphorical tendency in the elision of appetite and desire is reinforced by the more literal associations of excess. It is frequently the case that in depictions of the court, appetite and desire are associated in such a manner that the social consequences of consumption are foregrounded. *The Picture*, for instance, depicts two lecherous courtiers whose sexual and culinary indulgence threatens to undermine the strength of the nation. One expresses his displeasure at his own capacity to seduce virgins, declaring:

9 Perry argues that seditious voices in the period 'frequently imagined the influence of royal favourites in eroticised terms', and argues that these eroticised images of familiarity constituted the period's 'most important unofficial vehicle for exploring constitutional unease concerning the nature and limits of personal monarchy within the balanced English constitution' (Perry, 2006, p. 131; p. 1). Likewise, Linda Woodbridge argues that in revenge tragedy tyranny is 'usually sexual', with the sexual dimension functioning as 'synecdoche for other rights violations' (Woodbridge, 2010, p. 185; p. 179).

There's no beauty
But yeeldes ere it be summon'd, and as nature
Had sign'd me the monopolie of maidenheads,
There's none can buy till I have made my market,
Satiety cloyes me . . . (I.ii.44–8)

Although 'satiety' could signify the satisfaction of any appetite, it was primarily associated with food, including 'the feeling of disgust or surfeit caused by excess of food' (*OED*, 'satiety', def. 1a). Cloy, likewise, could signify 'to overload with food, so as to cause loathing' (*OED*, 'cloy', def. 7). These culinary images occur in tandem with parodic references to court practices. Ricardo holds a 'monopolie' on maidenheads, a practice associated with a wide range of goods, but particularly luxury comestibles. Sexual and culinary excess are invoked in conjunction with imagery rooted in courtly corruption. Indeed, the actions of the two courtiers are figured as destructive in a fundamentally material sense. The court advisor Eubulus declares that they 'have donne / More hurt to the Kingdome by superfluous braverie . . . then a war / Or a long famine' (II.ii.31–4). The speech deploys the imagery of scarcity and famine, constituting appetite symbolically as a threat to the social order. The space of the court is defined by appetites which, in both a literal and metaphorical sense, threaten to trigger instability. Excessive appetites, whether literal or sexual, are damaging, opposed to the virtuous moderation necessary for the correct running of the state. The physical connection between consumption and sexual desire grounds the depiction of appetite in the excess which increasingly appeared to dominate courtly life in the period.

The elision of sexual and culinary appetite provides a framework through which early modern drama could portray unrestrained desire and its consequences, but also manifests a tendency to present desire as an expression of inequitable power relations. At the domestic level, it is visible as petty tyranny, the reduction of women to the status of objects to be consumed. At the political level, it is an index of a tyrant's relationship to his people. The representation of what were believed to be very literal connections between excessive consumption and excessive desire locates these drives in spaces of courtly or urban indulgence, so that sexual profligacy becomes merely the most visible instance of a more general excess. At the same time, the deployment of culinary imagery has a vital role in making explicit the parasitical nature of courtly decadence, linking the moral concerns of sexual exploitation with the broader social consequences of unrestrained desire. Literal consumption of food elides with the metaphorical consumption of people. At its heart, the conjunction of appetite and desire foregrounds the capacity of the subject to act upon the world. By blurring the distinction between these drives, the early modern theatre asserts an image of sexual activity as the exertion of power.

## Hunger, Appetite and Resistance

If the deployment of culinary imagery to depict desire has a tendency to foreground the destructive power of excessive sexual appetite, it also has the capacity to imply a pronounced degree of vulnerability. Critics have tended to emphasise the masculine nature of these culinary and sexual appetites, but the effacement of female desire can hardly be assumed in the early modern period. As Lawrence Stone has explained, 'the capacity of the female for multiple orgasms far exceeding the male ability to keep pace was a well-known fact' (Stone, 1977, p. 495). Robert Burton, for instance, declared 'of womens vnnaturall, vnsatiable lust, what countrey, what village doth not complaine?' (Burton, 1621, p. 541). Indeed, early modern plays frequently deploy hunger and appetite to conceptualise a specifically female form of desire. In *As You Like It*, the pregnancy consequent on sexual activity is reconstituted by Celia as a cannibalistic desire to 'put a man in your belly' (III.ii.198). In plays such as *Blurt, Master Constable*, a courtesan's clients are described as 'picking meate' (Dekker, 1602, sig. $D1^r$), to be consumed. And in *The Honest Whore* (1604), Bellafront refers to her 'pretty servant [who] sees three court dishes before her, and not one good bit in them' (vi.149–50). As such, the translation of reciprocal sexual activity into the simple subject–object relationship of culinary consumption has the potential to introduce a marked ambiguity regarding the question of who is eating whom.

Furthermore, precisely because the broader elision of appetite and desire is so frequently rooted in depictions of tyrannous excess, female appetite has the potential to function as a mode of critique. The conjunction of the culinary and the sexual makes it possible for forms of resistance to be imagined. A significant example is Middleton and Dekker's *The Bloody Banquet*.[10] The play appears to have been performed in the wake of the Midland Revolt, and displays a repeated concern with both the plight of the poor and the excesses of the rich. In the primary plot, a young queen

[10] *The Bloody Banquet* was published in 1639, but the precise date of its original performance is unclear. Chris Meads hypothesises that the play may have originally been written in the late 1630s, and that it consequently functions as 'a splendid summation of the trends and tropes of all banquet scenes up to that point' (Meads, 2001, p. 154). Taylor, by contrast, identifies a series of contemporary references within the parodic clowning scene which lead him to situate the original date of performance in approximately 1609, shortly after the Midland Rising, though he acknowledges that the text received later revisions before publication (Taylor, 2001). Although Taylor's argument for the earlier date is more convincing, Meads's claim attests to the absolute significance of these depictions of courtly excess for the text.

seduces a courtier at her husband's court, inviting him to a lavish, masked banquet and embarks on an affair under condition of anonymity. When he uncovers her identity, she murders him. But her husband, who has been informed of the affair, promptly forces her to consume the flesh of her deceased lover. In its cannibalistic assertion of the equivalence of sexual and culinary appetites, the play appears to embody a relatively conventional association of two forms of elite excess. But it is also notable that the excessive appetites of the primary plot are juxtaposed with a subplot, in which the wife of the country's deposed former ruler is forced to wander a landscape defined by hunger and want. The play consequently emerges as deeply concerned with the interconnection of hunger, appetite and sexual desire. As Gary Taylor has argued, the two plots 'set in opposition to one another two social worlds, defined by their relationship to ingestion' (Taylor, 2001, p. 15). Less clear, however, is the precise nature of the connection between these two culinary worlds. For many critics, the play constitutes a relatively conventional attack on the excesses of the rich. Pannen, for instance, argues that 'lust and want for more, i.e. an insatiable appetite, are ... the reasons and catalysts for this tragedy' (Pannen, 2012, p. 99). Yet this understanding of the relationship between hunger and appetite is repeatedly placed in tension with an association of sexual desire not with appetite, but with hunger and resistance. The play's cannibalistic queen is an emblem of both elite decadence and the riotous appetites of the rebellious poor.

The equivalence of a predatory, proto-capitalist appetite and sexual desire is established early in the play, and appears with particular clarity in a lengthy satirical scene in which two clowns deliver a description of a world dominated by wolves, which they categorise, according to socio-geographic location, as court wolves, city wolves, country wolves and sea wolves. The resulting image of contemporary society resembles in many respects that of the fishermen in Shakespeare's *Pericles*, who decry a world in which, on both land and sea, 'the great ones eat up the little ones' (II.i.28–9). By contrast with Shakespeare's play, however, *The Bloody Banquet* explicitly links these ungoverned social appetites with female sexual ones. The clowns declare that the literal wolves they are attempting to trap 'by their greediness ... should be she-wolves, / For the belly of a she-wolf / Is never satisfied till it be dammed up' (II.i.16–18). In presenting appetite as a predominantly feminine drive, the play constructs proto-capitalist acquisition as effeminising. But the analogy also privileges female sexual rapaciousness, and reflects a contemporary tendency to construct women, especially prostitutes, as devouring men. In doing so, the play highlights female sexual appetite. The actions of the Young Queen, who satisfies first her sexual and then her literal appetite with the flesh of her lover, might therefore be understood as the emblem of the worst excesses of a broader, proto-capitalist drive to consume.

A similar elision of culinary and sexual desire defines the representation of the Young Queen's seduction of her lover Tymethes. Here, the play consciously co-opts the literary tradition of the court banquet. In Act III, the Young Queen Thetis arranges a masked entertainment, in which her prospective lover is tantalised with both exquisite dishes and the promise of the sexual intercourse which will follow. As such, this first banquet scene constitutes what Taylor has described as the 'visual correlative' of the offstage adultery (Taylor, 2001, p. 15). As the audience gazes on the onstage culinary consumption, they are encouraged to imagine the offstage sexual indulgence. Throughout, the ostensible emphasis of the scene is on the appetites of Tymethes. The pander Roxano declares:

> This banquet from her own hand received grace,
> Herself prepared it for you – as appears
> By the choice sweets it yields, able to move
> A man past sense to the delights of love.
> I bid you welcome as her most prized guest,
> First to this banquet, next to pleasure's feast. (III.iii.37–42)

Roxano's speech imbues Thetis's labour with erotic connotations. She becomes figured as the final course upon which Tymethes will feast. As Tymethes himself later notes, 'all this nothing was / To the delicious pleasures of her bed' (IV.i.4–5). The excess of the banquet is eclipsed by the excess of the bedroom. At the same time, the fact that the queen is presented in this productive culinary context is relatively unusual. Although in practice women in numerous households of varying degrees of status played a significant role in the preparation of food, on the stage this position is more normally associated with professional male cooks. At one level, of course, this position might be understood as situating the queen in a menial position of service. But the play's concerted emphasis upon the connections between culinary and erotic stimulation ensures that she is also placed in a position of power. As in Massinger's *The Picture*, the close connections between appetite and desire imbue the female figure that produces sustenance with a marked degree of agency. By controlling the supply of food, the queen implicitly exerts control over Tymethes' sexuality, enabling her to assume the traditionally masculine role of host.

This ambiguity is accentuated by the scene's marked degree of dramatic irony. Throughout, Tymethes' consumption is narrated by Roxano, who accompanies the meal with a series of moralistic asides. He declares:

> I would not taste of such a banquet to feel that which follows it for the love of an empress. 'Tis more dangerous to be a lecher than to enter upon a breach. Yet how securely he munches!
> His thoughts are sweeter than the very meats before him.
> He little dreams of his destruction,
> His horrid fearful ruin, which cannot be withstood. (III.iii.70–6)

Once again, the emphasis upon Tymethes' lecherous nature and excessive consumption ostensibly emphasises the role played by his personal appetites. The sweetness of the banquet implicitly pales in comparison with the imagined intercourse which follows. Yet that moment of present consumption is also repeatedly juxtaposed with images of Tymethes's eventual destruction. In a material sense, the emphasis reflects the presence of the court spy, Mazeres, who throughout the scene engages in a series of bungled attempts to poison Tymethes. But in a more general sense, the lines express the fact that Tymethes's indulgence of appetite, as he unknowingly enters into a relationship with his country's queen, in fact leaves him in a markedly vulnerable position. Roxano's moralising, with its repeated emphasis on the imagery of defiled food and corruption, forces recognition of an underlying ambiguity as to who is eating whom. By indulging in consumption, Tymethes makes inevitable the fact that he too will in turn be consumed.

The cannibalistic banquet with which the play concludes reinforces these tensions. Deprived of his revenge following the queen's murder of her lover, the Tyrant, Armatrites, forces his wife to feed on the body of Tymethes. For Taylor, the Young Queen's actions literalise the 'social cannibalism' implied by the clowns' earlier description of a society of wolves (Taylor, 2001, p. 17). As such, it can be said to constitute the primary instance of the unrestrained appetites which appear to dominate the play. Armatrites justifies his revenge in terms which insist upon the parallels between sex and cannibalism. His revenge is predicated upon the literal incorporation of Tymethes's body into that of the queen. He declares 'The lecher must be swallowed rib by rib. His flesh is sweet; it melts, it goes down merrily' (V.i.204–5). As Julia Gasper has noted, the sequence can be understood in the context of contemporary ideas regarding the sexual act. Semen was believed to be formed from blood, and excessive sexual intercourse was consequently believed to be potentially effeminising for men. The Young Queen's sexualised cannibalism is juxtaposed with the actions of the outlawed Old Queen, who nourishes her starving infants with her own milk. For Gasper, 'the young Queen feasts on men, while her virtuous antithesis feeds and nurtures them' (Gasper, 2007, p. 639). Cannibalism consequently constitutes the logical extension of her earlier desire. At the same time, the cannibal act is figured in ways which imply that the queen has appropriated specifically male forms of desire. Armatrites tells his wife 'Here's deer struck dead with thy own hand; / 'Tis venison for thy own tooth. Thou know'st the relish: / A dearer place hath been thy taster' (IV.iii.215–17). As Pannen has noted, the punning reference to what she holds dear, translated into deer to eat, reinforces the play's underlying 'combination of eating and sex', while the 'dearer place' links the queen's mouth with her vagina (Pannen, 2012, p. 101). But the deployment of the imagery of hunting also reverses the contemporary tendency to reduce women to food. In large part, the horror inherent in the play's grisly climax is a product of the extent to which it literalises the queen's appetite for men. The play's second banquet provides the answer to the ambiguities inherent in the first. In the final instance, it is Tymethes who is consumed.

Yet it must be acknowledged that the text resists a simple identification of lust and appetite. The queen is repeatedly associated not with excess, but with hunger. On her first appearance, her situation, surrounded by a retinue of servants in the pay of her jealous, tyrannical husband, is described by her future lover through the invocation of a contemporary proverb. Tymethes declares 'Hunger and lust will break through flesh and stones, / And like a whirlwind blows ope castle doors, / Italian padlocks' (I.iii.27–9). The conventional version of this claim, as it appears in texts such as *Coriolanus*, is simply 'Hunger breaks through stone walls'.[11] Taylor has argued that by fusing hunger to lust, the text 'yokes hunger to lust, and stone to flesh, making the two paired appetites equally uncontainable' (Taylor, 2001, p. 14). More significant, however, is the extent to which this relatively unconventional pairing associates the queen with the famished poor, rather than the indulgent rich. Her subsequent infidelity consequently retains the potential to emerge as an appetite born from deprivation, in a similar manner to the unruly appetites of the lower classes in plays such as *The Bashful Lover* or *2 Henry VI*. In part, this association may be read in sexual terms. Like that of Isabella in *Women Pleased*, the wife's hunger can be interpreted as a veiled reference to the husband's impotence.[12] But, in the more overtly political context of *The Bloody*

[11] For further examples see Tilley (1950, p. 333). [12] See Chapter 2.

*Banquet*, this shared emphasis on hunger also raises the possibility that the queen may function as a surrogate for the hungry poor. Sexual appetite has the potential to operate as the equivalent of the appetites of revolt.

Indeed, the queen's eventual cannibalism is figured as a product not of appetite, but of hunger. Armatrites declares 'This as a penance I enjoined her to: / To taste no other sustenance, no, nor airs / Till her love's body be consumed in hers' (V.i.180–2). The invocation of the language of penance parodically situates the queen's actions as a form of religious reparation, while the consumption of the beloved body risks emerging as a grotesque inversion of the Eucharist. The Tyrant's actions might be read as an irreligious incursion upon the divine. Yet the passage also asserts the compelling power of hunger. Faced with a choice between starvation and cannibalism, the queen chooses the latter. On one level, this might be said to absolve the Young Queen of responsibility. A more troubling possibility is that hunger has awakened the destructive appetites which she now willingly indulges. As Taylor has argued, by contrast with the source text 'this Queen apparently continues to dine, onstage, during fifty-four lines of dialogue' (Taylor, 2001, p. 30). Yet the sight of a woman feasting on her lover is surely also calculated to encourage parallels between the queen's situation and contemporary accounts of famine.[13] As such, the Tyrant's strategy seems implicitly to align the Young Queen with the poor existing outside the walls of the castle. Once again, the text seems to suggest that hunger and lust may be equivalents, rather than existing in opposition to each other.

These parallels are emphasised by the scene's parodic deployment of the language of hospitality. Also present at the cannibalistic feast are the deposed King and his courtiers, secretly returned from exile. Disguised as pilgrims, the fugitives are welcomed by the Tyrant, who tells them 'We are but stewards for such guests as you: / What we possess is yours, to your wants due. / We are only rich for your necessities' (V.i.137–9). To an extent, this parodic approach serves to insist on the presence of the poor beyond the walls of the court, reinforcing the sense of cannibalism as the final act of elite depravity. At the same time, however, the appearance of the feigned courtiers also asserts the shared bonds of hunger between supposed pilgrims and cannibalistic queen. Indeed, the structure of the play privileges the queen as subject of resistance. The traditional revenger figures are, for much of the play, offstage. And while it is the King and his followers who in the final instance execute the Tyrant, they are driven to do

[13] See Chapter 3.

so not by their own grievances, but by the plight of the Young Queen. It is she who brings down the stone walls of the Tyrant's oppression.

As such, it might be argued that the play is defined by a fundamental ambiguity. At one level, the Young Queen's shift from sexual intercourse to cannibalism functions as a critique of both elite decadence and a voracious female appetite. The onstage consumption of flesh makes explicit the cannibal dimensions inherent in the metaphorical elision of the bounds between appetite and sexual desire. At the same time, however, to focus only on the queen's appetite risks replicating the perspective of the Tyrant. While Armatrites may justify his actions with the blithe declaration 'Sweet was your lust; what can be bitter there?' (V.i.277), the audience is hardly encouraged to share this perspective. Indeed, attention to the queen's repeated association with hunger, rather than appetite, reveals the extent to which she emerges as surrogate for an entire world beyond the walls of the castle. The Young Queen's desire emerges alternatively as decadent excess and act of rebellion. The text establishes a complex inversion of dominant trends in the representation of appetite, desire and courtly excess. Women's desire threatens to disrupt or reverse unrestrained male appetite. Yet the emergence of appetite as a surrogate for tyrannous excess lends female sexual appetite the potential to acquire at least a partial degree of legitimacy.

## Profit and Corruption

The ambiguities over who is eating whom are compounded by tensions regarding the potentially debilitating or effeminising nature of the substances to be consumed. The conjunction of appetite and desire is deployed to express anxiety at disease, at impotence or at the consequences of cross-class desire. But it also, above all, functions to conceptualise the increasing intrusion of market forces into every aspect of early modern life. In order to understand this emphasis, it is necessary to consider the changing nature of conceptions of the body in the period, and in particular the changing status of the grotesque.[14] For Mikhail Bakhtin, the grotesque defines a body

[14] Bakhtin's concepts of the grotesque and carnivalesque have been deployed by a wide range of critics with reference to Renaissance literature. A central theme has been the relationship between popular carnival forms and the theatre as institution. Bristol argues that these collective traditions give rise to 'dramatic forms that are intensely critical and even experimental in their representation of social and political structure' (Bristol, 1985, p. 4). Bruster, by contrast, emphasises the commercial dimension, arguing that the playhouses constituted 'places of business [which] regularized and normalized carnival' (Bruster, 1992, p. 10). Significant work has been carried out which relates the porous nature of the grotesque body to contemporary humoral theory, with Gail Kern Paster arguing that the latter

which 'is not separated from the rest of the world ... is not a closed, completed unit ... is unfinished, outgrows itself, transgresses its own limits' (Bakhtin, 1984, p. 26). It is a body which 'discloses its essence as a principle of growth which exceeds its own limits only in copulation, pregnancy, childbirth, the throes of death, eating, drinking, or defecation' (Bakhtin, 1984, p. 26). The grotesque is most commonly situated in terms of the temporal phenomenon of carnival, but for Bakhtin it also has a spatial dimension. It is embodied in the marketplace, conceived as 'a world in itself, a world which was one; ... the centre of all that was unofficial'. This spatial dimension is significant because the 'market' was itself subject to pronounced change in this period. As Jean-Christophe Agnew has demonstrated, the market in early modern England was increasingly 'placeless' (Agnew, 1986, p. 59). It exceeded the limits of space and time, operating instead as a system of 'commodity circulation' which exerted a defining influence over society (Agnew, 1986, p. 50). The grotesque body is implicated in this shift, and the representation of culinary and sexual appetites in a grotesque register provided the early modern theatres with a significant means of understanding a market which increasingly seemed pervasive. The market as a space of popular celebration becomes displaced by the market as a system of exchange.

The definitive example of these tensions is Ben Jonson's *Bartholomew Fair*. Historically, the eponymous fair was a temporal event, occurring annually on 24 August. But it was also spatially defined, held at Smithfield, the site of the livestock market. The play depicts a group of citizens who find their puritanical hypocrisy exposed within this carnivalesque space. The structure, although broadly in accord with the classical unities of time and place, is far more fragmented than is typical of Jonson's plays. As such, the grotesque body of the pig-woman Ursula, whose booth stands at the heart of the fair, acquires significance as a unifying principle. In her shop, the sale of sex, food and beer occur in conjunction, typifying the appetites of the fair; her very corpulence embodies the play's consistent emphasis on the 'enormities' of the Bartholomew festivities (II.i.34). Jonson is a playwright who has long been associated not simply with food, but

offers 'historical corroboration of the Bakhtinian grotesque', while simultaneously providing an opportunity for 'critique and correction' of the paradigm's totalising tendencies. Critics have also attacked the model's utopian dimension (Paster, 1993, p. 15). Stallybrass and White warn against 'its nostalgia; its uncritical populism ... its failure to do away with the official dominant culture, its licensed complicity' (Stallybrass and White, 1986, p. 19). Cohen claims that the problem lies 'in overestimating the autonomy of the oppressed, in succumbing to populist voluntarism' (Cohen, 1985, p. 27).

with the bodily processes which accompany it, and in particular digestion and excretion.[15] *Bartholomew Fair* is a text in which the connections between bodily functions and comestibles assume an especially prominent position.[16] Critics have emphasised the unease with which the grotesque body is treated in the text. Gail Kern Paster argues that the play deploys the functions of the grotesque body to 'subordinate women as sexual objects', situating them within the context of 'early modern English culture's complex articulation of gender – the weaker vessel as leaky vessel' (Paster, 1993, pp. 53, 24). Lori Schroeder Haslem suggests that the play rejects the Bakhtinian model because 'the association between the digestive/excretory and the female sexual cannot be explained in ... wholly positive terms' (Haslem, 1995, p. 439). As such 'while ostensibly striking a carnivalesque attitude toward this association, [*Bartholomew Fair*] also advances a more negative attitude – one grounded in a rhetoric of the maternal body as diseased and in need of a purgative cure' (Haslem, 1995, p. 439). A similar ambiguity can be discerned in the play's treatment of female food production. For Huey-Ling Lee, the play embodies the extent to which a cook's gender 'determines whether the food he or she makes is nurturing or polluting' (Lee, 2006, p. 251). Keri Sanburn Behre, by contrast, argues that Ursula's role as producer of food has the potential to 'expose a crack in the patriarchal power structure and cultural anxiety about women's power' (Behre, 2018, p. 139). Yet whether focussing on the ambiguity of the grotesque body, or of female food production, it is necessary to acknowledge the extent to which the play's ambivalence springs from its implication in a system of exchange and commodification which is typified in, but by no means restricted to, the fair. Attention to the representation of sexual desire and appetite reveals a profound anxiety at the porous nature of the grotesque body. That anxiety springs, in the final instance, from the flux of the market itself.

Throughout, Jonson employs a calculated confusion between various forms of appetite. In the space of the fair, this intertwining of culinary and sexual appetites is clearly associated with a nascent capitalist economy. The citizens' trip to the fair is initially motivated by a desire to consume roast

[15] Bruce Boehrer has asserted Jonson's 'enduring fascination with alimentary matters', placing particular emphasis on the excretory dimension to Jonson's work (Boehrer, 1997, p. 3). In a similar manner, Andrew Moran claims that Jonson 'always remembered the privy behind the dining hall' (Moran, 2015, p. 23). Robert Appelbaum has noted that Jonson himself was 'an avid eater and drinker, even in defiance of the science of the day', and situates this biographical dimension in the context of Jonson's recurrent interest in 'the *social meanings* of food' (Appelbaum, 2010, pp. 315, 317).

[16] Moran notes that 'none of his comedies more revolves around bodily functions than does *Bartholomew Fair*' (Moran, 2015, p. 23).

pig. Yet the word pig is subjected to a profound instability in the play. Ursula, the 'oily pig-woman' (Ind.91–2), is not simply a vendor of roast meat, but has been 'punk, pinnace, and bawd, any time these two and twenty years', and runs an establishment where you 'may ha' your punk and your pig in state' (II.ii.60–1; II.v.33). References to Ursula's 'litter of pigs' and her role as 'mother o' the pigs' thus imply not simply the food she sells, but also the prostitutes who operate out of her booth (II.iii.2; II.v.57). In Act III, Scene II, the search for pig leads the citizens to Ursula's booth. There they encounter a pimp, the Irish Captain Whit, who by the end of the play has succeeded in persuading both Win and Madam Overdo to adopt the appearance and possibly the practices of prostitutes. He describes the food on offer, declaring:

> A delicate show-pig, little mistress, with shweet sauce, and crackling, like de bay-leaf i' de fire, la! Tou shalt ha' de clean side o' de table-clot, and di glass vash'd with phatersh of Dame Annesh Cleare. (III.ii.50–2)

As Tracy Thong has noted, 'There is ambiguity as to whether Whit is addressing Win or referring to her as a "delicate show-pig"' (Thong, 2007, p. 294). The reference to 'bay-leaf', which was, as Joan Fitzpatrick has noted, 'reputed to ward off disease' (Fitzpatrick, 2011, p. 33), implies preparation for exposure to sexually transmitted infections. Likewise, the scene includes reference to 'rosemary-branches' which, as Williams has noted, were believed to induce abortion (cf. Williams, 1994, III, p. 263). The same conjunction of images is deployed by Shakespeare, in *Pericles*, in which a Bawd tells the kidnapped Mariana, 'come up, my dish of chastity with rosemary and bays' (xix.172–6). The association of young women with these herbs serves simultaneously to alert the audience to the potential consequences of prostitution, and to figure the women's bodies as foods which require seasoning. If appetite is associated with sexual desire in the play, it is with a specific form of that desire which can only be satisfied through purchase. To satisfy an appetite for food is by implication to show a desire for sex, and vice versa.

Connections between food, sex, corruption and profit recur in the play. The fair is a space defined by the sale of degenerated foodstuffs, with gingerbread made from 'stale bread, rotten eggs, musty ginger, and dead honey' (II.ii.7). Yet as the reference to bay-leaves implies, prostitutes too can be rotten. When told he may receive both punk and pig 'piping hot' (II.v.34), Quarlous notes that he would 'rather ha'my punk cold' (II.v.35). The punning response implies the presence of venereal disease amongst the booth's prostitutes, so that they are hot from the pox. Likewise, Ursula hopes that the two gallants will be 'plagued one day – poxed they are already, I am sure – with lean playhouse poultry' (II.v.78–9) and later expresses a desire to see them 'poxed first, and pilled, and double piled' (II.v.101). The thinness of the imagined prostitutes, as Fouassier has noted, is not simply a product of hunger, but also of venereal diseases, while the baldness implied by the reference to 'double piled' is likewise a result of the pox (Fouassier, 2008, p. 33). Crucially, the parallels between the two types of corrupt commodities shown on stage serves to emphasise their connections to the fair's status as market. At a time when the early modern authorities were increasingly concerned with measures to prevent the adulteration of basic foodstuffs, the conjunction of rotten food with infected prostitutes marks both as indicative of the dangerous consequences of an emergent capitalist society.[17] This in turn imparts a pronounced element of vulnerability to the residual emphasis upon openness inherent in the grotesque body, for it implies that its porous nature opens it up to infection from the corrupting effects of exchange.

Ostensibly, the space outside the fair is distanced from this emphasis upon exchange and the grotesque. The puritan reverend Busy declares of appetite that it is 'the disease of longing, it is a disease, a carnal disease, or appetite, incident to women; and as it is carnal, and incident, it is natural, very natural' (I.vi.39–40). The word carnal can mean in this context simply fleshly or bodily, but also implies a specifically sexual longing. Busy's emphasis upon the importance of place, so that pork may be 'a meat that is nourishing, and may be longed for', but which when consumed in the fair acquires 'a spice of idolatry', recalls theological debate regarding the propriety of sexual desire in and out of the state of marriage (I.vi.41; I.vi.44). But it also serves to distinguish between the capitalist practices of the fair and those of the city. The flux of the market is notionally presented as other, a space outside the bounds of ordinary citizen life, yet *Bartholomew Fair*'s emphasis upon hypocrisy undermines this distinction. When the citizens arrive at Ursula's booth, she assumes that they lack the capacity to consume, and justifies this assumption precisely because they have come from the centre of London, declaring 'they are all sippers, sippers o' the city; they look as they would not drink off two penn'orth of bottle-ale amongst 'em' (III.ii.87–8). Yet Knockem responds that they are 'good guests, I say, right hypocrites, good gluttons' (III.ii.91). For all

[17] Cockayne emphasises the extent to which bread loaves 'could be deliberately adulterated with stones and other items to bulk them up' (Cockayne, 2007, p. 91). Diane Purkiss notes that 'the assize of bread was in force until the beginning of the nineteenth century and was only then abolished in London' (Purkiss, 2010, p. 16).

their puritanical pretensions, they remain driven by the same appetites as the inhabitants of the fair. The ostensible distinction which the play draws between consumption in the fair and consumption in the city is subjected to a profound degree of instability. The carnival of the suburbs reveals the inner logic of the city. It does so because Jonson's representation of the grotesque body retains that residual element of universality which coloured the levelling laughter of Bakhtin's carnivalesque.

Moreover, the commodification of women extends well beyond the space of the fair and is specifically figured through images of food and appetite. In the opening act, Littlewit describes his wife to the gallant Winwife, deploying what ostensibly appears to be a simplistic description of Mistress Littlewit. In a parodic imitation of the blazon tradition, he declares that she has 'a strawberry breath, cherry lips, apricot cheeks, and a soft velvet head, like a melocoton [peach]' (I.ii.11–13). Winwife, in response, tells Littlewit 'my taste . . . tends to fruit of a later kind: the sober matron, your wife's mother' (I.ii.16–17). The emphasis upon personal taste appears to focus the audiences upon pleasure, implying simply preference. Yet the significance of these fruit-based metaphors for an early modern audience would surely have been influenced by the anxiety with which fruit was treated in the period.[18] Indeed, Littlewit's references are, without exception, to soft or wall fruits, which as Liz Bellamy has demonstrated were notable in this period both for their expense and perceived unsuitability for the English climate (Bellamy, 2019, p. 52). Littlewit's description of his wife in these terms consequently prefigures her inscription within the fair's economy of prostitution. The female body is figured as sweet and alluring, but also prone to degeneration, becoming dangerous if consumed in excess. Likewise, Winwife's preference for 'fruit of a later kind' is consistently shown to be mercurial. He endeavours to secure the hand of the widow Purecraft for financial gain, while she is shown to be aware of her marketable value. She declares that she has 'been a wilful holy widow only to draw feasts and gifts from my entangled suitors', and is also 'a special maker of marriages for our decayed brethren with our rich widows' (V.ii.44–5; V.ii.46–7). She recognises her own status as a potential source of wealth and capitalises on it in a way that implicitly links her to the practices of contemporary prostitutes who, as Fouassier has noted, were known for the 'habit of being paid in foodstuff for their performance' (Fouassier, 2008, p. 31). Inside and outside the space of the fair, sexual desire is implicated in a network of commodification, of which the carnivalesque is an extension.

[18] See Chapter 1.

The propensity of exchange to exceed the bounds of the fair is emphasised by the ambiguous position of the theatre. Like the fair, the playhouse was a space where boundaries between the sale of food and sex could be elided. Stephen Gosson, for instance, claimed that 'The first building of Theaters was to ravish the sabines, and . . . they were continued in whordome ever after', and argued that women used the sale of apples as a cover for prostitution, remarking 'instead of pomegranates they give them pippines' (Gosson, 1582, sig. G5$^{v}$; sig. G6$^{r}$). Jonson appears to encourage the association between fair and theatre. *Bartholomew Fair* was originally performed at the Hope Theatre by the Lady Elizabeth's Men, a company comprised of various former child actors from troupes such as the Children of the Chapel and the Children of Paul's (cf. Munro, 2005, p. 2). The Hope was the last of the open-air amphitheatre playhouses to be constructed, and by contrast with the Globe, was conceived, as the contract for its construction relates, as a space 'bothe for players to playe in, and for the game of Beares and Bulls to be bayted in the same' ('Hope Contract', 2002, p. 209). In the Induction, Jonson scathingly deploys the unique space in which his play was performed to blur the boundaries between theatre and fair, noting that it provides the right setting because the bears and dogs made it 'as dirty as Smithfield, and as stinking every whit' (Ind.119–20). Indeed, the stage-keeper is accused of collecting the apples thrown by the audience, to feed 'the bears within' (Ind.39). The play is itself a commodity for sale, as shown in the Book-Keeper's joking references to connections between the price paid for a ticket and the degree to which audience members may criticise. This metatheatrical emphasis compromises any sense of distance from the networks of exchange in which both food and sex are implicated. The theatre, as perhaps the primary instance of the commodification of carnival forms in the early modern period, can hardly escape the commodification which it ostensibly satirises.

*Bartholomew Fair* stands as a significant example of the conjunction of appetite and sexual desire precisely because it shows that both were implicated in the representation of grotesque bodies which at this historical moment are firmly associated with a nascent capitalist system of exchange. The dominance of a market economy for food ensures the association of both appetites with money, credit and exchange. The relationship is at its most overt in the depiction of the marketplace of the fair. But the play's emphasis on hypocrisy attests to the capacity of these grotesque desires to escape the space of the fair, in a manner which embodies wider tensions regarding the shift from the market as space to the market as system. Indeed, the theatre is also situated within this system, asserting a wry sense of complicity on the part of the audience. Appetite provides a significant means of exploring these tensions because its recurrent nature, and association with pleasure, mark it as an inherent, if carnal and problematic, bodily function. The grotesque body emerges here detached from its association with harvest and seasonal renewal, becoming instead defined by its dangerous vulnerability and openness to market forms of exchange. The ambivalence of the theatre to the twin desires of the grotesque body must be read in the final instance as an embodiment of wider forces motivating a simultaneous attraction to and repulsion from the emergent capitalist system.

## Conclusion

The conjunction of appetite and desire is rooted in material and metaphorical connotations of excess. At times, that excess embodies characteristics of the grotesque body, implying an unabashed emphasis on sexual pleasure, opposed to restraint or authority. But in the majority of the early modern plays, it is the anti-social elements which are emphasised. The focus on excess in the face of plenty implies not the culinary and sexual celebrations of harvest time, but the unreasoning appetites of the tyrant, whether in the context of literal tyranny, or the implicitly tyrannical power of men over women. Just as the poor go hungry so that the rich may surfeit, so unrestrained sexual desire is figured as a threat to the social order which impinges on the rights of individual subjects. If it is true that sexual excess stands as an index for wider political violations, it is precisely through the imagery of appetite that the issues of social injustice are most vividly highlighted. The twin aspects of the representation of excess and desire are related, since the association of unbounded sexual and culinary appetites with the lower classes enhances the critique of those in power. The courtier who fails to master his appetite has reduced himself to the same status as the servant whose desire for 'meat' is placed in opposition to a conventional aristocratic restraint. Yet whereas the servant is defined primarily by a desire which can be neither acted upon nor satisfied, the courtier constitutes a problem for the social order because his unrestrained desire coincides with a disruptive and no less expansive power to enforce his ungoverned appetites.

At the same time, the deployment of a gustatory model of desire also introduces a marked degree of vulnerability to these expansive appetites. The reduction of the reciprocal act of sexual intercourse to the subject–object relationship of consumption introduces a troubling ambiguity, which the early modern theatre can deploy not only to stigmatise unruly feminine appetites, but also to imbue those appetites with transgressive potential. In a play such as *The Bloody Banquet*, the very strength of the association between sexual, culinary and political excess also creates the possibility for forms of imagined resistance. Desire emerges as the embodiment not only of the appetites of the rich, but also of the appetites of revolt. The Young Queen functions as both a representative of elite depravity and surrogate for the hungry poor. The play's complex reimagining of the conjunction of appetite and desire constitutes both the natural conclusion to, and a comment upon, revenge tragedy's implicit equation of women and the wider populace, making possible the depiction of unruly desires which operate in opposition to the dominant forces within society.

Yet perhaps more destabilising than these moments of rebellious consumption is the extent to which the conjunction of appetite and desire provides a means to explore the operation of exchange. Appetite provides a significant medium for these tensions not simply because of the more general parallels between the consumption of food and the sexual act, but rather because in early modern English society the issue of food consumption constituted the most significant example of market dominance. Food, as the most basic instance of commodification within early modern society, serves as a metaphor for the commodification of sexuality. In the final instance, appetite exposes how these forms threaten to undermine the ordered hierarchical nature of a society built upon residual principles of stability in both sexual and social terms. Food and sex emerge as commodities that must be bought, in a manner which increasingly foregrounds the inescapable nature of the market. It is frequently impossible for characters to detach themselves from a desire for either food or sex, yet the satisfaction of these desires is figured as contingent upon manipulation of a market which threatens to break down barriers and invest ostensibly natural practices with an illicit form.

# CHAPTER 5

# *Female Food Refusal*

Hunger can appear on the early modern stage as an instance of poverty, oppression or simple misfortune. It has the potential to be a character's defining characteristic, or a transitory state to be relieved by chance or a benevolent superior. Yet the theatre of the period also demonstrates a repeated concern with those who actively reject food, and who consequently embrace or resist the state of hunger. At times, these characters are misers such as Lopez in *Women Pleased*, figures whose food refusal is implicated within a more general tendency to privilege accumulation over consumption. But food refusal also emerges as a form of isolation and resistance which is specifically gendered female. In Shakespeare's *Hamlet* and *The Two Noble Kinsmen*, it functions as an index of disorderly mental and sexual states. In *The Broken Heart* and *A Woman Killed with Kindness*, it is a means of atonement and redemption. In *The Widow's Tears*, it is an expression of mourning. In the two most significant critical accounts of early modern food refusal, Nancy A. Gutierrez and Sasha Garwood have stressed its radical potential. Gutierrez argues that the self-starved female body emerges as 'a site of political apprehension and cultural change' (Gutierrez, 2003, p. 20). Garwood claims that food refusal 'always signifies a space where women can act outside cultural dominance' (Garwood, 2009, p. 108). However, the emphasis which these critics place upon male authors' attempts 'to reinscribe self-starvation within the bounds of patriarchal control' (Garwood, 2009, p. 108), has prompted a tendency to valorise an irreclaimable original act of food refusal, leaving the precise nature of its subversive properties decidedly ambiguous. Indeed, both critics acknowledge that accounts of food refusal are frequently defined by fidelity to gender norms.[1] This chapter argues that the

[1] Gutierrez notes that discursive representations of the act can 'interpret the action of food refusal in such a way that its inherent resistance is contained' (Gutierrez, 2003, p. 2). Garwood identifies a recurring tension between 'the elevation of dominant cultural ideologies (the importance of chastity) . . . and a supreme act of self-will' (Garwood, 2009, pp. 110–11).

potential radicalism of food refusal emerges not despite its fidelity to contemporary gender ideology, but rather because it carries that fidelity to a point of problematic excess. At its most subversive, food refusal develops as a form of almost parodic obedience which threatens to demonstrate the contradictory nature of the norms governing the lives of early modern women.

In order to understand this subversive conformity, it is first necessary to situate food refusal in the changing religious practices of the period. As Caroline Walker Bynum has demonstrated, women had long been associated with forms of religious practice rooted in fasting and abstinence.[2] In the medieval period, this constituted a significant part of contemporary worship since, as Albala has noted, 'it was taken for granted that physical self-abnegation, mortifying the flesh to bolster the spirit, was amongst the most praiseworthy of acts of devotion possible' (Albala, 2011, p. 43). But in the wake of the Reformation, these practices had acquired a far more marginal position within English religious thought. Although fasting might be endorsed as a means of encouraging reflection, its significance under the Church of England was increasingly secular. Weekly fish days were openly acknowledged to exist more for the purposes of strengthening England's navy and economy than for reasons of faith. And many in England viewed even these practices as worryingly Catholic.[3] The dominant principle with regard to fasting in sixteenth- and seventeenth-century England was moderation. Excessive abstinence from food was believed by many to be as problematic as gluttony, in part because 'excessive fasting was associated with the monastic life' (Fitzpatrick, 2007, p. 3). Furthermore, these anxieties could be particularly acute in the context of female bodies. Moffett, in a text originally written in 1595, cautioned 'maids and women' in particular, against 'consumeing their bodies with excessive abstinence', characterising the practice as 'a thing against nature and Godliness (which forbiddeth us to scourge or mark, and much more to consume our bodies)' (Moffett, 1655, p. 278). Female food refusal adopts a practice frequently endorsed in the period but carries it to an unacceptable degree. The excessive, sometimes terminal, fasts of the women depicted onstage had the potential to acquire pronounced Catholic undertones or to deploy theological justification for the act of self-slaughter.

[2] Bynum explores a range of female saints and mystics in the medieval period, arguing that for the women she considers, 'food, hunger, eating and feeding were far more vibrant and complex images than they ever were to male writers' (Bynum, 1987, p. 186). She identifies a wide range of food-based religious practices, noting that in these texts 'women fast, women feed others, and women eat (but never ordinary food)' (Bynum, 1987, p. 186).

[3] See Chapter 1.

The representation of female food refusal is also intimately connected to more secular concerns, most notably changing perceptions of the female body. As Gail Kern Paster has demonstrated, women in the period were frequently associated with a lack of bodily control, depicted as 'leaky vessels' incapable of mastering their disorderly bodies (Paster, 1993, p. 23). At times, the depiction of food refusal is implicated within this process, with self-starvation constituting an index of bodily subjugation. The characterisation of the jailor's daughter in *The Two Noble Kinsmen*, for instance, ties food refusal to the gendered condition of green-sickness. The implicitly medical emphasis has the potential to situate these women as slaves to their unruly bodies. At the same time, most of the plays depict the opposite, representing women who are capable of mastering the impulses of their bodies, ignoring or conquering the hunger drive. In rejecting sustenance these women work to close off the vulnerability of bodies which, as Paster notes, remained characterised 'by corporeal fluidity, openness and porous boundaries' (Paster, 1993, p. 8). Food refusal consequently has the potential to embody a state of absolute detachment from the world, in a manner which mimics the emerging, predominantly masculine model of the contained, self-sufficient body. The fascination of female food refusal stems in no small part from the extent to which it presents an uncharacteristic mastery of the humoral body, on the part of those more typically associated with openness, vulnerability and subjection.

Furthermore, food refusal acquires additional resonance from the changing nature of household production. Bynum has argued that the centrality of fasting and abstinence as a means of religious expression for medieval women stemmed in large part from the fact that they lacked the material power and independence necessary to engage in other forms of restraint. Their involvement in the provision of food in the household, whether as direct producers or in a supervisory role, lent a particular significance to acts of food refusal.[4] In the early modern period, however, women's relationship to domestic production was changing. As Natasha Korda has noted, 'household production was gradually being replaced by nascent capitalist industry', and thus 'it was becoming more economical for the housewife to purchase what she had once produced' (Korda, 2012, p. 36). For contemporary commentators, this constituted a disquieting source of

[4] Bynum argues that 'food is important to women religiously because it is important socially', and emphasises the extent to which in the medieval period 'the basic social responsibility for food preparation was woman's' (Bynum, 1987, pp. 189, 190). As a consequence, 'in periods such as the later Middle Ages in which world-denial was a favourite religious response, women found it easier to renounce food than anything else' (Bynum, 1987, p. 191).

corruption. Gervase Markham, for instance, decried reliance upon the 'furniture of the markets' (Markham, 1631, p. 4), warning of a taste for 'strangenesse and raritie' (Markham, 1631, p. 4) which risked awakening dangerous appetites that defy satisfaction. Yet as Korda has noted, Markham's own treatise gives the lie to his protestations, for it caters 'not only to the gentry's growing dependence on nascent capitalist industry, but its appetite for "strangenesse and raritie" as well' (Korda, 2012, p. 36). Where the food refusal of medieval women entailed the abdication of their own power and social role, that of early modern women constitutes a rejection of the corrupting force of exchange. In this context, food refusal emerges as the embodiment of a more general desire for absolute closure. Yet it is also a desire which, in the context of the pervasive nature of the market, was increasingly fruitless.

In order to explore these bodily, religious and domestic aspects to female food refusal, it is revealing to look beyond the space of the theatre, and consider the contemporary vogue for 'miraculous maid' pamphlets. These short texts recounted tales of young women who engaged in prodigious acts of food refusal. Here, a Catholic tradition of female food refusal is appropriated by the emergent ideals of militant Protestantism. But the sheer popularity of these texts also testifies to the commodity status of narratives of food refusal. And the texts' repeated concern with issues of deception reveal an underlying anxiety regarding the implicit control exhibited by the maids over their own bodies. A similar range of thematic concerns can be discerned in the theatre. The second section of this chapter will consider Thomas Heywood's *A Woman Killed with Kindness*, which places these tensions in the context of domestic tragedy and the increasing commodification of household consumption. But its depiction of female food refusal also enables the partial articulation of female agency in this context, for the character Anne Frankford moves from passivity to action only when she engages in self-starvation. Lastly, this chapter considers George Chapman's *The Widow's Tears*, a play in which food refusal leads not to death, but to the generation of uncontrolled appetite, in a manner which at first glance appears to embody the period's lurid stereotypes of lusty widowhood. Yet the play's pronounced emphasis on the central character's earlier hunger serves both to legitimise the eventual shift to appetite, and to articulate a series of anxiously parodic images of female community. In doing so, Chapman satirises the binary alternatives of wantonness and passivity which dominated contemporary gender ideology. Although these different texts deploy the image of food refusal in a variety of different contexts, they share a recurrent tendency to figure it as a form of excessive fidelity to dominant gender norms, carrying the implicit rules which governed female behaviour to a point where they threaten to collapse.

## 'Miraculous Maids'

In the second act of John Fletcher and Philip Massinger's *Love's Cure* the hungry servant Lazarillo and his master Pachieco discuss a 'miraculous maid in *Flanders* [who] liv'd three yeere without any other sustenance then the smell of a Rose' (II.i.23–7). The maid in question is Eve Fliegen, although as Hyder E. Rollins has noted the two playwrights appear to conflate elements of her story with that of Jane Balan, another 'miraculous maid' of the period.[5] An early account of Fliegen's tale had been published in English in 1611, and she is referenced not only in the work of Fletcher and Massinger, but also in plays by Jasper Mayne and William Davenant.[6] In *Love's Cure*, however, the miracle is reformulated into a carnivalesque image of monstrosity. Lazarillo declares: 'they say her guts shrunk all into Lute-strings, and her neather-parts cling'd together like a Serpents Taile, so that though she continued a woman still above the girdle, beneath that she was monster' (II.i.28–31). The conventional tale of miraculous resistance to hunger is reformulated as a grotesque image of the drive's effects upon the body. At one level, the humour might be situated as a product of the increasing medicalisation of food refusal, in a period in which the basic physical consequences of hunger received greater attention. At the same time, Fliegen's perceived monstrosity also embodies broader anxieties inherent in the contemporary obsession with women who refused food. By figuratively linking the notorious 'miraculous maid' to the sort of hybrid monsters found in contemporary fairs and carnivals, Lazarillo gestures to the parallels which existed between a 'miraculous maid' such as Fliegen, and the wider range of prodigies which contemporary pamphlet culture served up for the early modern public. Fliegen consequently emerges as simultaneously miracle and fraud; the object of both medical curiosity and popular fascination.

That element of notoriety is well attested by the proliferation of contemporary accounts of food refusal. Fliegen was only one of a wide range of

[5] Rollins notes that the length of the fast described mirrors that of Balan, who was purported to have survived without food for three years. (See Rollins, 1921, p. 357.)

[6] In Jasper Mayne's *The City Match* she is described as 'the Dutch Virgin that could live /By th' sent of Flowers' (Mayne, 1639, p. 16). In William Davenant's *News from Plymouth*, she is 'The maid of *Brabant*, that liv'd by her smell, / That din'd on a *Rose* and supt on a *Tulip*' (Davenant, 1673, sig. Aaaa2[r]).

'miraculous maids' in the period. A pamphlet published in 1589 reported the story of Katerin Cooper, from the village of Schmidweiler in the Palatinate, who 'for sundry yeeres neither eateth, drinketh, nor sleepeth, neyther auoydeth any excrements, and yet liueth' (*Notable and Prodigious*, 1589). In 1597, Veitken Johans, from the Dukedom of Gulische, was likewise reported to have abstained from both consumption and excretion for four years, while remaining 'faire, of a very good complection, and to all mens seeming of perfit health' (Gurth, 1597, *sig.* B1$^{r}$). George Hakewill, writing in 1635, recorded a series of miraculous fasts, including that of a ten-year-old girl named Margaret, who in 1539 abstained from all food for three years, but continued 'talking, and laughing, and sporting as other children of that age use to doe' (Hakewill, 1635, IV, p. 440). Fliegen herself, meanwhile, was the object of multiple pamphlets, in both Dutch and English, and her story was also disseminated in ballad form. Existing critical and historical approaches to this material have emphasised the increasing medicalisation of female food refusal. For Walter Vandereycken and Ron van Deth, these figures constitute a transitional state in a 'process of secularization', which served to make it 'decreasingly self-evident' that food refusal could be interpreted as a product of supernatural forces (Vandereycken and van Deth, 1994, p. 47).[7] Nancy Gutierrez, by contrast, deploys the resources of postcolonial theory, and reads the accounts as exercises in containment, which seek to close off the potentially subversive nature of female food refusal. Yet both approaches to the topic assume a relatively reductive model of the religious in the period, and fail to acknowledge the unique properties of the early modern pamphlet industry. Although Gutierrez's approach avoids a reductive historical teleology, the decision to deploy the resources of postcolonial theory risks effacing the specificity of female food refusal, reducing it to a somewhat nebulously defined category of 'transgression'. In order to properly understand the defining features of these seventeenth-century figures, it is necessary to situate them within the wider tradition of religious female food refusal, acknowledging the significant shifts which occur. By reading the 'miraculous maids' as both a Protestant appropriation of an existing Catholic trope, and a product of the nascent news industry, it becomes possible to discern some of the tensions and anxieties which surround the representation of female food refusal in the period, both on and off the contemporary stage.

[7] The work of Vandereycken and van Deth constitutes an extension of claims established by Rudolph Bell, who explores the food refusal of religious women in medieval Italy, demonstrating that 'some holy women in late medieval times were described in terms that were similar in important ways to clinical descriptions of modern-day sufferers of anorexia nervosa' (Bell, 1985, p. ix).

Indeed, the most significant aspect to the numerous 'miraculous maids' of the period is the fact that they are not fasting. As Bynum has noted, as early as the medieval period people 'were clear about the differences between choosing to renounce food, one of the pleasures of civilisation, and being in the throes of a behaviour pattern that made eating impossible' (Bynum, 1987, p. 197). In a number of cases, saints were described breaking their fasts in public, precisely in order to demonstrate that their refusal of food was not a compulsion, but rather a deliberate act of faith.[8] The 'miraculous maids' of the early seventeenth century, by contrast, are overwhelmingly associated with the involuntary refusal of food. Fliegen emerges from a background of poverty. She is 'of meane and poore parents' and endures 'the bitternesse of much hunger' (Wood, 1611, p. 3). It is as a consequence of this 'extremity of misery' that she prays to God to 'relieve her, from that daily hunger' (Wood, 1611, p. 3). She swiftly adopts a stance not simply of abstinence, but of revulsion. When Fliegen is induced to swallow a cherry, by the Countess of Meurs, she falls into a 'sodaine and violent passion of an extreme sicknesse' (Wood, 1611, p. 4). When encouraged by doctors to attempt a spoonful of buttermilk, she 'made offer to tast it, but could by no meanes take it down' (Wood, 1611, p. 4). In a similar manner, Katerin Cooper is described as losing, first, 'all plesure & appetite to warme meats', and later all appetite for any food whatsoever, so that 'neither meat or drink goe down her throte' (*Notable and Prodigious*, 1589, p. 4). And Jane Balan 'loathes and abhors mightily, both meates & drinks' (Citois, 1603, sig. D1$^{v}$). The shift in emphasis is significant. Where in the medieval period the absence of volition tended to marginalise the religious element to food refusal, Fliegen's capacity to resist sustenance is clearly framed as a form of divine intervention. Her divine resilience is manifested not as a mastery of her own body, but rather through the elimination of appetite. Fliegen's agency is effaced, through the focus on the physical nature of her response to the food. Her resistance to hunger and appetite is reconstituted as a supreme instance of subjection to the body. Finding herself 'afflicted by these tryals' (Wood, 1611, p. 4), she has little choice but to abandon the consumption of food altogether.

Nevertheless, the shift from volition to disgust is complex, for it serves to reconstitute the fundamental struggle at work in the act of food refusal as one not between soul and body, but rather between body and world. As

[8] Bynum notes that 'supposed saints such as John the Good of Mantua and Columba of Rieti sometimes ate before an audience to demonstrate that they *could* eat – i.e. that their abstinence was voluntary' (Bynum, 1987, p. 196).

Vandereycken and van Deth have noted, medieval saints and mystics were driven in large part by 'penance or mortification of the body in pursuit of becoming united with Christ' (Vandereycken and van Deth, 1994, p. 51). The 'miraculous maids', by effacing the mortification of flesh and prioritising a sense of bodily compulsion, simultaneously emphasise a sense of distinction from society: what is being controlled is no longer one's own body, but rather the external world with its various forms of sustenance. As Robert Douglas-Fairhurst has argued, disgust 'provides a means of dividing up the world according to established conceptual schemes, of separating the pure from the impure, the safe from the defiling' (Douglas-Fairhurst, 2008, p. 63). The revulsion of figures such as Fliegen evinces a generalised disgust, characterising all sustenance as impure, in a manner which focusses attention not on the famished body so much as the rejected food. By asserting the visceral nature of the rejection of outside sustenance, these texts elaborate a fantasy of supreme detachment from society. In doing so, they might be interpreted as carrying contemporary prescriptions regarding the behaviour of women to its natural extreme. At a time when women were encouraged to remove themselves from the world beyond the home, the 'miraculous maids' engage in a practice of absolute containment.

Yet the excessive nature of this closure is also the object of concern. These texts are defined by a fundamental uncertainty regarding the underlying cause of the events that they describe. For Hakewill, the fasts are 'wonderful works of God', and he notes approvingly that 'the greatest and most notable part of the examples alleaged have beene of the Protestant Religion' (Hakewill, 1635, IV, p. 441). However, many were less easily convinced of the divine provenance of such extreme food refusal. Vandereycken and van Deth note that 'some people called [Fliegen] a witch or believed her to be possessed by the devil' (Vandereycken and van Deth, 1994, p. 63). In the case of Jane Balan, the prefatory verses announce the case as a warning to gluttons and an example of 'Gods iudgements' (Citois, 1603, sig. A2$^{r}$). Yet the main body of the text emphasises an explanation rooted in humoral theory, arguing that 'if some body be presented, which hath but small store of heate, and much more naturall moisture . . . there is no neede at all of much nourishment' (Citois, 1603, sig. C1$^{r}$). Furthermore, for all the ostensible distance between the 'miraculous maids' and the Catholic saints and mystics which preceded them, they retain many characteristics that might easily be associated with Catholicism. Fliegen, for instance, is described in one pamphlet as sustained by sweetness, in a manner implying clear parallels to earlier stories of saints sustained by divine manna. The account of Katerin Cooper described how she had been visited by both 'Jesuites' and 'nuns', and had received letters 'written as it were to a holy virgin, whereby it appeareth they would make her a very Idoll, yea and in the end forme and practise some pilgrimage vnto her' (*Notable and Prodigious*, 1589, p. 9). At one level, this theological ambiguity marginalises specific issues of motivation, in favour of the prioritisation of the act itself. Ascribed to a multiplicity of possible causes, the actions of the maids become significant not in religious terms, but as a curiosity or marvel. At the same time, however, the excessive, uncontrollable nature of the apparent resilience to hunger exhibited by the 'miraculous maids' retains the potential to emerge as the subject of heretical religious interpretation.

Moreover, the sheer excess of the extra-natural resistance shown by the 'miraculous maids' also enables their reconstitution as commodities, which in large part undermines their apparent detachment from the world beyond the household. Gutierrez has emphasised the parallels which exist in these texts between 'the household's position as contact zone between private lives and public affairs and the body's position as the threshold between the perception of interior and exterior lives' (Gutierrez, 2003, p. 88). Yet there are opposed trajectories at play. For Fliegen's extra-natural resistance to hunger also enables her reconstitution as a form of commodity, which in turn necessitates a move beyond the space of the home. Fliegen appears as a 'strange wonder', whose exploits draw huge crowds to see her. She is visited by both the Duchess of Meurs and the Dutch Prince Maurice. This notoriety, in turn, prompts a move beyond the space of the home. Fliegen's condition is such that it 'drew not onely many people to see her, but also many tryals to be put vpon her' (Wood, 1611, p. 4). A trope of the genre is the necessity of removing the maids from the private domestic space, so that the possibility of deceit can be discounted. This dynamic is amplified by the textual circulation consequent on the maids' notoriety. The numerous texts in which Fliegen's account appeared testify to both the imaginative power of the 'miraculous maids' and the profits to be made by capitalising on that power. The 'miraculous maids'' absolute fidelity to principles of closure and isolation threatens to emerge as precisely the opposite: the material and textual circulation of the maids in a specifically public context.

The implications of the repeated emphasis upon surveillance within the texts are complex. The numerous trials deployed against the various maids serve in large part not as attempts to uncover deception, but rather to add credibility to the account. At the same time, the possibility of deception is never entirely effaced. On the one hand, the great mass of surveillance described supports the maids' cases. But on the other, it adds magnitude to the extent of the deception. As the exchange between the characters of

Fletcher and Massinger's play demonstrates, part of the notoriety of these characters springs from the impossibility of knowing conclusively that they are genuine. Fliegen, indeed, would eventually be unmasked as a fraud, although the account would appear only in Dutch narratives of the case, rather than in English translations. Her burial would be registered in a church book in Meurs as that of a woman 'who cheated the whole world by scandalous lies and blasphemy' (Vandereycken and van Deth, 1994, p. 65). Yet the discovery of her deception seems not to have extinguished her status as a marvel or curiosity. In a contemporary wax museum, built along the lines of Madame Tussauds, Fliegen appeared alongside figures of the nobility. Vandereycken and van Deth note that 'causing hilarity in the audience, one arm of the wax figure made a movement to wipe breadcrumbs from her mouth' (Vandereycken and van Deth, 1994, p. 62). The implicit juxtaposition of an apparent indifference to hunger with the enduring possibility of a voracious, but concealed, appetite constitutes an integral part of the fascination which the 'miraculous maids' elicited.

Hunger, in these texts, emerges as in one sense an empty signifier. The food refusal of the miracle maids can be inscribed with multiple competing meanings. It is an act riven by ambiguity, capable of being read as millenarian prophecy, as Catholic idolatry, as possession or as a grand deception. In part, this tension is produced by the underlying assumptions of the society within which the acts occurred. Food refusal emerges as the embodiment of principles of passivity and closure which were invariably valorised in contemporary conduct books. Yet the notoriety which accompanies the act of food refusal enacts the opposite motion. It enables the detachment of the woman from the home, and requires the interrogation of her motives, her divinity and her sincerity. The textual dissemination of these accounts, in one respect, marginalises their voices, but it also accentuates their notoriety. The apparent passivity of absolute food refusal is in constant tension with a pervasive suspicion of a hidden voracious appetite. The degree to which the actions of the miraculous maids embody orthodox understandings of women's behaviour ensures that these figures cannot simply be dismissed as aberrant or sinful. But at the same time, the element of excess which defines their actions introduces troubling aspects of ambiguity regarding their motivations, their prominence and the credibility of their claims.

## Privacy and the Household

In early modern drama, food refusal is presented in a relatively secular manner, detached from the miraculous context of the pamphlets. But it nevertheless embodies many of the same tensions regarding bodily control, the household and the possibility of deceit. These concerns are particularly prominent in *A Woman Killed with Kindness* (1603), by Thomas Heywood, a play which was performed by the Earl of Worcester's Men, probably at the Rose theatre. The main plot concerns the gentleman Frankford, who invites his friend Wendoll into his home. Wendoll proceeds to seduce Frankford's wife Anne, and, when the two are discovered, Frankford banishes his wife from his presence. Her response is to starve herself to death in an act of contrition, eliciting his forgiveness. Criticism of the play has explored both the causes of Anne's adultery and the legitimacy of Frankford's actions.[9] But of particular significance for an understanding of food refusal is a range of accounts which have scrutinised the play's attitude towards Anne's self-starvation.[10] While these accounts have provided insightful perspectives on the play's uneasy relationship with the contemporary discourse surrounding adultery, they have also tended to efface its investment with the changing material structures of the household.[11] Indeed, the title of the play is itself rooted in the tensions surrounding the consumption of food in the early modern household. The 'kindness' which leads to Anne's death is ostensibly the restrained behaviour of Frankford on discovering her adultery. But kindness in the period could mean 'kinship', linking Wendoll's entrance into their family unit with her downfall (*OED*, 'kindness', def. 3). It also signified a feeling of 'fondness' or 'affection' (*OED*, 'kindness', def. 2), implying a connection between Frankford's lavish treatment of both Wendoll and Anne, and their resulting act of adultery. The title channels a series of related concerns, which

[9] Frederick Kiefer suggests Frankford's treatment of Anne 'borders on the sadistic' (Kiefer, 1986, p. 94). For Kiefer, the motivation for Anne's adultery is intentionally obscure, since 'to have supplied a motive would have meant explaining and thus implicitly condoning Anne's transgression, something Heywood would not do' (Kiefer, 1986, p. 87). But for Paula McQuade the play 'provides a compelling critique of female subjection within marriage on the grounds that it prevents both men and women from acting as responsible moral agents' (McQuade, 2000, p. 233). And for Allison Hobgood the text functions as negative exemplar, 'a kind of homeopathic medical therapy that prescribed poison to treat poison' (Hobgood, 2014, p. 99).

[10] Atkinson, Kiefer and van Fossen have argued that her starvation constitutes a legitimate act of penance. But as Green has noted, death 'is not simply a side effect of Anne's penance but her goal', and for this reason it clearly has a disquieting dimension from the perspective of a contemporary audience (Green, 2005, p. 65). Indeed, as Jennifer Panek argues, whatever Anne's intentions, in the final instance she 'dies a suicide' (Panek, 1994, p. 373).

[11] A significant exception is the work of Allison Hobgood, who productively reads the play as 'a narrative about unsuccessful humoral governance and the dangers of unruly affection' (Hobgood, 2014, p. 103). But while a concern with the permeability of the humoral body is undoubtedly characteristic of the text, it is nevertheless necessary to assert the specific emphasis which the play places on the commodified nature of the foods which are ingested.

link the incursion of strangers into the home with a domestic excess produced by the incursion of commodities. 'Kindness' in this play is of a piece with the desire of the relatively modestly endowed Frankford to aspire towards aristocratic forms of largesse, leaving his household open to dangerous sexual incursion by aspirant outside influences.

Within the play Anne is explicitly described as receiving treatment from Frankford which does not accord with his position in society, and which stimulates appetite, rather than necessity. On discovering her infidelity, he asks her:

> Was it for want
> Thou play'dst the strumpet? Wast thou not suppli'd
> With every pleasure, fashion, and new toy, –
> Nay, even beyond my calling? (xiii.106–9)

Frankford can conceive of adultery as springing only from neglect, a 'want' which he himself has prevented, implying that Anne's behaviour defies explanation. 'Want' itself, with its implicit association with 'wantonness', raises the possibility that her transgression is inherent. For David Mann, the lines are typical of the play's tendency to present Anne's crime as 'inexplicable, monstrous, and entirely the woman's' (Mann, 2008, p. 135). Yet the speech hints at other, more troubling possibilities. In acknowledging the degree to which he has provided pleasures beyond his 'calling', Frankford reveals the extent to which his earlier actions have moved beyond the bounds of his rank. The reference to 'every pleasure, fashion, and new toy', meanwhile, implies a reliance upon the 'furniture of the market', which texts like Markham's *The Good Housewife* condemned. 'Suppli'd', in particular, figures the various pleasures to which Anne has access as emanating from her husband's funds, rather than the home's labour. Occurring in conjunction with the reference to Anne as a 'strumpet', which could signify prostitute, Frankford's speech links the commodification of household produce with the commodification of sexuality itself, and does so in a manner which asserts both his own complicity in this transformation and his own ignorance or disavowal of that fact. Anne's transgression is the product of an excessive liberality which extends beyond the bounds of both Frankford's home and the consumption appropriate to his rank. It is a 'kindness' which has been facilitated in the final instance by the insertion of the home into a market economy of 'pleasure', rather than necessity.

Furthermore, this emphasis on commodified consumption occurs in parallel with the marginalisation of Anne's agency within the household. When Frankford leaves the house, Wendoll tells Anne:

> I am husband now in Master Frankford's place
> And must command the house. My pleasure is
> We will not sup abroad so publicly,
> But in your private chamber, Mistress Frankford. (xi.89–92)

Wendoll's ability to act in this manner is reliant upon the position which he has acquired within the Frankford household. In essence, Wendoll gains this control over both the house and Anne simply because Frankford has given it to him. But as Panek has noted, this marginalisation of the woman was in fact atypical of the conventional middle-class family in the period. In reality 'it is Anne who by rights should have the command of the house, as her husband's deputy when he, the master, is away' (Panek, 1994, p. 366). It is significant, however, that it is in the context of culinary consumption that this transfer of authority is established. Anne is seduced in the private chamber of the house. The text raises the prospect of illicit acts which may take place behind the closed doors of private chambers in general, while also implying the particular impropriety of this withdrawal of Wendoll and Mistress Frankford. Indeed, the private space is imbued with erotic significance, with Anne's body figured as the household, while the private chamber in which Wendoll will 'sup' is her vagina. Both Anne's passivity and this form of sexualised consumption can be linked to the play's broader climate of commodification. As Susan Cahn has noted, the increasing dominance of commodity exchange tended to marginalise the role of women within the production of food. Where 'sixteenth-century women had made necessary objects, seventeenth-century women were more likely to purchase them' (Cahn, 1987, p. 63). Whereas the former had enabled the relative valorisation of women's labour as help-meets to their husband, the latter entailed reliance on the husband's income and the consequent reduction of the wives to mere consumers. Furthermore, a valorisation of that passivity emerged as a characteristic of upper echelons of society, becoming 'for a time, the price of upward social mobility' (Cahn, 1987, p. 7). The forms of commodified consumption which Frankford's household privileges appear in tandem with an aspirational desire to marginalise the authority of the wife, in a manner which leaves her a prey to the abuse of power by Frankford's male subordinate.

In the first instance, therefore, Anne's food refusal can be understood as a rejection of the upwardly mobile patterns of consumption which have defined her household. As Green has argued, her refusal of food is 'emblematic of her wish for complete physical closure: she will no longer "sup" with anyone, anywhere' (Green, 2005, p. 64). In particular, she rejects commodified consumption. She declares that she 'never will nor eat, nor drink, nor taste / Of any cates that may preserve my life' (xvi.101–2). Cates are defined in the *Oxford English Dictionary* as 'Provisions or victuals bought (as distinguished from, and usually more delicate or dainty than, those of home production)' (*OED*, 'cate', def. 1a). They are, as Natasha Korda has argued, 'by definition exchange-values – commodities, properly speaking – as opposed to use-values, or objects of home production' (Korda, 2012, p. 52). Anne detaches herself from a world of commodities and exchange, severing herself from the porous boundaries of bodies and households which have ceased to be open in a purely feudal sense, but have instead taken on the characteristics of a dangerous vulnerability to incursion from outside. In doing so, she appears to follow the spirit of the original punishment insisted upon by Frankford. In banishing her from his house he reverses the tendency towards openness which has hitherto dominated his household practice. He bars her entrance to his presence, and to that of her children, ensuring an absolute privacy. Yet Anne's food refusal, while it replicates the underlying logic of this closure, carries it to a point of excess. She threatens to enact her own martyrdom, stimulating precisely that fear which motivated the 'kindness' of Frankford's punishment in the first place. But her actions also focus the attention of the audience away from the issue of her own personal fallibility, and towards the exchange of men and commodities which Frankford himself has permitted. Anne's food refusal constitutes an excess of conformity to patriarchal authority which threatens to destabilise that authority.

Indeed, Anne's hunger enables not only closure, but also notoriety. As with the 'miraculous maid' pamphlets, her food refusal rapidly attracts the attention of the local community. Jenkins notes that 'Many gentlemen and gentlewomen of the country are come to comfort her' (xvii.35–7). When she is visited on her deathbed, by her brother and his associates, Maltby declares:

> Divers gentlemen,
> Your loving neighbours, with that just request
> Have moved and told him of your weak estate,
> Who, though with much ado to get belief,
> Examining of the general circumstance,
> Seeing your sorrow and your penitence
> And hearing therewithal the great desire
> You have to see him ere you left the world,
> He gave to us his faith to follow us,
> And sure he will be here immediately. (xvii.42–51)

In adopting a culinary practice which embodies isolation, Anne transforms herself into the object of reports and sympathy, thus counteracting the isolation upon which her initial punishment was predicated. Indeed, in a dramatic sense, her food refusal enables the conjunction of the primary and secondary plot. For the first time since the opening of the play, Anne encounters her brother, and other characters from beyond the Frankford home. Where Frankford's original punishment entailed her erasure from public life, her food refusal transforms her into a focus of notoriety and affective power. Furthermore, by dramatising the response of the onstage audience, the play simultaneously co-opts the sympathies of the audience in the theatre.

At the same time, there are elements of tension within the play which prevent the simple unification of fictional and actual audiences. Throughout, Anne's strategy of redemption is premised on a dangerous confusion of God's authority and her husband's. When the adultery is initially discovered, she claims that 'to whip but this scandal out, I would hazard / The rich and dear redemption of my soul' (xiii.136–7). Frankford's forgiveness is placed in a position of privilege above the redemptive force of God. Likewise, as Panek has argued, by the play's conclusion she 'no longer simply values Frankford's forgiveness above God's, but now conflates the two' (Panek, 1994, p. 373). She declares 'My fault so heinous is, / That if you in this world forgive it not, / Heaven will not clear it in the world to come' (xvii.85–7), and her final lines express confidence that 'Pardon'd on earth, soul, thou in heaven art free' (xvii.119). Anne undoubtedly believes that her suffering and hunger have guaranteed her salvation, but she does so largely because of a distinctly problematic equation of divine authority with that of her husband. Indeed, Anne's self-inflicted hunger operates within the play to ensure the forgiveness of her husband, precisely at the expense of her soul. The onstage audience raises no objection to this stance, and critics have tended to take them at their word. It is striking, however, that Anne's strategy for redemption is rooted in the same marginalisation of female agency which the play has foregrounded as lying at the root of Anne's initial adultery. As such, the play's kindness constitutes not a didactic model to be followed, but rather the supreme indication of Frankford's culpability.

It is the representation of food refusal, however, which enables this culpability to become visible. In *A Woman Killed with Kindness*, female food refusal emerges as a means of isolation and stability, in a world defined by the flux of commodity exchange. But it is also both product and commentary upon a more general marginalisation of female agency within the family home. Frankford's 'kindness' is problematic not only because it opens up his house to the forces of exchange, but because it occurs in tandem with an upwardly mobile desire for status which prompts the reduction of his wife to a position of passivity. Food refusal, to an extent, disrupts that state. In rejecting sustenance, Anne asserts her own agency, marshalling the local community in order to ensure that her husband bestows his forgiveness. At the same time, however, Anne's destructive self-starvation attests to her continuing dependence upon her husband. Food refusal is both the continuation of his orders for her, and a strategy predicated upon the equivalence of Frankford's judgement and God's. It is, in the final instance, a symptom of a decline in values consequent upon the spread of commodity exchange.

## *The Widow's Tears*

*A Woman Killed with Kindness* depicts food refusal in tragic mode, but the subject could also receive comic treatment. George Chapman's *The Widow's Tears* (1604; Chapman, 1975) depicts female self-starvation in the context of widowhood. The play appears to have been popular, produced at the Blackfriars, the Whitefriars and at Court. At its heart, the text is a reworking of one of the most significant classical models of female food refusal: the tale of the 'widow of Ephesus'. In the original, a young woman demonstrates her loyalty to her dead husband by refusing to abandon his tomb, and rejecting all offers of sustenance. But she undermines her protestations of grief by allowing herself first to be seduced by a young soldier, and then offering up her husband's body to help her new lover to escape responsibility for a crime. As Edward Wheatley has noted, the tale has 'a long and rich history of revision and augmentation in a number of different genres' (Wheatley, 2014, p. 628). In the medieval and early modern period, it emerged as a fundamental model for the stereotype of the 'lusty widow'. Chapman's text deploys this basic model of plot but complicates it in two significant ways. Firstly, he introduces a subplot, which dominates the action of the play's opening acts, depicting the remarriage of Eudora, another widow. Secondly, he complicates the primary plot by introducing an element of deceit on the part of the husband. Chapman's Lysander feigns death in order to test the sincerity of his wife Cynthia. The resulting reworking of the 'Widow of Ephesus' tale consequently prioritises issues of performance, but also provides a unique perspective on the uneasy status of the widow's hunger as symbol and guarantor of grief. Indeed, by effacing the presence of the husband's literal corpse, the play focusses the audience's attention not on the grisly aftermath of the widow's affair, but rather on the preceding act of food refusal and her eventual susceptibility to her disguised husband's culinary and sexual advances.

Cynthia's hunger is bound up with her apparent status as a widow. Widowhood in early modern England was, as many critics and historians have noted, an ambiguous and often threatening state. While the majority of contemporary women remained legally under the control of either husbands or fathers, widows had a degree of independence and this material power was frequently manifested as a disturbing degree of sexual agency. Lawrence Stone notes that, 'it was generally assumed that young widows, suddenly deprived of regular sexual satisfaction by the loss of a husband, were likely to be driven by lust in their search of a replacement' (Stone, 1977, p. 281). This was perceived as raising the worrying possibility that widows might seduce young men of lower social standing, thereby retaining after remarriage the power which they had attained through widowhood. Indeed, as Linda K. Neiberg has noted, contemporary beliefs regarding marriage emphasised the extent to which the widow's character was subsumed within that of her husband. So while the figure of the unattached widow embodied a threatening degree of female independence, 'remarriage posed an arguably greater threat to patriarchal values – that the dead husband would be erased from memory' (Neiberg, 2013, p. 179). *The Widow's Tears* ostensibly embodies many aspects of this ideology of widowhood. In both the subplot and the main plot, supposed widows assert their commitment to an ideal of grief and the memory of their dead husbands, which they rapidly abandon. Moreover, both Eudora and Cynthia choose as the objects of their affection men of significantly lower status, the first through marriage to her former servant, the second through her eventual response to the amorous advances of her husband, disguised as a common soldier. The primary motivation of the two women appears throughout as the conventional, overwhelming desire of the 'lusty widow'. Yet critical opinion has frequently differed over how far the play endorses the misogynist stance of many of its characters, and of early modern society more generally. For Neiberg, 'although the play initially appears to reproduce prevailing ideologies about the lustful widow, its female protagonist, Cynthia, instead gestures towards a self-determined future no longer circumscribed by conventional stereotypes' (Neiberg, 2013, p. 177). Likewise, Wheatley emphasises the extent to which deception and disruption emerge as male, rather than female, characteristics in the play, so that Chapman 'implicates the men as much as or more than the women' (Wheatley, 2014, p. 639). For Elizabeth Hodgson, these ambiguities are precisely the point: a consequence of the way Chapman's play 'interweaves the inscrutability assigned to womanly grief and the inscrutability of a theatrical performance' (Hodgson, 2009, p. 61). Attention to the representation of Cynthia's self-starvation provides a significant perspective on these concerns.

From the very beginning, Cynthia's food refusal is depicted as an act which exceeds the bounds of moderation. The Malcontent Tharsalio figures the immoderate nature of Cynthia's grief as itself a symbol of insincerity. He declares:

> This strain of mourning wi' th' sepulchre, like an overdoing actor, affects grossly, and is indeed so far forced from the life, that it bewrays itself to be altogether artificial. (IV.i.105–8)

Central to this concern is a metatheatrical emphasis, building upon the fourth act's central conceit,[12] where hunger emerges not in opposition to theatre, but rather as evidence for the performative nature of Cynthia's grief. The extent of her ability to overcome the natural impulses of hunger is deployed to assert the distance between her actions and those of a genuine griever. Just as performance is distanced 'from the life', so too is Cynthia's unnatural hunger. The use of the term 'grossly' enables a curious inversion of Cynthia's hunger. The term ostensibly signifies the insincerity of Cynthia's performance. But the word also retains fundamental material and culinary implications in the period, which imbue Cynthia's fast with connotations of excess. For some, it is true, this element of excess is itself the guarantor of sincerity. Lysander's friend, Lycus, for instance, asks 'Could she, if she dissembled, thus dally with hunger, be deaf to the barking of her appetite, not having these four days relieved nature with one dram of sustenance?' (IV.i.116–18). The pressure of necessity is figured as a drive which forecloses the possibility of deception. The act of abstinence is presented as fundamentally opposed to the impulses of 'nature' and it is precisely this distance which demonstrates the truthfulness of her grief. Cynthia's hunger is consequently figured as a necessary means for her to demonstrate her sincerity. Yet even here, Cynthia's fidelity

[12] As Elizabeth Hodgson has argued, the structure of Chapman's play foregrounds the issue of performance, with the graveyard scenes emerging as an extended metatheatrical sequence which 'questions whether anything can really be known about a widow's love through its analogy to dramatic performance itself' (Hodgson, 2009, p. 60). Earlier, when Lycus describes his own sympathetic tears to Tharsalio, Tharsalio dismisses his account, declaring 'So have I seen many a moist auditor do at a play, when the story was but a fiction' (IV.i.48–9).

is figured as dangerously destabilising. Lycus declares that Cynthia's grief was such that he 'was forced to turn woman, and bear a part with her' (IV.i.45–6). Her sorrow is conceived as both genuine, and dangerously destabilising to Lycus's masculine reserve, reducing him to tears. Food refusal is from the very beginning of the act associated with the transparent indication of grief. But it also presents Cynthia as a model or exemplar to be followed.

Indeed, Cynthia's ability to influence those around her is central to the representation of her food refusal. By contrast with other instances of female food refusal, *The Widow's Tears* depicts not a single woman, starving in isolation, but two. Tharsalio reports that Lysander's 'intolerable virtuous widow, for his love, and, for her love, Ero, her handmaid, are descended with his corpse into the vault' (IV.i.17–19). The ambiguous insertion of 'for her love' serves to disrupt the emphasis upon Cynthia's connection to her supposedly dead husband. The love of a widow for her husband is offset by the love of a servant for her female master. An ostensible act of grief emerges as the basis for the establishment of a potentially troubling female community. Furthermore, Ero explicitly frames their joint food refusal in terms of the notoriety which the two will acquire. She declares 'Sure I am the wonder's over, and 'twas only for that, that I endured this; and so, o' my conscience, did you' (IV.iii.33–5). Her reference to the temporally bounded 'wonder' refers to the commonplace proverbial expression 'a wonder lasts but nine days'.[13] In doing so, Ero makes explicit the parallels between the actions of her mistress and the contemporary vogue for 'miraculous maid' pamphlets. Yet the meaning of Cynthia's potential status as a 'wonder' is decidedly ambiguous. At one level, her wondrous status serves to situate her explicitly as an exception to the norm, as a character whose resilience to the culinary and sexual demands of the body is significant because it differs from that of other women. At the same time, Ero's assurance that both she and her mistress have engaged in food refusal only to gain the notoriety of the status of wonder serves to figure Cynthia's mourning itself as little more than performance. Cynthia consequently embodies not simply the fame of the 'miraculous maid' pamphlets, but also their association with the possibility of deception. The emphasis is placed not on the act of mourning itself, but rather on the reputation which Cynthia will gain through engaging in it. Hunger, through its association with the phenomenon of the wonder, risks embodying the very opposite of sincerity. Perhaps more significant than

[13] See Tilley (1950, p. 749).

the implication of insincerity, however, is the extent to which Ero's assessment of her mistress's situation reveals the potential notoriety which the act of food refusal lends her. Indeed, by translating an expression of mourning to a wondrous excess of resilience, Cynthia threatens to marginalise the significance of her initial motivation. As with the 'miraculous maids', the act of food refusal becomes of greater significance than the precise cause behind it. Cynthia is notable not for her grief, but for the simple fact of her ability to withstand hunger.

Furthermore, the potential consequences of Cynthia's excessive statement of grief are a cause of some disquiet within the text. Of particular significance is the potential of her food refusal to constitute a form of exemplum. Tharsalio declares:

> For this does she look to be deified, to have hymns made of her, nay to her; the tomb where she is to be no more reputed the ancient monument of our family, the Lysandri, but the new-erected altar of Cynthia, to which all the Paphian widows shall after their husbands' funerals offer their wet muckenders for monuments of the danger they have passed, as seamen do their wet garments at Neptune's temple after a shipwreck. (IV.i.119–26)

Tharsalio's speech deploys the associations which persisted in early modern culture between fasting and Catholicism. Cynthia's actions are figured as aspirations towards not simply saintliness, but apotheosis. At the same time, however, there is a striking conceptual slippage at work here. For it swiftly becomes clear that Tharsalio's fears centre not simply on idolatry. Cynthia's act of mourning threatens to supplant not God, but rather the patriarchal construct that is the Lysandri. The family tomb risks being reconstituted as a monument to female independence. Indeed, by the final line, Tharsalio imagines a succession of widows, whose ostensible symbols of grief, their 'wet muckenders' (handkerchiefs), are reworked as tokens of thanks for escaping the 'danger' of marriage. Here, the implications of celibacy inherent in the refusal of food are of absolute importance. Cynthia's ability to withstand hunger threatens to become less a demonstration of grief than an indication of her capacity to live without the material or sexual involvement of men in general. Her act of self-control, while ostensibly displaying unparalleled dedication to her husband, has the potential to metamorphose into the precise opposite of that reliance.

To an extent, of course, these tensions are alleviated by Cynthia's eventual descent into appetite. Garwood, for instance, argues that 'her abrupt abandonment of [food refusal] is used to prove the universal iniquity of the female sex' (Garwood, 2009, p. 107). Yet perhaps more significant than the fact that Cynthia eventually succumbs to appetite is the degree to which the attempts of her disguised husband to disrupt her food refusal centre principally upon her servant. Ero rapidly adopts many of the characteristics of the male domestic servant. She is promptly subjected to appetites which, as the character's name implies, are imbued with overt sexual implications. By contrast with the conventional opposition of servant to master, however, Cynthia proves vulnerable to almost identical appetites. The sexualised culinary desires of Ero, therefore, appear initially as a mark of class identity, but are arguably reworked as a symbol of female frailty. Indeed, the corrupting influence of these lower-class figures might be considered in the context of changing contemporary attitudes towards household management. As Cahn has noted, the early modern period was defined by an increasing emphasis on the extent to which women lacked the skills to adopt a position of power within, as well as outside, the contemporary household.[14] It is significant that in the subplot, too, Eudora's remarriage is in large part a consequence of her betrayal by a female retainer. In *The Widow's Tears*, the hierarchies of contemporary society emerge as a source of weakness for the two women. Unable to govern their subordinates, they rapidly find themselves unable to govern their own bodily urges.

At the same time, the underlying association between hunger and sexual activity serves to complicate this interpretation. The disguised Lysander declares:

> I would have you live, and she would have you live freely, without which life is but death. To live freely is to feast our appetites freely, without which humans are stones; to the satisfaction whereof I drink, lady. (IV.iii.63–7)

The parallels between the drives of appetite and desire assert a relatively conventional image of a woman who cannot control her own body. Lysander's image of a society in which all 'feast [their] appetites freely' recalls the warning of Ulysses in *Troilus and Cressida*, of a world without degree, in which 'appetite, an universal wolf . . . Must make perforce an universal prey / And last eat up himself' (I.iii.121–4). At the same time, however, Cynthia's susceptibility to her disguised husband's advances is a result not of an innate, uncontrollable desire, but of an appetite derived

[14] Cahn notes that in this period 'education in basic domestic skills once deemed necessary for housewives was limited as the role of the housewife was limited', and highlights the 'the increasing numbers of and visibility of women who did not know how to meet their families' needs without resort to the market' (Cahn, 1987, pp. 112, 114).

from hunger. Lysander, by figuring the opposition of hunger to appetite as one between life and death, asserts the universality of hunger. Through equating the sexual desire consequent upon widowhood with the universal force of hunger, the play normalises desire. But it also foregrounds the unattainable nature of the ideals to which Cynthia has been held.

The culpability for her failure lies not with Cynthia, but with her husband, and his foolishness in subjecting her to a needless test of her virtue. Indeed, this interpretation is reinforced by the text's deployment of classical allusion. Lysander is repeatedly compared to the Greek figure Acteon, who was transformed into a stag and torn apart by his own hounds, as punishment for spying upon the goddess Diana as she bathed. Early in the play, Tharsalio warns Lysander not to mirror the fate of a man who 'could not be content to adore Diana in her temple, but he must needs dog her to her retired pleasures, and see her in her nakedness' (I.iii.68–70). Later, Tharsalio imagines Lysander transformed by Diana, for the crime of curiosity, from a 'sober and staid gentleman . . . into a monkey' (II.i.28–30). The scheme of deception is likened explicitly to a hunt, with Lycus comparing the plans of the two brothers to those of men who 'hunt hares to death for their sports, but the poor beasts die in earnest' (IV.i.35–6). Furthermore, the name Cynthia was itself an occasional epithet for Diana. Lysander is consequently linked, metaphorically, to Acteon. Khamphommala has noted that in the plays of Shakespeare, Acteon is repeatedly deployed in a sexual context, and 'metaphorizes not only hunger as desire, but also seduction as hunt' (Khamphommala, 2008, p. 20). Acteon's transformation into a stag, and consequent acquisition of horns, ensures that he has the potential to function as an image of cuckoldry.[15] Yet, as Pamela Allen Brown has demonstrated, horns in this period could be associated not simply with literal cuckoldry, but also with the phenomenon of 'horn-madness', or excessive jealousy (Brown, 2003, p. 95). Indeed, in *The Widow's Tears* the emphasis is clearly placed on the crime of 'curiosity', and by extension on Acteon's culpability and foolishness. At one level, the use of this image lends a cannibalistic implication to Cynthia's eventual consumption of food. In indulging her appetite with what she believes is a new lover, she symbolically devours her former husband. But above all the image reinforces the culpability of Lysander. By creating a situation in which his wife is deprived of sustenance, both literal and sexual, he sows the seeds of his own undoing. Through its insistence on the links between hunger and appetite, the play presents Cynthia's eventual fall as

[15] As Claire McEachern notes, 'Renaissance cuckolds were often called "Actaeons"' (McEachern, 2008, p. 616).

a product not of an innate, lustful identity, but rather of her own husband's foolishness. Lysander risks being devoured by appetites that he himself has awakened.

*The Widow's Tears* ostensibly conforms to a relatively predictable model, asserting the insincerity of a widow's grief, and emphasising the power of her lust and appetite, at the expense of her bodily control. Cynthia's initial ability to master her hunger simply makes her eventual submission to sexual and culinary appetite all the more apparent. However, this perspective risks marginalising the overtly self-reflexive nature of the text's concern with the intersection of hunger, appetite and lust. In the first instance, Cynthia's restraint is figured as the basis for the development of female community, in a manner which threatens to offset the patriarchal drives of the play's overall trajectory. Secondly, the underlying equation of sexual and culinary appetite, through its association with Cynthia's hunger, is constructed as a natural, necessary drive. Far from stigmatising Cynthia's desire, the play instead appears to ridicule the delusion and entitlement of her husband, who seeks to extend marital control beyond his own apparent death. In doing so, the text threatens to highlight the paradoxical nature of contemporary gender norms. Cynthia faces a choice between appetite and hunger. The former incurs charges of hypocrisy. But her commitment to the latter can be demonstrated in the final instance only through her own death. By translating the sexual concerns of widowhood to the culinary level, the text asserts the untenable nature of the norms to which Cynthia is held.

## Conclusion

In the context of female food refusal, hunger detached from appetite is imbued with a radical potential which is notably absent in early modern drama more generally. When a servant such as Adam in *As You Like It* conquers appetite, their unsatisfied hunger becomes an emblem of good service. When misers such as Lopez, in *Women Pleased*, starve themselves, they are the object of dismissive mirth. But the representation of female food refusal is accompanied by a pronounced element of anxiety. This anxiety stems not from these women's violation of gender norms, per se, but rather because they make visible the unspoken dynamics of contemporary ideology. Food refusal emerges as an excess of closure. The ideal of the woman detached from society, isolated within the home, had become increasingly dominant in the period. More broadly food refusal embodies a desire and capacity for stability in the context of a world increasingly determined by flux. Female self-starvation thus emerges as the embodiment of a dominant impulse within society. Yet through the process of embodiment, the culture's overriding impulse towards female passivity threatens to emerge as fundamentally flawed. If in some circumstances, the emaciated female body can function as an ideal, it can also emerge as a parody or critique of that ideal. It is female passivity taken to its logical extent: an image of female identity which can end only in the absolute passivity of death. The intersection of the physical and metaphorical dimensions to the representation of hunger serve as a means of thinking through the depreciating material power of women within both the home and wider society.

Moreover, food refusal is repeatedly associated with a form of affective control. Its practitioners emerge as an object of fascination or pity, in a manner which frequently entails the exertion of material pressure upon other characters. In the case of the 'miraculous maid' pamphlets that fascination is, implicitly or explicitly, the basis for advancement within contemporary society. In *A Woman Killed with Kindness*, it ensures that Anne can obtain her husband's forgiveness, if not that of God. And in *The Widow's Tears*, it is the basis for fantasies of female community, in which husbands die unmourned and widowhood emerges as a state of dangerous liberation. In each case, however, there is a paradoxical invocation of absolute closure and passivity to ensure one or another form of change. These tensions are exacerbated on the early modern stage, because the depiction of these women enables reflexive consideration of the fascination of contemporary audiences with the phenomenon of self-starvation. Just as the pamphlet culture of early modern Europe amplified the notoriety of the 'miraculous maids', so the contemporary London theatres both participated in, and reflected upon, the anxious attention paid to the spectre of female food refusal.

These tensions are alleviated, in part at least, by the implicit spectre of fraud or deceit. The 'miraculous maid' pamphlets, in particular, are animated by the possibility of a voracious appetite concealed within the ostensibly self-contained and mastered body. An integral part of the popularity of these accounts is this underlying fear and fantasy of an unknowable female interiority. There are parallels between the depiction of these women and the representation of lower-class male figures, such as the hungry servant. The latter's visible appetite retains an ambiguous relationship to the hunger which it may or may not express. In the same manner, the self-inflicted hunger of food refusal may in practice mask a voracious, and satisfied, appetite. In this respect, *The Widow's Tears* emerges as a text of particular radicalism, precisely because it does not castigate Cynthia's eventual turn to consumption. Both her hunger and her eventual descent into appetite are figured as troubling for the patriarchal norms which govern the play's society. But by locating the source of both in the actions of her husband, the text detaches Cynthia from any sense of culpability, and foregrounds the critical component of the two drives. The hypocrisy, in this context, lies not with the play's heroine, but with the male characters who have orchestrated the predicament in which she finds herself.

# CHAPTER 6

# *Imperial Appetites*

One of the most significant material contexts for the study of hunger and appetite on the Renaissance stage is imperialism. Whether in the early settlements of Jacobean colonialism or the starving armies of the European wars, it was at sites of imperial conflict that hunger was at its most acute. Famine had, for the most part, been eliminated in England, but in the New World numerous settlers starved, fed on defiled foods and even engaged in cannibalism, with the representation of this colonial hunger emerging as a key means by which contemporary accounts contested the imperial project.[1] At the same time, England's presence within an increasingly global network of food raised issues not simply of want, but of plenty as well. In contemporary pamphlets war and empire recur as solutions to, rather than causes of, the problem of hunger, while in the theatre appetite emerges as a means of conceiving of and, at times, critiquing these expansionist desires. Existing critical material has explored the wider cultural and political significance of the 'starving time' in Virginia with a particular emphasis on Fletcher and Massinger's *The Sea Voyage* (1622).[2]

[1] In 1587–88, 1597 and 1623, the counties of Cumberland and Westmorland experienced outright famine (cf. Appleby, 1978, p.1). But the rest of England faced problems of dearth, rather than famine. In the New World, by contrast, famine was recurrent. Accounts by John Smith, George Percy and William Strachey recorded the extreme conditions of the 'starving time' of 1609–10, and alleged that settlers resorted to cannibalism. Although these claims have been disputed by many historians, archaeologists working at the Jamestown site in 2012 uncovered evidence for at least one case of cannibalism (cf. Horn et al., 2013).

[2] Gordon McMullan reads *The Sea Voyage* as a reworking of *The Tempest* which draws upon reports of the starving time in order to 'both analyse and mock the processes and dangers of colonial venture' (McMullan, 1994, p. 198). Anthony Parr emphasises the degree to which the inadequacies of the play's would-be settlers mirror 'failings amongst the early Virginia colonists' (Parr, 1995, pp. 24–5). Claire Jowitt argues that in both *The Sea Voyage* and *The City Madam* the spectre of starvation is deployed in order to highlight the degree to which 'the correct management of appetite [determines] commercial, sexual and social position and success' (Jowitt, 2003, p. 192). Other major studies of the significance of food for early modern colonial texts include Joan Fitzpatrick's 'I must eat my dinner' and her work on *Henry V*, *Macbeth* and *Pericles* in *Food in Shakespeare* (Fitzpatrick, 2010; Fitzpatrick, 2007).

And extensive historical work has been carried out on the role of food exchange in early modern colonial encounters.[3] Food has also played a key role in the recent critical and historical emphasis which has been placed on the significance of Old World conflict as a model for colonial expansion in the Americas.[4] In this chapter, I build upon this work to assert the vital significance of hunger and appetite to the issue of imperialist expansion at both a material and ideological level. I will explore the degree to which the control of empire was reliant on, and represented through, control of the food supply, with hunger emerging as motive and means for imperialist expansion. I will demonstrate how the twin drives of hunger and appetite emerge in the imperial context as a way of conceptualising a wide range of residual and emergent class subjects. Hunger and appetite are integral to how early modern theatres conceptualised the opportunities and threats inherent in England's nascent colonial project.

Early modern experience of the New World was mediated through textual accounts of the potential productiveness of the land, which was alternately envisaged as a source of abundance, a barren location defined by want or a space which required specifically European cultivation in order to release its natural plenty. The former is a dominant theme of colonial propaganda, with many accounts drawing parallels between the New World and the bounty of the Garden of Eden. Hakluyt's *Principal Navigations* is replete with descriptions of the Americas as a land which is 'the fairest, frutefullest, and pleausantest of all the worlde, aboundinge in honye, waxe, venison, wilde fowle', where there exists such 'great store of vynes, all as full of grapes as coulde be, that if any of our fellowes went on shoare they came home laden with them' (Hakluyt, 1889, XIII, pp. 183, 188). A similar preoccupation is found in literature, so that in Marvell's 'Bermudas', for example, the song

3 Michael LaCombe notes the 'ubiquitous' nature of food in contemporary textual accounts of colonial settlement, arguing that 'when Indians and English produced food, exchanged it, ate it, or described their experiences, they conveyed dense and interlaced messages about status, gender, civility, diplomacy, and authority' (LaCombe, 2012, p. 3). Walter Cohen has stressed the significance of luxury foods as the motive of imperial expansion, noting the 'probably decisive role of economics in overseas expansion' (Cohen, 2001, p. 128). John Wood Sweet argues for the 'crucial' role played by food as both a means of interaction and a cause of conflict between native tribes and early colonial settlers in Jamestown (Sweet, 2005, p. 2).

4 Recent historical work by Robert Appelbaum, Karen Kupperman and John Sweet has emphasised the degree to which the varied discourses of colonial activity in the period emerge from models of imperial expansion which were heavily indebted to more conventional, Old World warfare. Likewise, critics such as Ania Loomba and Martin Orkin have made similar arguments in the case of early modern theatre, noting, for example, that '*The Tempest* brings together histories of New as well as Old World contact' (Loomba and Orkin, 1998, p. 13). These parallels are of particular relevance to the case of hunger and appetite, because issues of inadequate food supply and starvation were prominent characteristics of both forms of conflict.

of the settlers asserts that God 'makes the figs our mouths to meet, / And throws down melons at our feet' (Marvell, 2003, p. 57). However, this plenty could also be the object of suspicion. LaCombe notes that many contemporary commentators 'warned that to live in a foreign climate and to subsist, even in part, on the foods it produced might transform English bodies, with a corresponding change in temperament' (LaCombe, 2012, p. 57). Figures such as William Bradford claimed that the 'change of air, diet and drinking water' which the colonists would encounter 'would infect their bodies with sore sicknesses and grievous diseases' (Bradford, 1952, p. 28). The fertile climates of the New World were perceived not only as a source of wealth, but also of degeneration.

Other accounts adopted a more sceptical approach, asserting that colonial plenty could only develop through European intervention. Sir George Peckham defined colonial expansion as the right of 'Emperours and Kings ... to plant, possesse, and subdue' (Peckham, 1583, p. xxxii). In 1598, a group of colonists expelled from Munster recommended genocide to Queen Elizabeth, arguing:

> Lett the feete of yore forces treade and trample downe these bryars that will not suffer yore plantes to prosper ... Lett them weare with theire heeles the very rootes out of the earth that they springe no more: soe shall you make Ireland a flourishing nursery for England. ('Supplication', 1995, p. 72)

In 1622, Sir Francis Wyatt, governor of Virginia, wrote that the main task of the settlers was 'expulsion of the Salvages to gaine the free range of the countrey for encrease of Cattle, swine &c' (Wyatt, 1926, p. 118). As accounts of the New World as a land of milk and honey came to be recognised as exaggerated, increasing emphasis was placed on the potential for plenty which it was suggested would exist, if the lands were subject to what was regarded as more sophisticated European management.[5] Both on and off the stage, imperial expansion could be imagined as a process of cultivation, a means to create the plenty necessary to satisfy expanding English appetites.

Yet in the early seventeenth century, imperial adventure was not all luxury goods and prosperity; there was also extreme hardship. Early English attempts at settlement in the Americas proved markedly unsuccessful. The Roanoke colony of 1587 was left without supplies due to the war with Spain and the colonists disappeared. Even the more successful

[5] Herrmann notes that 'Before the Starving Time, writers depicted America as an Edenic paradise where food was plentiful and required little labour. But the new, postlapsarian Virginia demanded hard work and perseverance to realize the land's bounty' (Herrmann, 2011, pp. 49–50).

1607 colony of Jamestown, in Virginia, faced significant problems. Poorly supplied, badly organised and showing little ability to grow their own food, the colonists experienced difficulties from the moment of their arrival. Between 1609 and 1610, following worsening relations with the native population, they reached crisis point. By the time the colony was relieved, in March 1610, only 60 of the original 240 inhabitants remained. Although in reality, as Robert Appelbaum has noted, the majority of deaths were a consequence of disease rather than starvation, hunger was nevertheless rife, and was assumed by contemporary observers to be the key cause of death (Appelbaum, 2006, p. 273). The destitution and suffering was such that on the arrival of Sir Thomas Gates in 1610, it was claimed that 'those wch weare Liveinge weare so maugre and Leane that itt was Lamentable to behowlde them for many throwe extreme hunger have Runne outt of their naked bedds beinge so Leane thatt they Looked Lyke anotamies Cryeinge owtt we are starved We are starved' (Percy, 1625, p. 269). Moreover, despite the colony's initial recovery, these problems continued for, as Sweet recounts, in 1622 'the colony was nearly wiped out by a well-coordinated attack', while 'in the months to come, many of the survivors who regrouped at Jamestown – and hundreds of new settlers sent to fortify the colony – died of disease and starvation' (Sweet, 2005, p. 1). For this reason, the representation of hunger has the power to function as a means of critiquing the colonial project. Colonial adventure is simultaneously a source of want and plenty. This lends a pronounced ambiguity to the representation of hunger and appetite within a colonial context.

In order to explore the significance of this ambiguity, I will first consider how depictions of hunger and appetite in a colonial context articulate a specific relationship to the land being colonised. I will then discuss how the representation of hunger and appetite enables interrogation of specific power relationships and processes of interaction inherent in the exchange of food between colonisers and colonised. The chapter will conclude with analysis of the representation of cannibalism, one of the most significant examples of hunger and appetite in contemporary depictions of the New World. Throughout, my primary focus will be on John Fletcher's *Bonduca* (*c.* 1613) and Fletcher and Massinger's *The Sea Voyage* (1622), plays which place concerted emphasis on hunger and appetite. They reveal a recurring opposition between resistance and subjection to these drives, but one which has special significance in a colonial setting. Indeed, the key characteristic of the colonial situation is the strain which it places on this apparent opposition, and on the ability of aristocrats to maintain a privileged position of detachment from the world which surrounds them. The plays show the role played by hunger and appetite as mechanisms for imagining the wider dangers associated with England's imperialist expansion, and this acquires resonance from the contemporary tendency to associate playing companies with attacks on the colonial project.[6] Yet there are also key differences in the associations which hunger and appetite accrue in this context. Although both are deployed as a means of critique, the former tends to expose the material difficulties which colonists encountered, whereas the latter becomes a means to question the colonial project.

## The Space of Colonisation

In the theatre of the period, hunger and appetite emerge in the first instance as drives which embody specific relationships with, and attitudes towards, the land of the New World. The basic parameters of this relationship emerge with particular clarity in Chapman, Jonson and Marston's *Eastward Ho!* (1605; Chapman, Jonson and Marston, 1994), a play in which a group of adventurers plan a voyage to Virginia. The language in which they describe the land they hope to colonise constitutes, as Allan H. Gilbert has noted, an overt parody of accounts of Virginia found in Hakluyt (Gilbert, 1918). This parodic element is fused with images reminiscent of the land of Cockaigne. Seagull declares that Virginia is 'temperate and full of all sorts of excellent viands. Wild boar is as common there as our tamest bacon is here, venison as mutton' (III.iii.37–9). The paradise he envisions is of plenty, but is defined by a pronounced element of upward social mobility. The foods which Virginia is believed to offer them are those of the upper classes.[7] And this culinary ambition is combined with the claim that the would-be colonists 'shall live freely there, without sergeants, or courtiers, or lawyers, or intelligencers' (III.iii.40–1). These images of levelling emphasise the dubious class basis of the characters' enterprise, which has been launched by a penniless knight and financed by the sale of his new wife's lands. Indeed, recognition

[6] Ralph Hamor, for example, in his *True Discourse of the Present Estate of Virginia* (1615) condemns the '*Papists* and *Plaires*, *Ammonites* and *Horonites*, the scumme and dregges of the people, [who] mocke at this holy Businesse' (Hamor, 1615, sig. A4$^r$); and William Crashaw's 'epistle dedicatory' to Alexander Whitaker's *Good Newes from Virginia* (1613) notes the 'many discouragements that have attended this glorious businesse of the Virginian plantation', which 'devised by the Divell, and set abroach by idle and base companions, are blowen abroad by Papists, Players and such like, till they have filled the vulgar eares' (Crashaw, 1613, sig. A2$^r$).

[7] Roger Manning notes that venison 'was considered a great delicacy among all social groups which had the means to procure it' (Manning, 1993, p. 11), but with the exception of events such as Kett's Rebellion of 1549, during which the poor slaughtered and ate large quantities of deer, few amongst the poor had access to the meat (Manning, 1993, p. 17).

of the upwardly mobile element within colonial expeditions is a frequent characteristic of contemporary travel plays.[8] But the most striking feature of the plenty and prosperity which the adventurers hope to encounter is its illusory nature: they soon find themselves shipwrecked, having failed even to leave the Thames, and are forced to return home hungry and penniless 'like so many masterless men' (IV.ii.102). The text crystallises an opposition between dreams of plenty and the reality of colonial hardship which constitutes a recurring characteristic of dramatic treatments of the New World. The representation of hunger functions as a critique of colonial propaganda. But no less notable is the degree to which the masterless appetites of the potential colonisers are the object of ridicule and concern.

Indeed, as the colonial project gains strength, the deployment of the conflicting imperatives of hunger and appetite acquire ever more unsettling dimensions. The two drives become a means not simply to ridicule expeditions to the New World, but to express fundamental anxieties about the potential consequences of an encounter with a foreign land. The latter is particularly apparent in John Fletcher's *Bonduca*, which was originally performed by the King's Men, *c.* 1613. The text depicts the Roman invasion of Britain, but in a manner which foregrounds the parallels between this conflict and contemporary events in Virginia.[9] It

8 Kupperman notes that travel plays tend to 'centre on men who . . . were not born to elite heroic roles, but who took on such leading roles in novel exotic locations. The new Atlantic scene made possible a kind of advancement unavailable at home' (Kupperman, 2005, p. xiv). There was no shortage of contemporary examples offstage, for the careers of men such as the overt self-publicist John Smith served to make evident the possibilities for advancement which the New World provided. As Michael LaCombe has argued, this was a period in which 'England's larger, younger population had a much harder time finding access to land and livelihoods than had previous generations, which contributed to unprecedented geographic mobility' (LaCombe, 2012, p. 27).

9 Critical approaches to the play have tended to ignore this dimension, focussing instead on the intersection of gender and power, and frequently reading the representation of the anachronistic alliance between Caratach and Bonduca as a comment upon the reigns of James and Elizabeth. Julie Crawford and Roland Boling, for example, emphasise the satirical dimension to the representation of Caratach, arguing that this constitutes a critique of James's court. Yet as Claire Jowitt has noted, the play deploys 'a series of resemblances between contemporary Virginia and pre-Christian Briton' alongside 'the dramatization of questions concerning the benefits and drawbacks of "Romanization"', in order to explore the merits of contemporary colonial practice (Jowitt, 2003, p. 475). The importance of these parallels is accentuated, moreover, by the wider significance of the Roman Empire in contemporary thought. As Sweet has argued, 'for many English political leaders and promoters of overseas colonization, an idealized view of ancient Rome helped them envision – and justify – what they wanted to do in America' (Sweet, 2005, p. 2). William Strachey, for instance, noted 'Were not wee our selves made and not borne civill in our Progenitors dayes? and were not Caesars Britaines as brutish as Virginians?' (Purchas, 1906, XIX, p. 62). By staging the Roman invasion of Britain, Fletcher is able to employ a complex poetics of imperialism, encouraging the audience to sympathise with both sides simultaneously, and complicating any one-dimensional view of cultural influence.

shows a changing balance of power, mediated primarily through control of the land and the food which it produces. In the opening two acts, the Roman soldiers are starving and without proper supplies. By the end of the play the British general Caratach has claimed that his country has been reduced to 'a wildernesse of wretches' (V.i.15), while he and his nephew are described by the Romans as 'a brace of bear-whelps, close, and crafty, / Sucking their fingers for their food' (V.ii.115–16). Hunger is an index of a lack of control, through which the theatre explores the success or failure of the colonial project. Crucially, the gradual process of seizing control of the land emerges in the text most clearly as a process of cultivation. In the opening scene of the play, Caratach describes the Roman advance, declaring:

> Those men, beside themselves, allow no neighbour;
> Those minds that where the day is claim inheritance,
> And where the sun makes ripe the fruits, their harvest,
> And where they march, but measure out more ground
> To add to *Rome*, and here i' th' bowels on us;
> It must not be; . . .
> That hardy *Romane*
> That hopes to graft himself into my stock,
> Must first begin his kindred under ground,
> And be alli'd in ashes. (I.i.163–74)

The speech establishes the war as one of conquest, in which the control of land becomes the dominant factor. The lexis of 'graft', 'stock' and 'harvest', alongside the reference to the addition of dead Romans to the country's soil, reveals the uncompromising nature of the Roman advance, but also evinces a fundamental anxiety over the racial and national intermingling which that advance may prompt. To tame the land requires a process of grafting oneself with the Other, raising the possibility that imperial expansion is defined not by cultural dominance, but by hybridity.

Yet *Bonduca* undermines the degree to which the Roman army is altered by this encounter with a foreign land. It deploys a conventional opposition of lower-class, appetite-driven soldiers and austere, upper-class officers which implies an element of permanence to their attitudes, implicitly disputing the capacity of a specific climate or land to effect change in the invading army. Throughout, the soldier Judas subscribes to the belief that 'Good bits afford good blows' (I.ii.101), asserting the necessity of sufficient provisions for military endeavour. But the officer Petillius ascribes Judas's appetite to his lower-class status, declaring that his service belongs 'In a Fish-market' and describing him as 'good man Cobler' (I.ii.93; I.ii.96). The class dimension is embodied with particular clarity through the representation of appetite. Petillius displays scorn for the common soldier, telling Judas that if he will not fight:

> You'll hang then,
> A sovereign help for hunger. Ye eating Rascals,
> Whose gods are Beef and Brewis, whose brave angers
> Do execution upon these, and Chibbals:
> Ye dogs heads i' the porridge pot; you fight no more?
> Does *Rome* depend upon your resolution
> For eating mouldy pie-crust? (I.ii.86–92)

Petillius defines the starving soldiers by figuring their appetite as of a specifically lower-class kind. Their gods are 'beef and brewis', a form of broth involving beef and vegetables, which as Fitzpatrick has noted 'would have been considered a modest dish' and has lower-class connotations in the period (Fitzpatrick, 2011, p. 58). In *Sir Thomas More*, for example, the foreigner Caveler robs the character Williamson of a brace of doves, declaring 'Beef and brewis may serve such hinds. Are pigeons meat for a coarse carpenter?' (i.23–4). Likewise, chibbals, a contemporary term for Welsh or spring onions, seem likely to have held lower-class connotations. *Via Recta* (1620) declares that they are 'much of the nature of Onions', and that they are 'best agreeable for cold constitutions, and for such as undergoe great labour, and exercise of body' (Venner, 1620, p. 144). The soldiers' consumption of both these foodstuffs is constructed as an assault upon the food, in a manner reminiscent of the martial feasting of apprentices in Dekker's *The Shoemaker's Holiday*. But here, the parallels between eating and fighting seem rather to suggest ridicule of Judas's belief that to fight well he must be well fed: the soldiers fight to fill their stomachs and not for the glory of Rome. Combined with Petillius's deployment of the proverbial phrase 'dogs heads i' the porridge pot', the speech seems to suggest an animal appetite that will be satisfied the moment his betters are not observing him.[10] Appetite emerges as an inherent property of the poor, rather than a product of their immediate situation. The text therefore appears to deny the significance of the material conditions in which the soldiers find themselves.

Yet at the same time, this natural appetite is aggravated by the colonial process. Later in the scene, Petillius tells his general:

[10] Tilley identifies the earliest printed example of this proverb to be in Francis Merbury's *The Marriage Between Wit and Wisdom, c.* 1579 (cf. Tilley, 1950, p. 312; Merbury, 1971).

Your clemency
Hath made their murmurs, mutinies; nay, rebellions:
Now, and they want but mustard, they're in uproars:
No oil but Candy, Lucitanian figs,
And wine from Lesbos, now can satisfie 'em;
The British waters are grown dull and muddy,
The fruit disgustful: Orontes must be sought for,
And apples from the happie Isles; the truth is,
They are more curious now in having nothing,
Than if the sea and land turn'd up their treasures.
This lost the colonies . . . (I.ii.165–76)

The speech lists a series of foods, all defined by their relationship to the settlements of imperial Rome. While some, such as Lusitania, loosely equivalent to modern-day Portugal, were overtly connected with the colonial exploits of antiquity, others, such as 'the happie Isles', combine classical and contemporary resonances. While the 'happy isles' could describe the afterlife, in Greek mythology, the term was also used in contemporary texts as synonymous with 'the Fortunate Isles' which, as Akhimie has noted, constituted 'a blend of myth and reality, [and] might have referred to the Canary Islands in the mid-Atlantic, or to various locations in the New World' (Akhimie, 2009, p. 157). These colonial locations are associated with decadence and luxury, with Lesbos, for example, recalling the homoerotic poetry of the Greek poet Sappho, prompting an elision of foreign customs with foreign foods. Rome's imperial conquests are figured as eroding both national identity and conventional military resistance to hunger and hardship in a manner which clearly recalls contemporary anxieties regarding the influx into Britain of luxury goods from abroad.[11] The 'mutinies' and 'rebellions' which constituted a frequent characteristic of early modern warfare are reconstituted not as a product of scarcity, but of luxury and decadence. In blurring the lines between the colonial territories of classical Rome and contemporary England, the passage asserts the troubling potential of imperial expansion.

Furthermore, hunger is also deployed in drama to explore the potential of the colonial landscape for compromising discrete European identities. This is particularly evident in Fletcher and Massinger's *The Sea Voyage*, a play originally performed by the King's Men in June 1622. The play reworks Shakespeare's *The Tempest*, but replaces the emphasis on magic

[11] Fitzpatrick argues that 'the recurrent association in the early modern period of foreign culinary appetites with physical and sexual degeneracy gave rise to the perception that foreign consumption was harmful to English natives' (Fitzpatrick, 2007, p. 83).

with a profound interest in the material conditions of colonial exploration.[12] It depicts various groups of pirate-colonists, who explore two islands, one defined by extreme natural bounty, the other by absolute want. Central to the action is the depiction of a group of shipwrecked would-be colonists, who find themselves faced with starvation and engage in a failed attempt at cannibalism. Claire Jowitt and Teresa Walters have argued that the play constitutes a response to the 1622 native uprising in Jamestown, but this seems unlikely, given the length of time which it took for the news to reach London (see Jowitt, 2003; Walters, 2002). Nevertheless, the text engages in a concerned manner with accounts of the earlier 'starving time', and without doubt its later performances acquired a more pronounced resonance as details of the uprising emerged. In this text, subjugation to hunger is deployed not merely satirically, but as a fundamental challenge to European identity.

Indeed, hunger is enacted from the outset in direct opposition to conventional images of colonial plenty. Stranded on the barren island, the Portuguese aristocrat Sebastian condemns the position he finds himself in, declaring:

> Nor meat nor quiet;
> No summer here, to promise any thing;
> Nor Autume, to make full the reapers hands;
> The earth obdurate to the teares of heaven,
> Let's nothing shoot but poysoned weeds.
> No Rivers, nor no pleasant Groves, no beasts;
> All that were made for man's use, flye this desart;
> No aëry fowle dares make his flight over it,
> It is so ominous.
> Serpents, and ugly things, the shames of nature,
> Roots of malignant tastes, foule standing waters;
> Sometimes we finde a fulsome Sea-root,
> And that's a delicate: a Rat sometimes,
> And that we hunt like Princes in their pleasure;
> And when we take a Toad, we make a Banquet. (I.iv.139–53)

[12] Gordon McMullan notes that 'the magical elements of *The Tempest* are conspicuous by their absence from *The Sea Voyage*' (McMullan, 1994, p. 241). In the place of the supernatural, Fletcher and Massinger insist on 'the possibility of starvation in paradise' and concentrate 'on the problems of practical government by human resources' (McMullan, 1994, p. 241). Although Parr has argued that 'the very abundance of analogy tends to suggest that, like *The Tempest*, this play refutes any attempt to tie it exclusively to a particular place or venture' (Parr, 1995, p. 22), Jowitt emphasises the relevance of the New World, arguing that 'the presence of European women on board Portuguese and French ships is significant in locating this play within a Western rather than an Eastern context, since the former was concerned with permanent settlement and the latter with temporary trading posts' (Jowitt, 2003, p. 193).

Where contemporary colonial propaganda sought to establish the New World as a new Eden, *The Sea Voyage* delivers an image of a fallen world of 'serpents', with the earth explicitly opposed to divine intervention, remaining 'obdurate to the teares of heaven'. This irredeemable nature places the island in explicit opposition to the wider tendencies within colonial discourse which, as Patricia Akhimie has noted, 'frequently imagined the globe as a series of potential country estates, waiting to be claimed and cultivated' (Akhimie, 2009, p. 154). Here, that tendency receives an ironic inflection. The island is a space which is constituted as resistant in every way to the project of colonial improvement. The references to rats as the object of hunts, seaweed as a 'delicate', and a Toad as a 'banquet' constitutes the island as the inversion of the aristocratic lifestyle that writers such as Ralegh and Smith imagined might be established within the New World. Hunger emerges as a visceral critique of plans for colonial settlement and the most overt manifestation of the land's physical resistance to the project of improvement.

Moreover, this hunger threatens the identity of the afflicted colonists. When Sebastian and Nicusa are first encountered by Albert's crew, for example, they are described in terms which question their humanity. Aminta draws attention to their 'sunk eyes' which 'are crept in, as if they had been frighted!' (I.iv.104; I.iv.105). Albert questions whether they are alive or are merely 'wandring shaddows' (I.iv.110). The image fuses the consequences of hunger with the supernatural, imbuing them with a ghost-like quality. John Smythe describes how 'sicke and starued Souldiors' returning from the Low Countries were reduced to the condition of 'miserable and pitiful ghosts or rather shadowes of men' (Smythe, 1590, p. xxi), but in *The Sea Voyage*, the characters who are subjected to this degenerative process are not common soldiers, but aristocrats. The text establishes hunger as a force which can corrupt identity, making the elite monstrous and reducing them to the same status as the 'shames of nature' who inhabit the island (I.iv.148). Sebastian's response to the pirates' queries is to assert the enduring power of his rank, telling them 'Onely our miseries make us *seem* monsters' (I.iv.103; my emphasis). Yet his immediate shift towards duplicitous behaviour, stealing the pirates' ship while they search for gold, implies that this seeming affects not simply the elites' outward appearance, but also their actions. The result is to emphasise not their capacity to withstand hunger, but the degree to which an aristocratic identity is reliant on a certain standard of material well-being and, more importantly, a public perception of that well-being.

Hunger and appetite therefore express a relationship with the land which is primarily defined by vulnerability. Whether the plays depict colonial bounty or extreme scarcity, they imply that culinary encounters with the Other are potentially degenerative. Yet the precise nature of the degeneration depends on the type of drive on which the play focusses. In the case of appetite, the colonists' vulnerability is a product of what is being consumed. It raises the prospect of a permanent shift in character. But appetite is primarily a characteristic of the lower classes, implying an ability on the part of the elite to detach themselves from the corrupting influences of the land. Hunger, by contrast, is more clearly associated with the precariousness of colonial enterprise. In *The Sea Voyage*, the effects of scarcity are wide-ranging, corrupting the elite and reducing their actions to the level of the lower classes. Yet hunger operates on a contingent and temporary basis. The result is that where *The Sea Voyage* deploys hunger to comment on the potential setbacks that a colonial voyage may encounter, *Bonduca* uses appetite to explore the more worrying possibilities inherent in imperialist expansion as a whole.

## Hunger, Appetite and Interaction

The material difficulties of the early settlers made interaction with the native population unavoidable, as the colonisers sought access to food. In English accounts, descriptions of native hospitality could function as a rhetorical tool to show the decline of similar customs amongst the English. William Wood, for example, noted that the natives 'are as willing to part with their Mite in poverty, as treasure in plenty' (Wood, 1634, p. 69), while Roger Williams declared that 'it is a strange truth, that a man shall generally finde more free entertainment and refreshing amongst these Barbarians, then amongst thousands that call themselves Christians' (Williams, 1643, p. 16). Elsewhere, an ability to secure food from the natives is used as a sign of the negotiating skills of the narrator, with John Smith's *Proceedings of the English Colony* (1612), for example, emphasising his ability to win the favour of the Algonquians, to such a degree that 'every other day brought such plenty of bread, fish, turkies, squirrels, deare, and other wild beasts, part they gave him as presents from the king; the rest, hee as their market clarke set the price how they should sell' (Smith, 1986, I, p. 214). Most significantly, eating with the natives emerges as a symbol of a worrying dependency on the part of the colonisers. Key examples occurred during the 'starving time' in Virginia when, as George Percy noted, 'To eate many our men this starveinge Tyme did Runn away unto the Salvages whome we never heard of after' (Percy, 1625, p. 267). In these times of scarcity, as LaCombe has argued, 'Hunger regularly trumped fears of hybridity' (LaCombe, 2012, p. 50). It is this unsettling aspect to these interactions which emerges most forcefully in dramatic treatments of the subject.

In *Bonduca*, these tensions emerge most clearly in Act II, Scene III, when Judas and his hungry soldiers attempt to steal food from the enemy camp. Initially threatened with torture and death by Bonduca's daughters, they are rescued by Caratach, and presented with food.[13] The subsequent depiction of natives and lower-class colonisers united through the consumption of food echoes the basic dynamic of Shakespeare's *The Tempest*, which, as Paul Brown has argued, raises the prospect of an alliance between the savage Caliban and the masterless Trinculo and Stefano as 'a threat around which the governing classes might mobilise, that is, around which they might recognise their common class position' (Brown, 1994, p. 52). On his return to the Roman camp, Judas recounts their encounter in terms highly favourable to Caratach. He tells the officers he has been:

> [With] *Caratach*.
> Shake now, and say, we have done something worthie!
> Mark me; with *Caratach*: by this –, *Caratach*:
> Do you as much now, and you dare: sweet *Caratach*.
> Ye talk of a good fellow, of true drinking;
> Well, go thy waies, old Caratach: besides the drink Captain,
> The bravest running banquet of black puddings,
> Peeces of glorious beef . . . (II.iv.56–62)

The repetition of Caratach elides praise of the food with praise of the man who provided it, turning Judas's speech into something akin to a hymn of praise for the enemy general. The speech lends a homoerotic dimension to the play's depiction of men bonding through food, an effect which is accentuated by the emphasis which the text has earlier placed on Caratach's disdain for Bonduca and her daughters. But this sexualised male bonding also contains an implication of rebellion, for Decius claims that they are 'turn'd Rebels all' (II.iv.65). Appetite, as a force which unites both natives and the lower class, is situated in direct opposition to the colonial project.

[13] The episode has ostensible parallels with the stance adopted by the Duke of Bourbon in Shakespeare's *Henry V*, who suggests that the French should 'send [the English] dinners and fresh suits / And give their fasting horses provender, / And after fight with them' (IV.ii.57–9). Yet where Bourbon merely ridicules the spent nature of the English army, Caratach follows through on his promises, presenting the soldiers with meat and wine.

Of course, the text tends to avoid the explicit statement of cooperation between the lower-class soldiers and Caratach's native resistance. Caratach demands not their loyalty, but rather 'In recompence of this good . . . A sound knock in the battell' (II.iii.94–5). He feeds them to ensure honour for himself. On his return to the camp, Judas asserts that he must 'kill *Caratach*, / That's all he ask'd us for our entertainment' (II.iv.70–1). But the Roman is also presented as judiciously employing the possibility of his support for the enemy for specifically material ends. When the officers claim that he and his men have drunk enough, he declares 'no wine, no fighting. / There's one call'd *Caratach*, that has wine' (II.iv.82–3). Caratach's acts have opened up the potential for collaboration between lower-class Romans and the native inhabitants of the island, and while this alliance is never in fact enacted, the power which it lends Judas is evident in the immediate capitulation of Decius to his demands. Indeed, the implied danger of intermingling between coloniser and colonised is accentuated by the name of Judas himself, for its associations with Jewry references earlier Roman conquests, emphasising the degree to which empire entails the dissolution of ostensibly rigid boundaries between different peoples and nations. Whereas in *The Tempest* the threat of collusion between natives and the masterless poor is fundamentally comic, in Fletcher's text the power which the prospect of intermingling lends the soldier Judas embodies far more profound anxieties over the potential consequences of colonial appetites.

In *The Sea Voyage*, hunger drives not only the lower classes, but also the elite, into processes of interaction. The stranded sailors are rescued from the barren island by a group of Portuguese women who have adopted the life of an Amazonian tribe. The ability of these Amazons to control the food supply places them in a position of power over the newly arrived Europeans. Tibault declares 'Be they Devils: Devils of flesh and blood; / After so long a Lent, and tedious voyage, / To me they are Angels' (III.i.210–12). His sense of morality is entirely dictated by hunger. The capacity of the extreme hunger produced by the colonial setting to prompt such blasphemous thoughts was well attested, with Percy recording that during the 'starving time' a man named Hugh Price:

> Did come openly into the markett place Blaspheameinge exclameinge and cryeinge owtt that there was noe god. Alledgeinge that if there were A god he wolde nott suffer his creatures whom he had made and framed to indure those miseries. (Percy, 1625, p. 269)

In *The Sea Voyage*, the result is not atheism, but an inclination towards worship of their seemingly native rescuers. Likewise, Juletta describes her ability to dictate the actions of the settlers, telling her companions 'Show 'em a crust of bread / They'll saint me presently, and skip like apes / For a sup of Wine' (IV.ii.40–3). Hunger forces them into a position of subjection which mirrors that of the soldiers in *Bonduca*. Yet here, the appetites which hunger has created are not simply products of want, but tantamount to idolatry. Although in *Bonduca* the process of intermingling is predominantly confined to those of lower rank, in the later work no one seems immune from the corrupting effects of the colonial terrain.

Of course, the supposed Amazons are in fact Europeans and Parr has argued that 'by creating a landscape empty of natives, *The Sea Voyage* sustains the common myth that what was discovered in the New World was virgin land, and that the only question to be decided was which colonising power held legitimate title to it' (Parr, 1995, p. 25). Yet while the native inhabitants are never presented on stage, there are allusions to them. Rosellia reminds her followers that the island was 'Inhabited heretofore by warlike women, / That kept men in subjection' and that they themselves resolved 'by their example ... here to plant our selves' (II.ii.203–6). The text is therefore situated after a process of intermingling which parallels that portrayed in the play, and which has apparently occurred for much the same reason: the necessity induced by the experience of hunger. Rosellia notes that:

> Necessity
> Taught us those arts not usual to our Sex;
> And the fertile earth yielding abundance to us
> We did resolve, thus shaped like Amazons
> To end our lives. (V.iv.41–5)

The text deploys the implied presence of both hunger and appetite to explore the process of hybridisation which has prompted the Europeans to assume the role of Amazons. The description of 'the fertile earth yielding abundance' is reminiscent of colonial propaganda, an image of bounty which stands in opposition to the simple fact of 'necessity'. Here the process of cultivation has been effected precisely by the sacrifice of a conventional European identity.

Attention to how these plays depict interactions with the native population makes clear the extent to which hunger and appetite on the Renaissance stage articulate fears of degeneration. As with the land, hunger and appetite imply relationships with the native population that embody wider fears of the vulnerability inherent in English colonial expansion. In large part, the power of these representations owes its origin to the wider significance of hospitable practice within early modern culture. Given the significance of this tradition as a tool 'deployed by the aristocracy for its dual function of promoting social harmony while reinforcing their influence within a deeply hierarchical society' (Heal, 1984, p. 90), it is unsurprising that the representation of European colonisers placed in a position of subjugation causes a dangerous inversion of the perceived natural order. The representation of these processes of interaction therefore calls into question the supposed superiority of European culture. Once again, however, appetite and hunger are shown to operate in distinct but related ways. Appetite remains predominantly associated with the lower classes, raising the prospect of a dangerous alliance between the masses of England and the native populations they might encounter. In place of the process of *translatio imperii*, Fletcher and Massinger present colonisation as a fusion of two cultures. Hunger, by contrast, embodies fears of a precarity which is more wide-ranging in class terms, but also a temporary predicament. If hunger embodies fears of the temporary subjugation of English colonial forces, appetite establishes the possibility not simply of defeat, but of hybridity and cross-cultural disorder.

## Cannibal Appetites

One of the most potent images through which the early modern theatre explored the degenerative effects of hunger was cannibalism. Although anthropophagy and cannibal imagery are recurrent features of these texts, they acquire added significance in the colonial context. Early anthropological and historical work on cannibalism placed great emphasis on whether or not cannibalism actually occurred, with a general tendency to read early reports of cannibalism as a process of legitimation, through which European colonisers justified their subjugation of native peoples.[14] Increasingly, however, critics have emphasised the degree to which images of cannibalism in early modern literature drew upon a dual tradition, with recent work acknowledging the significance of cannibalism in the Old World, as well as the New.[15] The presence of these dual traditions means

[14] In *The Man-Eating Myth*, for example, William Arens asserts the absence of 'adequate documentation' for socially sanctioned anthropophagy in any existing society (Arens, 1979, p. 21). Yet as Hulme has noted 'even for the sceptics, cannibalism does exist: it exists as a term within colonial discourse to describe the ferocious devouring of human flesh supposedly practised by some savages' (Hulme, 1998, p. 4). As Rachel Herrmann has argued, 'long before English colonization began, fantasies of cannibals infused textual and visual representation of the New World' (Herrmann, 2011, p. 68).

[15] Louise Noble, for example, highlights the tradition of medicinal anthropophagy, noting that 'paradoxically, while charges of cannibalism were being levelled at the geographically distant Other, cannibalism was being practiced at home' (Noble, 2003, p. 679). Raymond J. Rice,

that even when cannibalism is figured as a characteristic of the natives of the New World, it can be deployed to comment upon Europe. Indeed, the most significant example of cannibalism within a New World context for an early modern audience would undoubtedly have been the European cannibalism which had occurred during the 'starving time' in Jamestown.[16] Percy claims that settlers dug up 'dead corpses outt of graves' and 'licked upp the Bloode which ha(d) fallen from their weake fellowes' (Percy, 1625, p. 267). Most notoriously, one colonist was said to have murdered his wife for the purpose of eating her. Percy recorded how 'one of our Colline murdered his wyfe Ripped the childe outt of her woambe and threw itt into the River and after chopped the Mother in pieces and salted her for his foode' (Percy, 1625, p. 267). In the latter case, a central point of discussion was the extent to which the act was motivated by hunger, or by a depraved appetite for human flesh. William Strachey, for example, claims that the man killed her simply 'to satisfie his own pleasure and appetite', noting that a search of the man's house revealed he was already in possession of food (Purchas, 1906, IV, p. 1757). For those sympathetic to the Virginia Company's propagandist aims, it was necessary to dispute the extent to which starvation lay at the root of the cannibal act. As with the appetites of the soldiers in *Bonduca*, the transformation of hunger into appetite undermines the significance of want, associating cannibalism with an inherent voraciousness, rather than the material circumstances of the 'starving time'.

There is a similar ambiguity over the roles of hunger and appetite in the representation of cannibalism in *The Sea Voyage*. Here, anthropophagy ostensibly emerges as a product of extreme hunger. The text deploys what Herman Pleij has described as a 'hunger topos' (Pleij, 1997, p. 107), typical of contemporary accounts of famine, where cannibalism is suggested only after a variety of other forms of tainted appetite. The sailors consider trying mud and bark, then medical supplies and finally human flesh. The steady progression mirrors accounts of the 'starving time', such as Percy's claim that 'having fed upon horses and other beasts as long as they lasted, we were

meanwhile, reads European cannibalism as a specifically gendered discourse, with the Renaissance theatre defined by the 'need to displace the anxiety of cannibalism onto the body of the woman' (Rice, 2004, p. 301).

16 In a series of accounts of the starving time, John Smith, George Percy and William Strachey noted the existence of cannibalism. Although these accounts were published shortly after the performance of *The Sea Voyage*, the fact that they were preceded by the account of the Virginia Company, which strenuously denied rumours of cannibalism induced by hunger, makes evident the large degree of public knowledge of events in Virginia (cf. Percy, 1625; Purchas, 1906; Smith, 1986; Virginia Company, 1610).

glad to make shift with vermin, as dogs, cats and mice' (Percy, 1625, p. 267). In the case of *The Sea Voyage*, the shift between the defiled foods to human flesh is initiated when Franville asks the surgeon:

> Wher's the great Wen
> Thou cutst from *Hugh* the saylers shoulder?
> That would serve now for a most Princely banquet. (III.i.52–4)

The 'wen', signifying a lump, protuberance or tumour, is transformed into a 'Princely banquet' (*OED*, 'wen', def. 1a, 1b). The impact on the audience of this juxtaposition of their enthusiasm and anxieties surrounding corrupted flesh and the incorporation of another body seems calculated to inspire humour, but also disgust. This disgust is in part contained by the dramatic irony within the scene. The audience is aware that Albert has already secured a promise of food for his starving companions, but the effect is nonetheless to situate cannibalism as an act of desperation, arising from necessity.

However, when the sailors decide to eat Aminta, their female captive, the representation of cannibalism acquires a very different inflection. Aminta becomes not simply sustenance, but a delicacy. She is 'young and tydie' and will 'eate delicatly / Just like young Porke a little lean' (III.i.106; III.i.107–8). The position of disgust from which the audience observes their culinary cravings is highlighted at the precise moment when the settlers turn from necessity to desire and pleasure. Moreover, Aminta is described as 'unrosted' and 'unsod' (III.i.109), with the latter signifying that she has not yet been boiled. She has been turned into an ingredient, in language which distinguishes the sophisticated appetites of the settlers from contemporary accounts of cannibalism amongst native tribes, which stressed the simplicity of their customs. Later, the sailors discuss the possibility of salting Aminta's body, declaring 'we shall want Salt' and 'Tush, she needs no powdering' (III.i.111–12). The obvious pun on make-up makes explicit the parallel between the different means by which women can be consumed: as objects of sexual desire, or as literal foodstuffs. The reference to 'powdering' the body is also significant in the context of later reports of events in Virginia, the majority of which note that the man who ate his wife also salted the body to preserve it. As Robert Appelbaum has argued, 'the mutilation of the corpse, along with application of the culturally "cooked" process of salting the body parts – in other words, daring to act on barbarous impulses with all the Providence that civility demanded – is perhaps what most offended his executioners' (Appelbaum, 2006, p. 274). In precisely the same manner, *The Sea Voyage*'s representation of cannibalism constructs it as not simply the degeneration of European identity into that of the colonial Other, but a parody of the very elements of sophistication which notionally distinguished the two. Cannibalism is a product of the hunger inflicted on the pirate-colonists by a barren land, but it is also a manifestation of their European appetite for delicacies.

A significant motivating force behind the sailors' move towards cannibalism is frustration at the failure of their colonial project. Although hunger affects characters across the social spectrum in *The Sea Voyage*, it is notable that those who attempt to engage in cannibalism are those who are, as Parr has argued, 'modelled on the younger sons of minor gentry who hoped to find in the colonies the wealth and status denied them at home, and who proved in many cases to be maladjusted and workshy' (Parr, 1995, p. 21). In *The Sea Voyage*, the expectations of these aspirant characters aggravate the hunger which the barren land inflicts upon them, becoming the source of cannibal desires. Franville declares:

> True we were bound yee all know,
> For happy places, and most fertill islands,
> Where we had constant promises of all things,
> She turn'd the Captains minde . . . (III.i.88–91)

Aminta is a fitting object for their cannibalistic appetites precisely because she is believed to be responsible for their current plight and the consequent failure of their imperial ambitions. The opposition of images of fertility and abundance to the experience of hunger and poverty connects their expansionist desires with more literal appetites. Robbed of the original object of their desire, they rapidly shift their attention to the body of Aminta. The devouring of Aminta is described in the language of the colonial project. They plan to 'cut her throate, / And then divide her, every Man his share' (III.i.118–19), and worry that her 'hinder parts' 'will not fall to every Man's share' (III.i.141–3). As Wrightson notes, a key model of colonialist expansion in the period was the joint-stock company, which constituted 'associations of capital, open to any investor', in which trade 'was conducted by the directors on behalf of the company, and the proceeds were shared among investors' (Wrightson, 2000, p. 179). These companies not only constituted, as Hill has argued, 'a great advance in the capitalist organization of English society', but were also the model used by theatre companies such as the King's Men (Hill, 1967, p. 57). Fletcher and Massinger link the implicit connections between imperial project and cannibalism to an instance of actual Virginian anthropophagy. The depiction of the colonists' tainted appetites is deployed to explore the destructive potential of imperialist expansion.

The use of colonial cannibalism to comment on the state of European society springs from the wider significance of cannibal imagery in the period as a figure for an emergent ideology of bourgeois individualism. Even when cannibalism is more overtly presented as a characteristic of the native Other, it retains this capacity to function as a comment upon European social practices. In Jonson's *The Staple of News* (1626), for example, the cook Lickfinger describes his comic plan to send an expedition of cooks to the New World to convert the cannibals into 'good eating Christians' (III.ii.157). The text implicitly parodies the attempts of colonists to impose Christian civility on the natives of the New World. At the same time, the power of his cookery is demonstrated through its supposed ability:

> To make such sauces for the savages
> And cook their meats with those enticing steams,
> As it would make our cannibal-Christians
> Forbear the mutual eating one another,
> Which they do do more cunningly than the wild
> Anthropophagi that snatch only strangers,
> Like my old patron's dogs there. (III.ii.174–80)

Like Montaigne's 'Of the Cannibals', with its claim that 'there is more barbarity in eating a man alive, than in eating him dead' (Montaigne, 1991, p. 234), Jonson deploys New World cannibalism as a means to satirise an emergent capitalist economy. His text participates in a wider tradition which figured non-native cannibalisms as the modus operandi of European society. Here, the power of this image derives in large part from its inversion of the previous, parodic dichotomy between civilised colonisers and barbarous colonised.

In *The Sea Voyage*, the reflexive capacity inherent in the representation of the cannibal act is accentuated by the metatheatrical emphasis on the colonists' actions. The distance between audience and characters is severely compromised by the degree to which cannibalism is justified with reference to its textual legacy in early modern culture. Morillat declares he has 'read in stories-' (III.i.109), while Lamure responds 'Of such restoring meates, / We have examples; Thousand examples' (III.i.100–1). Lamure's comments constitute an interjection in Morillat's sentence, continuing the sense and amplifying the implied textual presence of cannibalism, creating the impression of a communal literary tradition which they intend to act upon. As Parr notes, audiences within the Blackfriars would undoubtedly have possessed:

> A sense of familiarity with the issues that a play about voyaging would be likely to raise, and an expectation that the standard *topoi* of 'colonial' writing – wilderness, promised land, cannibalism, gold hunger, savage customs – will be deployed to create a deft and topical entertainment. (Parr, 1995, p. 31)

Yet the degree to which the existence of these topoi are deployed to justify the practice of anthropophagy blurs the line between passive audience member and active character. The result is to suggest that the difference between the lurid appreciation and enthusiastic practice of cannibalism is simply a product of material circumstance. The barren islands of the failed colonial project provide space for the activation of a tradition which is widespread, and to which the play itself is contributing.

Although ostensibly associated with foreign practices and cultures, the case of *The Sea Voyage* makes clear the more complex connotations of cannibalism within the period. The force which drives the colonists to attempt to kill, cook and eat Aminta is not hunger alone, but hunger in conjunction with appetites which, through the text's emphasis upon her potential status as a delicacy and object of colonial 'sharing', are clearly presented as owing their origin to the society from which they have come. In conjunction with the text's wider emphasis upon the fragility of European identity, this comic scene raises the worrying prospect that frustrated imperial hopes may make manifest the troubling undercurrents within the colonising, rather than the colonised, society. Through its stress upon the ambiguity of the dividing line between text and practice, *The Sea Voyage* insists upon the possibility that these forces may exist within the audience, calling into question the spectator's potential for complacency or critical distance. Hunger makes possible the activation of unnatural appetites lurking within contemporary European civilisation, and the representation of cannibalism crystallises wider tensions which can be discerned in the theatre's use of both hunger and appetite to conceptualise the relationship between colonisers and the New World.

## Conclusion

Analysis of the representation of hunger and appetite within the context of imperialism highlights the degree to which these drives are implicated in the formation of identity. Specific attitudes towards the consumption of food, and a wider tendency to resist or to be subdued by hunger and appetite, are integral to the manner in which class and race are constructed in these plays. Appetite recurs as a characteristic of the poor, the upwardly mobile and the racially Other, and becomes a means to raise the troubling spectre of collaboration between these different groups. Yet the use of hunger and appetite to explore these identities consistently emphasises a relational model of identity, since the two drives emerge as a means of conceptualising the relationship between individuals and their world. In the case of colony and empire, the nature of identity belies the capacity of specific subjects to withdraw from the material and social contexts in which they are situated. This dimension is particularly visible within a colonial context because the lands and societies which these characters encounter are constructed as threatening. But this network of relationships also acquires significance because the material factors governing imperial expansion in the period made visible wider processes of social change.

Indeed, attention to the representation of hunger and appetite in a colonial context reveals their power as a form of political critique. In the case of hunger, this negative appraisal of colonialism most obviously constitutes a debunking of the propaganda produced by vested interests such as the Virginia Company. The frequency with which lists of defiled foods recur in these plays highlights the centrality of hunger and appetite to contemporary debates over imperialist expansion and the extent to which that debate remained highly contested. But hunger also provides playing companies with a means to problematise the assumptions of those who believe that the process of colonial exploration will be a simple matter of civilising docile natives. While this form of criticism should not be elided with more modern attacks upon the immorality of imperialism, it nevertheless constitutes a significant challenge to nascent forms of colonial expansion. Residual paradigms for understanding the body such as humoral theory provide the basic structure for writers to conceptualise the interactive nature of the colonial experience, indicating how the process operated upon the colonists themselves. In doing so, these plays make clear the fragility of the ideological models through which the English legitimised their imperial expansion. The theatre constitutes a significant forum for discussion and consideration, lending imaginative form and substance to the wider body of rumours which circulated about the various crises of the Virginian colonies.

In the case of appetite, by contrast, susceptibility to change is a product, in the first instance, of eating, and of the liminal characteristics of the consumption of food. This element of vulnerability is aggravated by the specific nature of early modern beliefs regarding food consumption. It emerges particularly clearly in plays depicting imperial adventure, because colonisation necessarily requires encounters with, and consumption of, the unknown. Yet this dangerous element of openness helps to explain the anxiety which invariably defines the representation of appetite. Excessive consumption can be read not simply in moralistic terms, but as a readiness to consume that which may effect change. Appetite is troubling because its metaphorical and literal senses threaten to coincide, forcing elision of the act of eating exotic foodstuffs, the act of obtaining those foodstuffs through unsettling processes of interaction, and the class tensions and expansionist desires which produce the desire for the exotic in the first place. The experience of empire foregrounds the association of appetite with the elements which Korsmeyer has identified as central to the process of eating: a 'liminal activity, occurring at the threshold between "inside" and "outside" the body' (Korsmeyer, 2005, p. 5). Whereas the colonial propaganda of the period seek to stimulate this appetite for foreign lands and foods, in plays such as *Bonduca* appetite is the object of a pronounced anxiety. The troubling aspects to appetite are highlighted by the colonial context because it embodies a dangerous fascination with the products of a colonial Other which, through a process of consumption, threaten to become incorporated within the imperial body. In doing so, these foreign foods and peoples challenge the identity of the colonists themselves, in a manner which manifests the wider reliance of early modern colonists upon the land and resources of those that they sought to conquer.

CHAPTER 7

# *Revolt*

A consistent thread running through the representation of hunger and appetite on the early modern stage is the possibility of lower-class violence. In depictions of service, hospitality, sexuality and imperialism, the spectre of hunger reveals a pervasive ruling-class fear that the collapse of hierarchy may produce disorder and rebellion. Yet plays which represent the act of revolt often treat these connections with caution. Prompted, perhaps, by the potentially seditious nature of the material, many playing companies seem anxious to detach onstage revolts from the issue of hunger. *Gorboduc* (1561) features a rebellion of the commons against the monarchy, in response to the queen's murder of her son. But the rebellion is depicted only in dumb show, ensuring that the rebels are not given voice on stage and their actions are associated with the impersonal prompting of the furies. Heywood's *1 Edward IV* (1599) portrays a revolt by the illegitimate royal Falconbridge against the eponymous monarch. Although it is predominantly presented as lower-class in nature, Falconbridge declares that he and his followers do not rise 'for mending measures, or the price of corn, / or for some common in the weald of Kent, / That's by some greedy cormorant enclosed' (ii.30–2). In *George a Green* (1599), the Earl of Kendall claims to rise with the intention 'to relieue the poore, or dye myselfe' (I.i.15), but soon proves to be more concerned with looting the surrounding countryside than with protecting the poor. Fletcher and Massinger's *Beggars' Bush* (1622) and Massinger's *The Bondsman* (1623) emphasise the participation of disguised noblemen in what ostensibly appear to be lower-class revolts. Although the former gives a prominent role to masterless vagabonds, they are depicted in a romanticised manner which detaches their position from a lived experience of hunger.

There are, however, exceptions to this trend. In this chapter, I will focus on three plays in which hunger and appetite are significant as drives which motivate revolt and as the means through which revolt is represented. *The Life and Death of Jack Straw* (1593) and Shakespeare and Marlowe's *2 Henry*

*VI* (1594) participate in the general vogue for history plays which defined the 1590s. The former is an anonymous play, possibly written by George Peele, and probably performed not in the public theatres, but as part of a city pageant.[1] It has received critical attention primarily for its relationship with Shakespeare and Marlowe's play and has generally been painted in an unfavourable light.[2] Although *2 Henry VI* has invariably been characterised as a more sophisticated work, critics have debated whether audiences would have responded sympathetically to its representation of rebellion.[3] Both plays depict rural revolts which begin as relatively justifiable responses to injustice and hunger, but which are increasingly defined by rebellious excess. *Coriolanus* (1608), by contrast, is a later play, written shortly after the Midland Rising. Its urban setting and investment in the political structures of Republican Rome distinguish it from the earlier plays, but it shares their concern with the transition from initial injustice to the process and consequences of revolt. Critical readings have situated the play in the context of both the uprising which preceded its performance and its Republican setting, while significant work has also considered the play's treatment of the imagery of feeding.[4] By positioning *Coriolanus* in

1 Irving Ribner notes that there is 'no record of its having been performed on any public stage or at court' (Ribner, 1965, p. 72). He argues that it 'appears almost certainly to have been written for a city pageant' (Ribner, 1965, p. 72), stressing that it comprises only four acts and amplifies the role of the Lord Mayor, William Walworth, whose descendant was also Lord Mayor in 1590–1.

2 Ribner argues for its historical significance, but acknowledges that 'small claim can be made for its literary value' (Ribner, 1965, p. 71). Richard Helgerson notes that the mere act of representing rebel grievances on stage is 'a matter of some consequence', but nevertheless argues that in both *Jack Straw* and *2 Henry VI*, the rebels are 'aggressively discredited' (Helgerson, 2003, p. 34).

3 Rackin suggests that by 'giving public voice to the grievances they shared with actual rebels in Shakespeare's England, the actors threatened to produce in the real time of the audience the same disorder they enacted in the fictive time represented on stage' (Rackin, 1990, p. 208). William Carroll, on the other hand, acknowledges that 'Cade's complaints were real ones, frequently heard outside the theatres', but argues that 'this representation of Cade tends to subvert their political and ideological power' (Carroll, 1996, p. 155). Likewise, Craig A. Bernthal has argued that 'the contradictions in Cade's program of reformation are comically obvious' (Bernthal, 2002, p. 259).

4 Critics such as David George and Steve Hindle situate the hunger of the plebeians in the context of the Midland uprising of 1607 (George, 2000; Hindle, 2008). Richard Wilson, by contrast, dates the text slightly earlier, but nevertheless asserts the relevance of contemporary lower-class rebellion and the increasing dominance of the market for an understanding of the play's treatment of the plebeian uprising (Wilson, 1993). Critics have placed particular emphasis on Coriolanus's attempts to assert his ability to transcend hunger. Janet Adelman situates this tendency as the product of the absence of maternal nourishment, arguing that 'If the spectre of a multitude of hungry mouths, ready to rise and demand their own, is the exciting cause of *Coriolanus*, the image of the mother who has not fed her children enough is at its centre' (Adelman, 1992, p. 355). Joan Fitzpatrick reads Coriolanus's resistance to hunger as a critique of his wider disdain for the plebeians, noting that it suggests 'that a man out of touch with his body can become out of touch with ordinary (hungry) people, ending up with so little sense of cultural identity that Rome's arch-enemy, Aufidius, becomes his friend' (Fitzpatrick, 2007, p. 96). And in a similar vein, Stanley Cavell has emphasised the degree to which hunger is implicated in Coriolanus's aspiration to a quasi-deified status, arguing that 'what

the context of the theatre's wider deployment of hunger and appetite, it is possible to discern the complex ways the play rewrites the concerns of both *Jack Straw* and *2 Henry VI*.

In focussing on these three relatively exceptional plays, I aim to discern the characteristics associated with revolt when it is depicted through the representation of hunger and appetite. The conjunction of hunger and violence emerges not simply as an implicit threat, but rather as a represented practice which acknowledges, even as it frequently condemns, the agency of the poor. These onstage revolts entail the representation of injustice, but also contain dreams and fantasies of a better world. At every stage, the process of depicting revolt is bound up with hunger and appetite, with the act of rebellion figured not simply as lack, but also as consumption and excess. They embody, therefore, the fundamental interrelationship of suffering and utopian impulse, a relationship which in this period finds its most evocative expression in hunger and appetite.

The emphasis which these plays place upon hunger as the stimulus of revolt is arguably an accurate manifestation of contemporary lower-class disorder. The early modern period was defined by a series of uprisings, which varied dramatically in extent and efficacy. Of particular significance were the London riots of 1595, an abortive rising attempted in Oxfordshire in 1596, and the Midland Revolt of 1607. But throughout the period, there were numerous small-scale riots which, while never reaching the level of overt insurrection, attested to the constant possibility that resentment might spill over into outright revolt. Hunger played a significant role in these riots, which invariably occurred in periods defined by bad harvests and dearth. Historians and critics have linked these uprisings to the tensions caused by the transition to a capitalist mode of production.[5] They have stressed the pressure on early modern society exerted by popular protest, which often restricted the process of transition.[6] Increasingly, however, they have also argued that the late sixteenth and early seventeenth

he incessantly hungers for is ... not to hunger, not to desire, that is, not to be mortal' (Cavell, 1983, p. 5).

5 Roger Manning, for instance, links revolt to the period's 'sequence of harvest failures, dearth, and food riots, as well as unemployment in the clothing trades', and emphasises the significance of anti-enclosure riots as a means by which the poor restricted the expansion of the newly capitalised form of agriculture (Manning, 1988, p. 157).

6 Key texts include Keith Wrightson's *English Society* (1982), Andy Wood's *Riot, Rebellion and Popular Politics* (2002) and *The 1549 Rebellions and the Making of Early Modern England* (2007) and John Walter's *Crowds and Popular Politics in Early Modern England* (2006). Drawing heavily on anthropological methods, and strongly influenced by early work from E. P. Thompson, Natalie Davis and Peter Burke, these historians pioneered a form of history that attempted to understand popular protest on its own terms. As Andy Wood has argued, while 'traditional political history viewed the

centuries were defined by a reduction in the efficacy and power of lower-class protest. Historians such as John Walter, Ian Archer, Steve Hindle, Keith Wrightson and Andy Wood have claimed that by comparison with Kett's Rebellion and the 'commotion time' of 1549, late-Elizabethan and early-Jacobean uprisings were relatively minor.[7] The downturn has been linked to the increasing integration of local elites within the power structures of the early modern state, in conjunction with a growing tendency to associate revolt with specifically proletarian elements within the lower classes.[8] The drama must be understood in the context of this relative decline and the changing class-composition of contemporary uprisings. But it is also important to acknowledge that the theatre, as a space of both performed fantasy and ruling-class propaganda, retained the capacity to extend beyond the contemporary lived experience of revolt and embody the latent, rebellious possibilities inherent in a society in flux.

Terminology is central to understanding the conjunction of hunger, appetite and armed resistance. I will use the term 'revolt', defined by the *OED* as 'an act of renouncing allegiance to established authority, esp. through collective armed rebellion; an insurrection, an uprising' (*OED*, 'revolt', def. 1a). This will avoid the cross-class, feudal connotations of 'rebellion', and the implication of systemic change inherent in the word 'revolution'.[9] The Renaissance stage features innumerable examples of

early modern period from the lofty heights of elite institutions, social historians preferred a more gritty, local perspective' (Wood, 2002, p. ix).

7 Wrightson has highlighted 'the realignment of the vitally important middling group in rural communities' who 'as the beneficiaries of economic change . . . had become increasingly distanced in their interests from their poor neighbours' (Wrightson, 1982, p. 181). Andy Wood argues that by the late sixteenth century 'the profound legitimation crisis that had been opened up by the early reformation was resolved through the incorporation of wealthier social fractions, via the medium of office-holding, into state structures' (Wood, 2007, p. 188).

8 Events such as the Peasants' Revolt of 1381 had long attested to the power of hunger to motivate resistance from below. But revolts of this sort had been the exception to a more general tendency for lower-class discontent to be manipulated by various factions within the elite. By the late sixteenth century, however, as James has argued, 'the notion that risings were necessarily "of the commons" . . . implied a changed attitude to dissidence on the part of those who had traditionally led rebellions and revolts' (James, 1986, p. 356).

9 All three terms have, of course, frequently been used as synonyms. But rebellion has tended to be associated in early modern English history with the uprisings of 1549, 1569 and 1601, all of which are defined by a regional, cross-class dimension which distinguishes them from the purely lower-class disorder which characterises revolts of this period which were motivated by hunger and want. The difference between revolt and revolution, meanwhile, is of course frequently ambiguous. As Jack Goldstone notes 'how do we tell, amid the swirl of current events, whether an outburst of violence is a passing storm or the beginning of a cataclysm? In other words, how can we tell when a state is truly threatened by revolution?' (Goldstone, 1991, p. xxi). By focussing on revolts, I aim to highlight the emphasis upon the agency of a nascent proletariat which tends to define the onstage representation of hunger and of violent, collective resistance to the state.

armed resistance to the state, but the conjunction of hunger and insurrection is almost exclusively a feature of lower-class resistance. By contrast with baronial rebellions, which imply a continued allegiance to feudal structures of authority and retainership, and which are depicted on the early modern stage in plays such as Shakespeare's *Richard II*, the revolts of the early modern theatre are firmly associated with hunger and lower-class agency devoid of aristocratic leadership. The representation of hunger and revolt is bound up with the emergence of a distinctive class subject. This lends an unprecedented significance to the plays of the early modern period as spaces in which the nature and aspirations of an emergent rural proletariat could be imagined. In reinscribing the histories of earlier, far more wide-ranging revolts into the specific socio-economic terrain of early modern England, the theatre invests this nascent subject with a power which extended far beyond the reality of contemporary revolt.

The specific dramatic significance of these onstage revolts can only be understood by moving beyond the alternately dichotomous and hierarchical conceptions of revolt currently dominant in the study of Renaissance theatre. The enduring legacy of New Historicism and Cultural Materialism has confined many accounts within a reductive model of contemporary society which occludes the specificity of political discourse in favour of a model which implicitly opposes the rich to the poor.[10] It is therefore significant that recent work by Jeffrey Doty, Oliver Arnold and Chris Fitter has paid more attention to the complexity of class forces in the period, and the specific content of popular political movements.[11] This critical perspective has highlighted the

[10] Cultural Materialist and New Historicist attention to the representation of revolt has tended to focus upon concepts of masterlessness. Stephen Greenblatt, for example, characterises such masterless men as 'the very types of Elizabethan subversion' (Greenblatt, 1994, p. 30). Yet, this emphasis tends to ignore the complex, fractured nature of both upper and lower classes in the period. Reducing these complex and shifting class identities to a dichotomy of masters and masterless tends to produce a reading of the theatre which is either voluntarist or pessimistically conservative. One marginal exception is Paul Brown's consideration of *The Tempest*, in which he argues that the masterless rebellion of Trinculo, Caliban and Stefano is 'a threat around which the governing classes might mobilise, that is, around which they might recognise their common class position' (Brown, 1994, p. 52). Brown recognises that the basic dichotomy of masters to masterless is precisely constructed by the period's theatre, but nevertheless he remains convinced that all the insurgency achieves is to 'bind the rulers together in hegemony' (Brown, 1994, p. 53).

[11] This more recent work is also significant for the emphasis which critics have placed both on the relevance of Shakespeare's own views and on their changing nature. Patterson, for example, identifies a transition from an early Shakespeare, 'hopeful' about the potential for reconciling class difference within early modern society, to the increasingly pessimistic playwright of the later plays. Fitter and Hadfield, on the other hand, argue respectively for a more radical or republican Shakespeare in the turbulent decade of the 1590s, by contrast with the increasing conservatism or defeatism of his later work. Peter Holbrook declares that 'in respect of social relations, mid-to-late Shakespeare is better

potentially monarchist sympathies of the Shakespearean crowd, with Doty arguing that 'early modern popular politics were not . . . exclusively radical and were rarely antimonarchical' (Doty, 2013, p. 162). Attention to the complex sympathies of rebellious subjects therefore 'pressures the conservative versus progressive binary through which most critics discuss Shakespeare's politics' (Doty, 2013, p. 162). Yet if Cultural Materialism tends to overstress the opposition of rich to poor, recent attention to monarcho-populism risks eliminating this dimension altogether. A model recognising the class dichotomy of rich and poor, and the fractured nature of the ruling classes at a time of sweeping social change, can provide a more nuanced understanding of the intersection of hunger, appetite and revolt. Indeed, attention to the role played by hunger and appetite enables an approach which recognises the fundamentally rational nature of revolt in early modern society, without accepting the assumption of an unquestioning fealty to monarcho-populist ideology amongst on- and offstage rebels.

To understand the interrelation of hierarchy and class in the representation of hunger and revolt, it is necessary to analyse these plays as depictions of processes, rather than events. The onstage revolts of the early modern theatre are defined by a recognisable structure, which moves from initial injustice to outright rebellion and eventual defeat, in a manner which is strikingly reminiscent of Ernst Bloch's model of 'rebellious' hunger.[12] I will therefore emphasise the structural significance of this model, while at the same time exploring the possibilities for disruption and 'reading against the grain' which inhere therein. I will first consider the role played by hunger and appetite in depicting the motivation for revolt. In the plays under consideration, it is rarely hunger alone which precipitates revolt, but rather hunger which exists in opposition to unrestrained ruling-class appetites. Secondly, I will explore how the process of rebellion is portrayed on the stage. Lower-class revolt is repeatedly depicted through the representation of appetite, with the rebels' hunger translated into an unrestrained desire to

than early . . . *The Comedy of Errors*, for instance, is more committed to traditional notions of social hierarchy than later plays' (Holbrook, 2003, p. 74).

12 Bloch argues that:

> If [hunger] increases uninterrupted, satisfied by no certain bread, then it suddenly changes. The body-ego then becomes rebellious, does not go out in search of food merely within the old framework. It seeks to change the situation which has caused its empty stomach, its hanging self. The No to the bad situation which exists, the Yes to the better life that hovers ahead, is incorporated by the deprived into *revolutionary interest*. (Bloch, 1995, p. 75 [Bloch's italics])

Bloch articulates a dialectic of hunger, whereby deprivation prompts not simply a negative response to present injustice, but rather a desire to reorder contemporary society in its entirety.

consume. In my last section, I will argue that in the early modern theatre, this period of excess would have been multivalent. In the complex conditions of original theatrical performance, the staging of the rebels' appetites raises the possibility that the audience will endorse this unrestrained consumption, creating a space for the imagining of a proto-communist and, within the context of the period's mode of production, utopian vision of a society without class.

## Injustice

The significance of hunger as a force driving revolt was widely acknowledged in the early modern period. In 1549, an anonymous treatise had queried 'What Faith and allegiance will those men observe towards their prince and governor which have their children famished at home for want of meat?' (Tawney and Power, 1924, III, p. 336). By 1597, Francis Bacon could confidently declare that 'the rebellions of the belly are the worst' (Bacon, 1985, p. 103). Hunger was perceived as a state of desperation, with unprecedented power as the source of revolts. It was, for Bacon, the quintessential example of those elements of grievance which 'in offending people, joineth and knitteth them in a common cause' (Bacon, 1985, p. 104). A similar emphasis can be discerned in the theatre. The citizens of *Coriolanus* resolve 'rather to die, than to famish' (I.i.4–5). The peasants of *The Life and Death of Jack Straw* declare 'before wele lacke / Wele stuffe the Gallowes till it cracke' (i.108–9). Want emerges as the force which propels them into collective action in a manner which embodies that element of liberatory compulsion which Bloch defines as 'the No to the bad situation which exists' (Bloch, 1995, p. 75). Yet the connections between hunger and revolt are complex. Hunger is no unitary phenomenon, but a possible consequence of a wide variety of social and physical factors, the interpretation of which is invariably contested. Bacon may have acknowledged that hunger is the primary motivation for revolt, but he situates that hunger as itself a product of appetite.[13] He argues that the chief means by which a state might prevent rebellion is 'the repressing of waste, and excess' and the prevention of 'the multiplying of nobility, and other degrees of quality, in an over proportion to the common people' (Bacon, 1985, p. 104). In a period when concepts of growth and expansion were largely foreign to economic theory, hunger emerges as a product not simply of circumstance, but of the acts and appetites

[13] Appetite, here, embodies the characteristics which Bloch associates with 'the rich and sated', a product of the fact that man, 'if he has what is necessary', is subjected to 'new desires . . . which torment him differently, but no less intensely than the previous naked privation' (Bloch, 1995, p. 49).

of the elite. To understand how the causes of lower-class rebellion are represented in the early modern theatre, it is therefore necessary first to consider the precise significance of hunger in this period, and second to acknowledge its integral relationship with the appetites of the rich.

On the Renaissance stage, hunger signifies not simply desperation, but exclusion. It implies figures who exist outside the structures of reciprocity and hierarchy which ensure stability within contemporary England. It can on occasion emerge as characteristic of aristocratic, as well as lower-class rebels. In the first act of Shakespeare's *Julius Caesar* the eponymous ruler declares:

> Let me have men about me that are fat,
> Sleek-headed men and such as sleep a-nights.
> Yond Cassius has a lean and hungry look.
> He thinks too much: such men are dangerous. (I.ii.191–4)

Caesar's wariness is well founded. The lean and hungry Cassius convinces the less famished Brutus to join him in a conspiracy which culminates in Caesar's assassination and an eventual civil war. But the explicit connection which the play draws between a lean body and a rebellious mind merits consideration. In part, it appears to speak to Caesar's superstition, typical of a man who 'loves to hear / That unicorns may be betrayed with trees. / And bears with glasses' (II.i.202–4). Yet Caesar's concern can be understood as extending beyond irrationality. For Caesar, an indulged appetite is associated with meekness. The adjective 'sleek', could mean smooth or healthy, but could also imply a sense of fawning docility, as in the allusion to 'sleek Flattery' in Jonson's *Cynthia's Revels* (I.ii.37), or Wolsey's characterisation of Suffolk as 'sleek and wanton' in Shakespeare's *Henry VIII* (III.ii.241). To eschew such food is to reject docility and to risk thinking too much. As a member of the patrician class, the hunger which Cassius experiences is not the result of lack of means. Instead, his 'hungry look' suggests social alienation. As in the case of Appemantus in *Timon of Athens*, Cassius's hunger implies he exists outside the structures of feasting and hospitality that constituted a central component of the social hierarchy in both classical Rome and early modern England. In associating Cassius with a self-inflicted hunger, Shakespeare's text embodies wider tensions resulting from the increasing inefficacy of hospitable practice as a tool of social control.[14] In a play in which the plebeians are controlled by Lupercal festivities and the beneficence of Caesar's supposed will, Cassius's hunger symbolises a man who cannot be bought.

[14] See Chapter 3.

When hunger is associated with lower-class revolt, this sense of exclusion implies a more radical failure on the part of the rich. The entire fourth act of *2 Henry VI* is dominated by a revolt, but the basis of this outburst of lower-class activity is established much earlier, in the infighting and indifference of the elite. In one significant scene, three petitioners approach the Duke of Suffolk, under the mistaken belief that he is the Lord Protector. It emerges that one of the petitions is against the duke himself, for 'enclosing the commons of Long Melford' (I.iii.20–2). The queen, Suffolk's lover, dismisses the petitioner and one of his companions as men 'that love to be protected / Under the wings of our Protector's grace' (I.iii.38–9). She promptly destroys the petition, and instructs them, 'Begin your suits anew' (I.iii.40). As Carroll has indicated, the episode was an addition by the playwrights and is 'not present in any of the sources' (Carroll, 1996, p. 138). It reflects the practice of revolt in early modern England, which invariably followed unsuccessful attempts by the commons to seek redress through peaceful means such as petitions.[15] The revolt, when it comes, is a symptom of the rich's unwillingness to alleviate the hunger of the poor. It is this sense of a broken contract which has been identified by recent critics as evidence of a monarcho-populist discourse in which violent means are deployed for relatively conservative ends. Doty, for example, argues that 'an understanding of popular politics equips one to read Shakespeare's crowds not as irrational lovers of violence but rather as stewards of the commonwealth or conscious agents of their own material interests' (Doty, 2013, p. 162). Hunger can be characterised as symptomatic of the failure of the elite, and it is those failings which are responsible for revolt.

Furthermore, the failings are repeatedly conceptualised through images of appetite. In *Coriolanus*, the hunger of the plebeians finds its most powerful expression in their condemnation of the Roman senate as the 'cormorant belly'. The bird was widely considered a creature of insatiable appetite, 'Whose Crawes with eating will be never full' (Baxter, 1606, sig. H2$^{v}$). The image of the cormorant recurs in descriptions of enclosers and engrossers of corn.[16] The phrase implicitly links the hunger of the plebeians

[15] Holstun notes that these discursive forms 'originated in a hierarchical and medieval world' implying 'in its very structure a *local* appeal from low to high', but argues that by the 1640s they had become 'larger in scope and ambition . . . a medium more of lateral *association* than of hierarchical *appeal*' (Holstun, 2000, p. 107).

[16] Adams, for example, declares that 'the churlish Cormorant is a mischicuous *Rider:* hee sits on a black Iade, Couetousnesse; and rides onely from market to market, to buy vp graine, when hee hath store to sell: and so hatcheth vp dearth in a yere of plenty' (Adams, 1619, p. 172). As Kevin de Ornellas has argued, whereas early incarnations of this image are predominantly used to imply simply an uncontrollable appetite, 'toward the end of the sixteenth century, the cormorant becomes a familiar emblem not only of greed but

with acts of enclosure carried out by a contemporary elite, embodying the theatre's tendency to emphasise the connections between rebellion and the excesses of certain sections of the ruling class. Likewise, at the height of the rebellion in *2 Henry VI*, the King is told that 'All scholars, lawyers, courtiers, gentlemen, / They call false caterpillars and intend their death' (IV.iv.35–6). The image of parasitical feeding was a common one. Thomas Adams, following Pliny, claimed that caterpillars were:

> Litle wormes bred in the green leaves of plants, [which] prove in three dayes catterpillars & eate up those plants. The Countrey breeds, these covetous wretches, and they devour her. [Pliny] writes also that Catterpillars are bred by a dew, incrassated and thicked by the heate of the Sun. It is the warmth of prospertie, that breedes and feeds our usurers. Others say, that they come of butterflies egs, the which heate of the Sunne hatcheth, working so fit a passive matter to the forme of a catterpillar. So commonly your usurer hatcheth, his riches out of the Butterflies egs, laid abroad by prodigall young gallants. (Adams, 1619, p. 323)

The caterpillar is an image, most obviously, of parasitical feeding, which must be destroyed lest it endanger the plant, or society, upon which it subsists. Yet particularly striking is its association with excess and 'the warmth of prospertie'. The unruly appetites of 'prodigall young gallants' are the products of an excess of usury and the generalised spread of capitalist praxis, at the expense of the traditional structures and conventions of feudal society. Lower-class revolt emerges as a means to curb the excesses of those members of the elite who have abandoned their responsibilities.

These images of parasitism are defined by a marked lack of specificity. Appetite emerges as a floating signifier, which can be invested with a diverse range of political meanings. In *Sir Thomas More* (1600), for example, it is associated not with English elites, but with London's immigrant population.[17] To a degree, this is unsurprising, for urban uprisings

also of covetousness', so that by the end of the century, it tends to suggest 'not only their insatiate lust for material excess but also the desire to deprive other men of their possessions' (Ornellas, 2007, p. 39). The deployment of the cormorant as a justification for revolt constitutes the culmination of this process, but it should be noted that the shift might potentially be understood not in terms of the symbolic properties of the bird, but rather as evidence of the changing significance of appetite more generally.

17 The play has received critical attention primarily as a consequence of the fact that Shakespeare may have collaborated in its production. But it also constitutes one of the most significant examples of contemporary censorship, with Edward Tilney, Master of the Revels, instructing the company to 'leave out the insurrection and the cause thereof' (*More*, Tilney, 1–2). John Jowett links the play to the contemporary vogue for plays 'dealing with the lives of the friends and advisers of kings' (Jowett, 2011, p. 29). Yet it arguably, and to the displeasure of the censor, aimed also to satisfy the audience demand for depictions of rebellion and revolt, evident not only in *Jack Straw* and *2 Henry VI*, but also the likes of *George a Green* and *1 Edward IV*.

were frequently associated with anti-alien sentiment.[18] Immigrants were attacked, and their workshops looted, in the 'Evil May Day' riots of 1517. Hatred of strangers was a significant, if not a dominant, theme of the events of 1595, with an explicitly anti-alien riot taking place on 12 June. In the play, however, the hatred of strangers is explicitly formulated with reference to hunger and appetite. As Joan Fitzpatrick has noted, the play's opening depiction of the strangers' offences elides literal and sexual appetites, so that 'accusations of foreigners' gluttony are accompanied by accusations of their voracious sexual appetite', with the implication that 'foreign appetites must be controlled in order that English national security be maintained' (Fitzpatrick, 2007, p. 83). Conventional attacks, for example on the impact of foreigners on the availability of employment, are in large part displaced by an emphasis upon their uncontrollable appetites. The rioters fear that they will 'see a red herring at a Harry groat, butter at elevenpence a pound, meal at nine shillings a bushel, and beef at four nobles a stone' if 'strangers be suffered' (vi.1–4). Their bill of wrongs claims that 'aliens and strangers eat the bread from the fatherless children, and take the living from all the artificers and the intercourse from all the merchants' (i.123–6). Indeed, the elite acknowledge the extent of the problem, with Shrewsbury claiming that foreigners are 'fattened with the traffic of our country' (iii.14). Even when removed from specific issues of enclosure and engrossment, hunger and appetite retain their function as the key means for figuring the injustice which motivates revolt.

Nevertheless, the basic opposition of hunger to appetite had the potential to highlight inequality in a way which could prompt more radical action. The issue emerges particularly clearly in Shakespeare's *Coriolanus*, which opens with a plebeian uprising during the early years of Republican Rome. In the first scene, the patrician Menenius Agrippa confronts a group of starving and rebellious citizens, attempting to persuade them to abandon their insurrection. Hunger is presented as an undeniable fact, made visible on their bodies. The first citizen notes that 'the leanness that afflicts us' is 'the object of our misery' (I.i.17–18).[19] The ensuing debate focusses on the origin of that hunger. The first citizen claims that 'What authority

[18] Archer has argued that 'the anxieties of the aldermen centred on relations between the citizens and the alien population', rather than class-based discontent, and notes that 'Evil May Day haunted the consciousness of the late-sixteenth century metropolitan magistrate' (Archer, 1991, p. 4).

[19] Object, in this period, could signify 'The presentation of something to the eye or perception' (*OED*, 'object', def. 1b), and the line asserts the commonly held understanding that hunger is self-evident, a truth which cannot be concealed. Similar concerns define Cleon's description of the effects of famine in *Pericles* (see Chapter 3).

surfeits on would relieve us' (I.i.14), and declares that their misery 'is as an inventory to particularise their abundance' (I.i.1–19). The implications are manifold. The reference to surfeit implies the indulgence of appetite to the point of saturation. But the notion of poverty as an inventory goes further, seeming to some extent to deny the pleasure principle, in favour of a misery which exists solely for the sake of maintaining a regressive class system. Menenius, by contrast, seeks to detach the experience of hunger from the fact of injustice. He claims that 'For the dearth, / The gods, not the patricians make it' (I.i.67–8), and tells the citizens that they 'may as well / Strike at the heaven with your staves, as lift them / Against the Roman state' (I.i.62–4). Hunger is a force imposed from outside society, a divine judgement which rebellion will not only fail to alter, but may actually make worse. Revolt implies, therefore, a population which attributes hunger to interior, socially constructed causes. As such, it can be argued that hunger and appetite function as a common framework of images which must be imbued with specific political content. But they are also derived from the material facts of exploitation and inequality, at a period of apparent polarisation. It is their lack of inherent meaning which ensures their potential utility as bearers of a more radical political message than that which constitutes monarcho-populism.

The radical potential of this process is accentuated by the anachronism which has long been acknowledged as a defining feature of the period's representation of revolt. Rackin argues that *2 Henry VI* 'loads the rebels' speeches with anachronistic references to current grievances and literal places that serve to localise the action in sixteenth-century England' (Rackin, 1990, pp. 214–15). Steve Hindle notes that in his reimagining of the account of the plebeian rebellion given in Plutarch, Shakespeare 'conflated two historical rebellions (the usury riots which led to the creation of the Roman tribunate in 494 BC and the corn riots of 491 BC) into a single fictional one which, like the Midland Rising, was caused fundamentally by dearth' (Hindle, 2008, p. 41). These anachronistic changes have various consequences. They establish the rebels' hunger as the product of nascent capitalism, which was undermining traditional structures of reciprocal hierarchy. The plays therefore manifest an ambiguity comparable to that evident in the representation of hunger and appetite more generally. Instances of enclosure or engrossment can be interpreted as either specific actions by individuals, or in class terms as an inherent opposition of rich to poor. At the same time, by aligning past revolts with the audience's experience of present injustice, the plays contribute to the creation of what Annabel Patterson has called a 'cultural tradition of protest' (Patterson, 1989, p. 38), encouraging the concept of a continuous conflict between the appetite-driven rich and the hungry poor.

Yet the deployment of hunger and appetite in this context acquires a complexity which extends beyond the element of immediate injustice which prompts revolt, creating a means of understanding the underlying dynamic of the period. Hunger constitutes an index not simply of misery, but of exclusion. It becomes a symbol for the breakdown of social structures designed to ensure stability. In this sense, revolt indicates failure on the part of the elite. It implies a broken contract which exposes the presence within early modern society of forces which can be termed broadly capitalist in nature. The representation of revolt might therefore function to obscure the more radical dimension to hunger which Bloch's model implies. Nevertheless, this conservative dimension is always in tension with a more basic opposition, which opposes not the benevolent landowner to the ravenous encloser, but rather the hungry and excluded to the well-fed rich. It is the uneasy tension between these two dichotomies which determines the complex representation of revolt in the period. To understand these contradictions more thoroughly, it is necessary to consider not simply the causes of revolt, but how the process of rebellion is portrayed.

## Excess

There was fairly widespread acceptance that rebels might have legitimate grievances. The problem was not so much the motivation as the act of revolt itself. *A Students Lamentation*, published in the wake of the 1595 riots, claimed that Jack Cade, Jack Straw and the like 'would be Reformers, & wrongs forsooth they went about to right: but when they had got head, what wrong did they not count right?' (1595, p. 7). As Greenblatt has argued, 'radical protest ... appealed not to perceptions utterly alien to those expressed in official circles, but rather drew unacceptable conclusions from those same perceptions' (Greenblatt, 1988, p. 21). Crucially, the transition from initial injustice to uncontrollable revolt was frequently conveyed through the representation of hunger and appetite. Alexander Neville, in his account of Kett's Rebellion, described how 'besides Swannes, Geese, Hennes, Ducks, and all kind of fowles without number, about three thousand Bullocks, and twenty thousand Sheepe, were royotously spent in the Campe within few dayes' (Neville, 1615, sig. D3$^{r}$). For Neville, the rebels were 'drowned in drink, and excesse ... overcharged with meat', a group of 'miserable common people' unable to control their own appetites (Neville, 1615, sig. C4$^{r}$). A similar emphasis is to be found in the 'Homily Against Disobedience'. The text explicitly compares this notion of rebellious excess to the appetites of the rich, declaring:

> Where other gluttons and drunkardes take to muche of suche meates and drynkes as are served to tables, rebelles waste and consume in short space al corne in barnes, feeldes, orels wher, whole garners, whole storehouses, whole cellers, devour whole flockes of sheepe, whole droves of oxen and kyne . . . (Church of England, 1571, p. 577)

Revolt is constructed not as the antithesis of the appetites of the rich, but rather as their extension, a form of reckless consumption which dwarfs the gluttony of the elite. As the homily expresses it, 'hunger and famine . . . are the peculiar companions of rebellion', since 'rebels do in short tyme spoyle and consume al corne and necessarie provision' with the consequence that 'extreame famine and hunger must needes shortly ensue and folowe rebellion' (Church of England, 1571, pp. 578–9). The dominant discourses of the period disrupt the opposition of hunger to appetite which constitutes the basis of rebellion, ensuring that revolt and rebellion recur as forces associated not with redistribution, but with the gratuitous consumption of food.

It is this element of excess which defines the acts of the rebels in plays such as *2 Henry VI*. Cade's very first demand is that:

> There shall be in England, seven half-penny loaves sold for a penny; the three-hooped pot shall have ten hoops, and I will make it felony to drink small beer. All the realm shall be in common, and in Cheapside shall my palfrey go to grass. (IV.ii.60–4)

In a similar manner, Cade will later demand that 'at the city's cost, the Pissing Conduit run nothing but claret wine this first year of our reign' (IV.vi.2–4). The very name Cade, as his followers themselves note, recalls a 'cade', or barrel, of herrings (IV.ii.30). This emphasis upon consumption is multifaceted. In the first place, it effects a shift in the representation of revolt; whereas before the hunger of the poor is placed in opposition to the appetites of the rich, the process of revolt emerges as simply the opposition of competing forms of appetite. Like the 'Homily Against Disobedience', *2 Henry VI* figures revolt as merely another form of consumption. Indeed, these unrestrained appetites are explicitly associated with the hypocrisy of the rebels, and the inadequacy of their supposedly egalitarian plans. In Act IV, Scene III, Cade praises the Butcher for the skill with which he slaughters his enemies, declaring:

> They fell before thee like sheep and oxen, and thou behaved'st thyself as if thou hadst been in thine own slaughter-house. Therefore thus will I reward

> thee – the Lent shall be as long again as it is; thou shalt have licence to kill for a hundred lacking one. (IV.iii.3–7)

The exchange has multiple functions. Firstly, as Ronda Arab has noted, the animal imagery serves to imply the potentially ferocious nature of the lower classes, who bereft of upper-class leadership 'could reduce high men to animals, to the beasts upon which their lowly trades operated' (Arab, 2005, p. 11). Yet the very nature of the Butcher's reward also emphasises the contradictory nature of Cade's egalitarian claims. He promises the Butcher that he will not only retain the strict rules regarding the sale of meat in Lent, but will extend them, ensuring that his follower will receive a monopoly as a reward for his service. The communal fantasies with which he motivates the commons of Kent are displaced by a vigorous attraction to the rule of profit.

This element of gratuitous consumption coincides with an apparent tendency to emphasise not simply the excessive nature of the rebels' consumption, but also the base nature of their aims. When it is declared that the laws of England will issue only from the mouth of Cade himself, his followers note that 'it will be a stinking law, for his breath stinks with eating toasted cheese' (IV.vii.9–10). As Joan Thirsk has suggested, in the early 1600s, cheese would increasingly become a food consumed by the rich, but at this point it was firmly associated with the poor. Even in 1607, De Mediolano could declare 'The poorer sort when other meat is scant, / For hunger eate it to releeve their want' (De Mediolano, 1607, sig. $B2^{v}$). The stench of Cade's breath is an index of a lower-class voraciousness, which remains intact despite his ascent to power. Likewise, in *The Life and Death of Jack Straw*, the appetites of the rebels are most obviously embodied in Scene V, when the clown figure Miller steals a goose to feed the camp. He declares:

> And in faith as long as this Goose lasts wele not starve:
> And as many good fellows as will come to the eating of
> Her, come and welcome.
> For in faith I cam lightly by her,
> And lightly come lightly gone,
> We Captaines are Lords within our selves,
> And if the world hold out we shalbe Kings shortly[.] (v.395–400)

Maya Mathur notes that 'his speech emphasises the disproportion between the food he has stolen – one goose – and the number of people it is meant to feed' (Mathur, 2007, p. 38). Miller's speech constitutes a farcical counterpart to the biblical story of the loaves and the fishes, a ludicrous attempt to make a fixed amount of food suffice for an entire army. The goose, a conventional symbol of foolishness, functions metonymically for the hapless Miller. Indeed, even as he speaks, another rebel enters the stage, steals the goose and leaves Miller holding only the head. The rebels' earlier pretensions to ideals of justice and equality are reduced to the spectacle of thieves squabbling over scraps.

The appeal of these fantasies of communal consumption is undermined by the failure which invariably accompanies such lower-class revolts on the stage. The key example is once again *2 Henry VI*. By the end of the fourth act, the defeated Cade is starving. Chris Fitter observes that 'Nothing in the chronicles had suggested a Cade famished at his death: the condition is pure Shakespearean invention' (Fitter, 2012, p. 76). The play consciously foregrounds his final hunger, to the extent that Cade, with his dying words, declares that he is vanquished 'by famine, not by valour' (IV.ix.74).[20] The trajectory of the play entails a movement from hunger to appetite, and back to hunger again. This representation of the rebel can be usefully explored in the context of medieval notions of vice. Catherine Belsey argues that 'the role of the Vice . . . is to entice the human hero to damnation' (Belsey, 1985, p. 36) and its attractive and exciting nature is precisely the point. Paula Neuss suggests that in plays such as *Mankind* the audience was positively encouraged to identify with the vices, so that in the end they could be forced to recognise the seductive quality of vice and their complicity in the threatened damnation (Neuss, 1973, p. 65). Belsey, and earlier Bernard Spivack, have shown the indebtedness of characters such as Richard III to the traditional vice figure of medieval moralities, yet these characteristics seem far more pronounced in rebels such as Jack Straw and Cade. In *The Life and Death of Jack Straw* and *2 Henry VI* it is by allowing the audience to identify with the rebels' slogans and seditious promises, only to show where such actions would eventually lead, that the plays demonstrate that rebellion is an illegitimate response to hardship.

Yet the plays' depictions of reckless excess attest not simply to the flawed nature of these rebellions, but also to their power. The emphasis on the connections between the hunger which prompts rebellion and the appetite

[20] Critical attention to the play has frequently focussed on the scene. For Fitter, the passage speaks to the experience of deserting soldiers in the period. But despite Cade's original identity as a soldier in the Irish wars, the degree to which he has become identified with rebellion implies that his final famished position embodies a more general emphasis upon the connections between hunger and revolt.

which it generates ensures that these revolts are associated with the commons themselves. Attention to the intersection of appetite and excess in the theatre's representation of the process of revolt exposes the potential power of these uprisings, unrestrained by the moderating influence of local elites. In *2 Henry VI*, the aristocrat York ostensibly appears to use the rebel Jack Cade as a provocateur, seeking to destabilise the realm for his own factional ends. He claims to have 'seduced a headstrong Kentishman ... To make commotion as full well he can, / Under the title of John Mortimer' (III.i.356–9). Many critics have accepted York's belief in his ability to control Cade. Phyllis Rackin, for example, has argued that 'Cade does not finally or fully speak for himself. As York's pawn and alter ego, he follows a scenario of York's devising' (Rackin, 1990, p. 219). Yet while York plans to 'reap the harvest which that coistrel sowed' (III.i.381), there is a telling ambiguity in the line 'This devil here shall be my substitute' (III.i.371). Substitute had long signified 'person endowed with the authority to act on behalf of a superior in his or her absence' (*OED*, 'substitute', def. 1a), but by the end of the sixteenth century, it could also mean 'An object, practice, action, etc., which takes the place of another' (*OED*, 'substitute', def. 3). It is the latter meaning which seems most accurately to define Cade's actions within the play.[21] Cade, describing his fabricated royal lineage, is told 'the Duke of York hath taught you this' (IV.iii.146); his response in an aside is simply, 'He lies, for I invented it myself' (IV.iii.147). The laughter the line seems designed to elicit endorses Cade's position as a clowning figure capable of acting in his own right. Far from following York's script, there seems little evidence that Cade is not very serious in his attempts to form his own commonwealth. The possibility that he might succeed is central to the politics of the play. The emphasis upon consumption extends further than its effect upon the lower-class members of the audience, for it also implies a political stance towards the elite, emerging not simply as a plea that the poor refrain from rebellion, but also as a warning to those amongst the rich who might engage in either oppressive acts or political machination. The destructive forces which rebellion embodies function as a critique of its effects, but also of its perceived causes. The onstage violence operates in a manner not dissimilar from that which critics have discerned in the monarcho-populist uprising more generally. It serves to hold the elite to account, demonstrating the perspicacity of abiding by the traditional relief of the poor and

[21] Indeed, this scepticism pervades the play as a whole. In the opening act, Suffolk declares that he was charged 'To marry Princess Margaret for your grace' (I.i.4). The erotic relationship between Margaret and Suffolk makes evident the play's thorough anxiety regarding the theme of substitutes and factors.

loyalty to the monarch. The element of excess is significant for its effect on any putative rebels in the audience, but also, in varying ways, on every level of society.

The application of onstage revolts as cautionary tales for both upper- and lower-class members of the audience is accentuated by socio-geographic factors. The history plays of the 1590s tend to portray uprisings which originate outside the city.[22] It is therefore possible to characterise these insurrections, as several critics have noted, as an attack not upon the ruling classes, but upon London itself. Alexander Leggatt has noted that towards the end of the fourth act of *2 Henry VI* 'The energy becomes threatening, and the first London audiences must have felt the threat more sharply as it crept towards familiar places' (Leggatt, 1988, p. 17).[23] In *The Life and Death of Jack Straw*, the pillaging of the city by rural rebels is explicitly portrayed through the depiction of appetite. The aristocrat Spencer declares that the rebel army comprises 'sufficient mouthes inough / At highest tide to have drawen the Thames drie' (v.469–70). The metonymic reduction of the rebel army to a collection of mouths reflects the wider notion of the many-headed monster.[24] But the voracious consumption is specifically identified with one of London's defining geographical features. The appetites of the rebels risk consuming the city itself. Here, the juxtaposition of the full bellies of the theatre audiences with the gaping mouths of rural migrants is of absolute significance. This was a period in which migration from the countryside to London was at unprecedented levels.[25] Food riots and uprisings prompted by dearth and enclosure were almost without exception a rural phenomenon, as hunger rarely constituted

[22] This is the case not only with the depiction of lower-class revolts, but also in plays which involve more avowedly feudal forms of rebellion, such as *1 Edward IV*.

[23] Likewise, Rackin argues that Shakespeare's London audience were unlikely to sympathise with Cade's plans as he 'threatens to destroy their city's famous monuments' (Rackin, 1990, p. 214). The same strategy can be seen at work in Act I of *1 Edward IV*. Falconbridge delivers a long speech in which he details the many prizes London has to offer. As Dillon has argued, the speech shows Falconbridge to be 'simultaneously familiar with the significance of various parts of London and insolently determined to wrest that significance into new forms' (Dillon, 2000, p. 49). The result is that 'civic pride and patriotism are called into place to intensify hostility to the rebels' (Dillon, 2000, p. 49).

[24] The image was one which, as Peter Linebaugh and Marcus Rediker have argued, 'expressed the fear and justified the violence of the ruling classes' with regard to a wide range of rebellious subjects in the period from the Renaissance to the Industrial Revolution (Linebaugh and Rediker, 2000, p. 6). It draws on the Greek myth of the Hydra and consequently implies not only the complex mixture of individualism and collective action which defines the mob, but also its resilience, for in classical mythology the Hydra was a beast from which, for every head destroyed, 'two new ones grew in its place' (Linebaugh and Rediker, 2000, p. 6).

[25] A. L. Beier notes that 'The overall metropolitan population was about 12,000 in 1550, and rose to 200,000 in 1600, and no less than 375,000 in 1650' (Beier, 1985, p. 40).

the primary motivation for disorder in London.[26] Along with the rate of migration, this may well have prompted a certain distrust of and detachment from the onstage rebels, and while this may not have effaced the element of class-based identification, it may have come into conflict with it. The spectacle of a rural populace destroying the urban centre also has the potential to accentuate the monarcho-populist dimension to these plays. At a time when the elite were increasingly condemned for abandoning their rural estates in favour of city life, the play raises the spectre of the possible consequences of the absentee landlords' disregard for the rural poor. For every section of the audience, the fact that these plays portray assaults upon the city heightens their political and dramatic impact.

It is therefore significant that the later *Coriolanus* depicts a revolt which is urban in origin. Indeed, the word 'city' occurs thirty-six times in the text, which, as Jan Blits has noted, is more than in any other Shakespearean play (Blits, 1981, p. 44). The play represents the process of revolt as one which transforms hunger into appetite. Menenius comments that the wolf loves the lamb, because it desires to 'devour him, as the hungry plebeians would the noble Marcius' (II.i.9–10). The tribunes are described as 'The tongues o' th' common mouth' (III.i.22). Coriolanus is entreated to be 'humble as the ripest mulberry / That will not hold the handling' (III.ii.80–1), with the image implying not only Coriolanus's delicacy, but also the extent to which, reduced to the status of a foodstuff, he risks being swallowed up by the plebeians. But there are significant differences between the transition from hunger to appetite in this urban setting, and that in the earlier rural revolts. Firstly, the appetite of the plebeians is predominantly metaphorical, expressing a desire and capacity for political power, rather than literal consumption. The initial uprising prompts the distribution of corn, rather than the carnivalesque excesses of *2 Henry VI*. Secondly, their appetite is presented not as a threat to the city, but as Rome's inherent characteristic. In Act III, Scene I, for example, it is not the plebeians alone but Rome as a whole which is figured as consuming Coriolanus, for it becomes a city which may 'like an unnatural dam . . . now eat up her own'

[26] Although the city was disrupted by numerous riots and attempted uprisings, they were predominantly associated with attacks upon the administration of justice, fights between apprentices and the gentry and, in later years, moralistic attacks upon theatres and brothels. Manning argues that there was a shift in the nature of rioting in London during the early modern period. Elizabethan rioting was predominantly located in the city of London, and frequently targeted the city authorities. In the Jacobean period, by contrast, rioting increasingly occurred in the suburbs, and acquired a more festive character, with fifteen riots occurring on Shrove Tuesday, targeting local theatres and brothels (Manning, 1988, p. 211). Manning identifies only two food riots in London in this period, both of which occurred during the wider disturbances of 1595 (Manning, 1988, p. 204).

(III.i.294–5). As the citizens declare, 'the people are the city' (III.i.200). Although *Coriolanus* retains the element of power which defines the translation of hunger into appetite, the play mitigates the destructive element of that transition. The plebeians aim to devour not Rome, but Coriolanus.

The deployment of appetite as a dramatic expression of nascent revolutionary processes at work in the peasant revolt can therefore be said to be multifaceted. For the lower-class members of the audience, it functions in a similar manner to the medieval morality play. Rather than deny the legitimacy of the grievances which the onstage rebels express, the theatre asserts the destructive nature of the probable consequences. The identification with their initial plight which the audience experiences is precisely the point, ensuring a sense of implication in the eventual excesses which threaten not simply the social order, but also the city of London. Yet no less significant is the effect of these rebellious cravings on the elite of the audience. For these plays imply that the danger of allowing their own consumption to go unrestrained is that it may prompt and enable the destructive appetites of rebellion. As such, the representation of rebellion might be said to embody a stance akin to that of mid-sixteenth-century reformers such as Robert Crowley, who had argued in his 1550 text *The Way to Wealth* that 'men that would leave nothing for others, . . . Cormerauntes, greedy gulles, yea men that would eat up menne women and children are the causes of Sedition' (Crowley, 1852, p. 132). This depiction of excess embodies, and condemns, that element of revolutionary potential which Bloch identifies as characteristic of the politics of hunger. To focus solely on the element of condemnation is to ignore the extent to which the excesses of rebellion chastise also the increasingly capitalist impulses of the contemporary ruling classes.

## Utopia

The representation of rebellion on the Renaissance stage can therefore be said to be defined by a general tendency to move from hunger to excess in a manner which castigates the causes of revolt, while simultaneously rejecting the act of rebellion. Yet appetite, like hunger, remains a fundamentally contested subject in the context of popular protest. Andy Wood has demonstrated the extent to which popular memory of revolt centred on the consumption of food, with Kett's Rebellion described as a 'camping time', when the poor were 'eating of mutton' and 'roste meat' (Norfolk Record Office, Quarter Session Files, 1549–1554, fols. $9^{v}$–$10^{r}$;

Wood, 2007, p. 213). As writers such as Pierro Camporesi and Robert Appelbaum stress, images of fantastic plenty are notable in this period for their capacity to function as the basis of plebeian aspiration. They form an integral part of what Roy Porter describes as 'the central importance of hunger as a moving force in history', which must be understood not simply in terms of deprivation but as 'the stimulus to fantasy, to rebellion, to utopias – the idea of a land of Cockayne, where none will any longer be hungry' (Porter, 1980, pp. 10–11). If, as Camporesi asserts, 'the flight of the ragged and starving masses of the modern era into artificial paradises, worlds turned upside down and impossible dreams of compensation originates from the unbearability of the real world' (Camporesi, 1980, p. 17), it is nevertheless the case that the theatre, by dramatising rebel dreams of plenty, stages the possibility that these dreams may, in fact, be attainable within contemporary society. At this point, these texts acquire a markedly utopian dimension.

Utopian writing has often been understood in generic terms, but recent criticism has increasingly emphasised the broader significance of imagining the ideal society.[27] Robert Appelbaum argues for a discourse of 'ideal politics', existing 'in any number of forms' and which 'generates the image of an ideal society – a society that exists predominantly in the imagination and usually in the shape of an optimal alternative to a real society in the here and now' (Appelbaum, 2004, p. 1). It is this carnivalesque, utopian dimension which potentially inheres in the dramatic representation of rebellious consumption. If appetite is the unavoidable characteristic of revolt in the period, the implicitly temporal nature of these excesses is far less determined. The very process of dramatising revolt raises the possibility that the audience may respond to depictions of rebellious, unrestrained consumption not with castigation or fear, but with approval and good humour.

The primary terrain for this utopian impulse is religion. This is perhaps unsurprising, since as Robert Appelbaum has noted, 'in an age when revealed religion was still the primary framework of social thought, many of the most radical political fantasies were derived from the Bible' (Appelbaum, 2004, p. 5). One of the most evocative instances of this tendency occurs in the opening act of *The Life and Death of Jack Straw*,

[27] Religion provides one source of these utopian imaginings, but so too does carnival, which as Christopher Kendrick has noted, is both an influence upon literary representations of utopia and, 'a species of utopian representation in its own right, . . . the vehicle, the material source and referent, of the literary genre of *Cokaygne*' (Kendrick, 2004, p. 76).

when contemporary oppression is juxtaposed with a prelapsarian past of communal plenty. The rebellious Parson, John Ball, tells the crowd:

> England is growne to such a passe of late
> That rich men triumph to see the poore beg at their gate
> But I am able by good scripture to prove,
> That God doth not this dealing allow nor love.
> But when Adam delved, and Eve span,
> Who was then a Gentleman. (i.58–63)

The text shifts between the injustice of a contemporary present, an idyllic past and a communal future. The opening reference to the poor begging at the gate evokes the biblical story of the beggar Lazarus, who arrives at the gate of a rich man, 'desired to be refreshed with the crumbs that fell from the rich man's table' (Luke 16.21). It recalls, also, the stock image of hospitality literature, in which the poor man arrives at a great house, only to be refused entrance or to discover that the house has been boarded up because the master has moved to London.[28] In the biblical story, heavenly rewards legitimise earthly inequality, with the rich man told 'thou in thy lifetime receivedst thy pleasures, and likewise Lazarus pains; now therefore is he comforted, and thou art tormented' (Luke 16:25). But in the marginal notes to the Geneva Bible, more radical aspects of the passage are emphasised, with the text noting 'what punishment they shall have, which live deliciously and neglect the poor' and arguing that Abraham's use of 'son' to address the tortured rich man 'taunteth his vain boasting, who in his life vaunted himself to be the son of Abraham; warning us also hereby how little glorious titles avail' (Luke 16:19, n.*; Luke 16:25, n.*). Similar preoccupations appear in the play, for these images of biblical and contemporary inequality are juxtaposed with a vision of Edenic equality. This argument was not inherently radical. The system of degree was widely acknowledged to be a product of the Fall, springing from man's essentially sinful nature. But by contrast with the biblical story of Lazarus, Ball proposes instigating communality on earth, declaring 'Brethren, brethren, it were better to have this communitie / Then to have this difference in degrees' (i.64–5). Hunger emerges as a symbol of the Fall, but a fall which, in conjunction with the socially constructed nature of hunger, begins to emerge as soluble in the contemporary present.

This utopian impulse is far from confined to lower-class rebels in the period. As Appelbaum comments, 'the wishful image of the utopian food

[28] See Chapter 3.

of wishes expressed the aspirations of whole classes of people in the premodern world' (Appelbaum, 2006, p. 122). Utopia was a contested concept, a 'phenomenon over which a surprising number of people thought it important to contest proprietorship' (Appelbaum, 2004, p. 2). Revolt, therefore, might be interpreted as, in the final instance, a contest between competing utopian impulses. A key example occurs in the final scene of Act IV in *2 Henry VI*, when the starving Cade breaks into the private garden of Iden. Throughout the act, Cade's revolt has been rooted in imagery of the Land of Cockayne, a popular fantasy of a land in which vast quantities of food are readily available. In the garden scene, Cade's utopian fantasies are placed in opposition to a ruling-class utopia. Iden's name implicitly associates the space with Eden. The garden contrasts with the 'turmoiled' life of the court, a place of seclusion which is 'worth a monarchy' (IV.x.16; IV.x.19). It is ostensibly a space of charity, from which Iden 'sends the poor well pleased' (IV.x.23). Yet it is also implicitly associated with enclosure. In the Quarto version of the text, Iden claims that Cade 'hast broke my hedges / And enterd into my ground without the leave of me the owner' (Shakespeare, 1594, sig. G4$^{5}$). If the scene of Cade's death ostensibly chastises revolt, associating it with a base hunger, it simultaneously marks the re-emergence of the issue of injustice. Revolt is once again situated in relation to the opposition of hunger and appetite, in a manner which has the potential both to legitimise Cade and delegitimise the earthly paradise which Iden has created.

Of course, the radical potential of the utopian dimension to revolt is almost invariably compromised by its very impracticality. The word utopia signifies, etymologically, 'no place', and that element of impossibility colours most rebellious dreams in the theatre of the period. One significant exception, however, is *Coriolanus*. In this play, the rebels are notable for their apparent success in establishing a commonwealth in which labour is rewarded. The tribunes declare that the friends of the exiled nobleman Coriolanus 'Blush that the world goes well' and present an image of 'tradesmen singing in their shops, and going / About their functions friendly' (IV.vi.5; IV.vi.8–9). Here, the destructive element of excess and rebellion is arguably present, but has been translated from the commons to the aristocracy. When Coriolanus returns to Rome at the head of an army dispatched by a rival city state, he rejects the pleas of his former friends in terms which embody that element of wanton destruction which is elsewhere characteristic of rebellion. He is reported as declaring that:

> He could not stay to pick them in a pile
> Of noisome musty chaff: he said 'twas folly,
> For one poor grain or two, to leave unburnt
> And still to nose the offence. (V.i.25–8)

The threat to the commonwealth comes not from the excesses of the plebeians, whose initial rebellious acts have been to some degree successful. Instead, the text repeatedly transforms the seditious properties of hunger from the initially starving commons onto the socially excluded Coriolanus. It is he who figuratively becomes a vagabond 'pent to linger / But with a grain a day' (III.iii.88–9) and his metaphorical hunger prompts him to engage in destructive acts far more usually associated with a rebellious rural peasantry.

The representation of revolt is inseparable from the depiction of a utopian impulse, which even in the absence of the relative success depicted in *Coriolanus*, remains inherent in onstage revolt at the level of possibility. This utopian potential was accentuated by the conditions of performance in the early modern theatre, partly as a consequence of the theatre's reliance on the sale of tickets to the public. For as Thomas Cartelli has noted:

> Even when Marlowe and Shakespeare attempted to encourage their audiences to resist the theatrical appeal of such morally unsavoury characters as Faustus and Richard of Gloucester, they can hardly have hoped to erase entirely the psychological residue of the audience's probable engagement with them. (Cartelli, 1991, p. 16)

In such a situation, the playwright 'cannot finally command the outcome of the competition he has evoked' (Cartelli, 1991, p. 28). The emergence of this nascent class-based identification is particularly evident in the theatre's repeated deployment of humour in the representation of rebellion. This comic dimension has frequently been assumed to compromise the radicalism of the onstage rebel. Phyllis Rackin, for example, argues that in the first tetralogy, lower-class characters 'can rebel against oppression, but can never finally transcend the conventions of comic representation that keep them in their social place and mark their separation from the serious world of their betters' (Rackin, 1990, p. 221). Yet this interpretation appears to underestimate the complex significance of laughter in the early modern theatre.

A case in point is provided by the death of Cade in *2 Henry VI*, for the chastening dimension to Cade's famished demise is surely compromised by his repeated clowning on the subject of his own hunger. Climbing over a wall into an enclosed garden, he is reduced to such a degree of starvation that he is forced to eat grass. The scene ostensibly depicts a punishment of biblical proportions, echoing as it does the fate of the Babylonian monarch Nebuchadnezzar, who as punishment for his pride 'was driven from men, and did eat grass as oxen' (Daniel 4:33). Nevertheless, the power of this dehumanising image is compromised by the repeated comic transformations through which he describes the grass he eats. He declares that he has:

> Climbed into this garden to see if I can eat grass or pick a sallet another while, which is not amiss to cool a man's stomach this hot weather. And I think this word sallet was born to do me good; for many a time, but for a sallet, my brain pan had been cleft with a brown bill; and many time, when I have been dry and bravely marching, it hath served me instead of a quart pot to drink in; and now the word 'sallet' must serve me to feed on. (IV. ix.6–13)

Cade mimics conventional medical theories regarding the properties of foods deemed to be 'cold', implicitly asserting an elite status for himself, refiguring his present predicament as a choice and retaining the self-fashioning ability which he has displayed throughout. Sallet, meanwhile, which could mean either a literal salad, or a helmet, manifests a punning resilience which, as Chris Fitter has noted, simultaneously reminds the audience of his military past and implicitly links him with the scores of discharged soldiers who roamed London's streets in the period (Fitter, 2012, p. 76). Most significantly, Cade's claim that he may feed simply on the 'word' sallet, implies a strength of will which is in other plays almost universally the property of the elite. Cade's final, famished humour serves multiple purposes. It establishes him as the subject, rather than the object of humour, encouraging the audience to laugh with him, in the face of his upper-class enemies. It asserts his own defiance, implying a self-fashioning ability to claim an aristocratic identity which survives his various defeats unscathed. As such, his humour works to undermine any sense in which his final, hungry end might be said to castigate his earlier rebellion. It opens a space for the audience to endorse, even in the space of defeat, his rebellious attempt to satisfy the appetites of his peasant followers.

Furthermore, like carnival, the humorous levelling which characterises the representation of onstage rebels such as Cade and Straw has the potential to acquire a far more serious dimension. Forse suggests that, for the authorities, 'daily gatherings at theatres of groups of people whose numbers approached one percent of the total population must have seemed overwhelmingly frightening' (Forse, 1993, p. 18). Likewise, Manning has indicated that these large crowds were inclined to riot, even without the added incentive of inflammatory material onstage.[29] Within this context, the onstage transition from hunger to appetite acquires seditious potential. *The Life and Death of Jack Straw* is widely considered a reactionary text, even though the rebels dominate the stage and deliver many of the most sophisticated speeches. Walter Cohen, for instance, argues that the play is so obviously reductive that this material could be delivered 'in the serene confidence that it will be contemptuously dismissed' (Cohen, 1985, p. 228). Yet this approach may underestimate the radical implications of placing these oppositional statements on the public stage. From John Ball's rhetorical question 'when *Adam* delved and *Eve* span, / Who was then a Gentleman' (p. 4), to the assertion of Cade's followers that 'it was never merry world in England since gentlemen came up' (IV.ii.6–7), the theatre's depiction of rebellion is repeatedly defined by the vocalisation of proverbs and sentiments which had played a prominent role in the practice of historical revolts and in their wider memorialisation (cf. Wood, 2007, p. 182).[30] In doing so, the theatre channels the grievances of its audiences, forcing an identification with the hunger of the onstage rebels which threatens to overcome the boundaries of the morality formula, into a fully fledged endorsement of the radical appetites which rebellion unleashes. Furthermore, the reaction of an audience depends not only on class and status, but also on specific contemporary circumstances. This is most evident in *2 Henry VI*, first performed in approximately 1590, before the major uprisings of 1595, 1596 and 1607. Although rioting was not uncommon, there had been no real insurrection by the commons since Kett's Rebellion of 1549. Perhaps most significantly, during the 1595 riots, hunger once again became a significant motivating force driving Londoners towards disorder, with the first food riots since the 1520s. The staging of an uprising, complete with the vocalisation of rebel speech, would therefore have been far less subversive during the original performance than in the revivals of the subsequent twenty years, when revolt was a very real

[29] On 11 June 1591, for example, a large group of felt makers assembled on the pretext of attending the theatre, and attempted to break into the Marshalsea prison in order to rescue a fellow guild member. When the Privy Council discovered that further disturbances were planned, they took the precaution of closing the theatres, in order to prevent the gathering together of large crowds (Manning, 1988, p. 207). In the Jacobean period, Shrove Tuesday riots directed at theatres and bawdy houses became the norm, with the theatres functioning as both the pretext and object of assembling riotous crowds of apprentices.

[30] As Alessandra Petrina and Laura Tosi have noted, 'to speak of a "merry world in England" is to invoke explicitly a popular cultural image of the nation, one mocked by Protestant writings as a Catholic yearning for the past' (Petrina and Tosi, 2011, p. 215; cf. *OED*, 'merry', def. P1e; Tilley, 1950, p. 3).

possibility.[31] In the context of famine and disorder, rebellions of the belly may have started to seem more attractive than unbending loyalty to the state.

Attention to the representation of hunger and appetite in the context of revolt therefore reinforces the need to engage with the contingency of political meaning within the context of dramatic performance, while at the same time acknowledging the absolute significance of underlying structures of class and the productive forces. Perhaps more than is the case with any other literary form, a dramatic script is dependent for the creation of political meaning on a specific conjunction of material and ideological factors. Plays such as *The Life and Death of Jack Straw* and *2 Henry VI* engage with a popular tradition of protest which was itself contested. They appeal to an audience which was markedly heterogeneous in terms of class and profession, and which may well have contained many spectators who would participate in the riots and disorder which shook London during the turbulent 1590s. They operate within a tradition of the theatre which, for all that playwrights might deny it, encourages the generation of political meaning through networks of allusion and the creation of explicit parallels with contemporary figures and events. The theatre creates a space in which the slogans and ideas of a popular tradition of protest and rebellion can be staged. It dramatises the transition from hunger to rebellion, the intimate relationship between 'The No to the bad situation which exists, the Yes to the better life' (Bloch, 1995, p. 75). Yet particularly significant is the extent to which in doing so, it draws upon a much wider logic of the relationship between want and excess. It feeds upon a generalised politics of hunger and appetite which exists in the period, but proffers a solution to this basic contradiction which extends beyond the moralising of most contemporary observers.

## Conclusion

The depiction of revolt on the early modern stage is rooted in the representation of hunger and appetite. In the first instance, hunger announces the desperation of the rebels, and their exclusion from the failing structures of contemporary society. It embodies the neglect of traditional institutions, such as hospitality and the paternalistic structures of an idealised feudal

31 It might be argued that these changing circumstances prompted the alterations that were made to the later version of *2 Henry VI*. As William Carroll has argued, the removal of the reference to broken hedges in the folio text 'ensures that Iden will be seen not as a potential encloser' (Carroll, 1996, p. 138). The presence of these alterations raises the possibility that the play may have become rather more controversial than originally intended.

England. It implies, moreover, a form of revolt which is qualitatively different from the rebellious acts of upper-class discontent on and off the period's stage. Yet hunger alone is rarely presented as the origin of revolt. The depiction of the grievances which spur these lower-class rebels invariably depends upon explicit reference to the appetites of the rich. Nevertheless, the depiction of those appetites is always contested. On the one hand, they embody the destructive forces of a nascent capitalism; on the other, they retain a potential to stand for the generalised excesses of the rich. As a consequence, the plays' depiction of revolt is governed by a crucial element of indeterminacy. At times, the rebel cause emerges in terms of a radical opposition of want to plenty which requires systematic social change for its solution. More often, this radical dimension is subsumed within a conservative politics which condemns both the rebels and the actions of those sections of early modern society which provoke them.

No less significant, however, is the extent to which the depiction of appetite manifests wider anxieties regarding the nature of revolt. The spectacle of consumption operates in a manner which overtly distances it from the comparatively restrained approach of elite rebels such as *Richard II*'s Henry Bolingbroke. The voracious mouths of the many-headed monster deploy the spectre of plebeian unruliness to discipline those members of the ruling classes who might, after the fashion of Essex, attempt to draw on lower-class discontent to seize power for themselves. Yet the use of this fear is itself an acknowledgement of the power of the lower classes. In the wake of uprisings such as Kett's Rebellion of 1549, this power was widely recognised, and fear of the lower classes was to become an ever more significant factor in national politics in the years preceding the English revolution. As Christopher Hill has argued 'Both Charles I and the Parliamentary leaders expected this social anxiety to bring the other side to accept their terms in the Civil War' (Hill, 2002, p. 27). The fear of what might be unleashed by conflict at the top of society became a significant weapon in the factional struggles which precipitated the Civil War. The flowering of radical activity which occurred during the war shows the legitimacy of these claims.

Perhaps more strikingly, these texts also reveal the power of this nascent proletarian vision. The acts of ventriloquism within these texts give voice to grievances and aspirations which enable a specifically proletarian political perspective to emerge on stage. Depictions of appetite also function as a significant means of channelling class outrage and legitimising revolt. The theatre emerges as a forum for debate on one of the most pressing, and radical, political issues of the period. The representation of revolt allows the wider political issues inherent in the representation of hunger and appetite to emerge in crystallised form, explicitly linking theatre's wider association between appetite and an emergent capitalism with a revolutionary violence which seeks to resolve the fundamental opposition between want and excess, hunger and appetite, within early modern English society. Margot Heinemann articulates the traditional Marxist argument that the 'apprentices and law students who stood in the yard of the Globe to watch *A Game of Chess* would still have been youngish men when the barricades went up to bar the City to the troops of Charles I' (Heinemann, 1980, p. 3). This perhaps implies an excessive degree of causality, but it is nevertheless the case that a comparable configuration of drives would form the basis for many of the radical projects which emerged during the English revolution. At its heart, the representation of hunger and appetite could emerge as that most fundamental opposition of contradictory elements which constitutes the basis of revolutionary change. This is not a characteristic limited to the dramatic representation of literal revolts. Rather, these onstage uprisings constitute the most explicit expression of tensions which recur throughout the period's theatre of hunger and appetite. It is through these drives that contemporary playing companies and theatre audiences sought to understand the changing nature of their society. It is also through the representation of these drives that this understanding could, potentially, emerge in its most radical and oppositional manner. Hunger and appetite are manifested as a combination of despair and utopia, want and excess, which retain its power to mobilise and inspire.

# *Conclusion*

This book has asserted the centrality of hunger and appetite for an understanding of the politics of the Renaissance stage. Their representation is bound up with the depiction of the 'pathological symptoms' of the period's underlying socio-economic changes, focussing critical attention on the relationship between cultural texts and the material base of society (Wrightson, 1982, p. 157). The depiction of these drives also provided the theatres with a means of conceptualising those changes and of interrogating the forces which motivated them, in a manner which frequently allowed an unprecedented recognition of agency on the part of specific classes, genders, nations or individuals. Attention to the representation of hunger and appetite provides a framework to understand not simply contemporary political discussion in general, but also the specific conditions in which political meaning could be generated in the theatre as an institution, and thereby to acknowledge its role as the purveyor of foods and fantasies to a range of heterogeneous audiences. Perhaps most significantly, analysis of hunger and appetite provides a way of exploring the role of want and need within social and ideological structures, in a manner which acquires a particular significance in the context of a modern world which remains riven by scarcity and inequality.

One of the fundamental issues with which the theatre grapples is the question of what imbues specific subjects with appetite, and how best to restrain their desires. This emerges as a question of political importance precisely because appetite in the early modern theatre is almost always figured as a threat to the status quo. It embodies an urge to act upon society. It is a drive which is expansive, and which requires change for its often continuously forestalled satisfaction. On the one hand, the theatre is defined by a tendency to essentialise appetite. It appears as a trait which drives subjects to consume, in a manner which has little to do with the contents of their bellies. The precise nature of the subject with which appetite is associated varies dramatically. Different playing companies, writers and plays situate the forces threatening the status quo of early modern England as characteristics of a wide variety of different subjects within contemporary society. At times, the essentialising model of appetite functions as part of a process of mystification, figuring the domestic servant, or even the poor in general, as defined by an uncontrollable appetite which must be kept in check by the restraints imposed upon them by the state or the elite. Yet the rich too can be associated with an essentialising model of appetite. In popular political discourse, whether in the form of ballads or on the stage in the complaints of lower-class rebels, to be rich is often of necessity to be governed by a reckless, anti-social appetite which threatens society as a whole and which, once again, can only be held in check by the threat or exaction of violence. The specific subjects with which appetite is associated imply differing political strategies. But the uniting tendency is to read this drive as, in and of itself, a threat to the hierarchical structures of early modern society.

At the same time, the theatre can rarely detach itself from the notion that appetite is a universal characteristic of human subjects. The parallels between appetite and sexual desire, for instance, are reliant in great part on the inevitability of both forms of craving. In a similar manner, the theatre treats those characters who consciously encourage their own hunger, and consequently resist appetite, with a great degree of suspicion. Appetite is both base and universal. It provides a powerful means of considering not only the fallen or irredeemable nature of man in a religious sense, but also the fragility of specific identities. The appetites of domestic servants appear to distance them from the elevated concerns of their masters, but the theatres frequently dismantle this distinction, asserting instead a fundamental element of similitude. The very fact that appetite is imbued with such power to differentiate subjects simultaneously ensures that it retains the potential to comment upon the fragility of the lines which divide them. As a consequence, appetite can also be represented as a product of circumstance. In *The Sea Voyage* (1622), the cannibalistic appetites of the sailors may be indicative of their wider investment in a capitalised form of colonial expansion. But they also spring from the immediate circumstance of starvation, following the crew's shipwreck on a barren island. Likewise, contemporary ideas about appetite ensure that the feasting of Timon's guests could be interpreted as either an inherent propensity to consume, or as a product of the lavish manner in which Timon has distributed gifts. Appetite is caught between the totalising and the contingent: between appetite as characteristic and appetite as product of specific material circumstances. It is these twin aspects of appetite which lend it efficacy as a means to consider change within the totality.

It is only by acknowledging these associations that the representation of hunger in the early modern theatres can be understood. Within certain bounds, hunger is portrayed as not simply inevitable, but rather as desirable to ensure stability in society. When visible as a temporary need that is detached from appetite, it retains a certain power as a mechanism for the maintenance of social order. The power of traditions of charity and hospitality, for instance, is reliant upon the existence of hunger. Even in the case of famine, it is not hunger alone, but the implicit transformation of hunger into appetite characteristic of the process of revolt which constitutes a threat to the status quo. Episodes such as the distribution of food gifts by Pericles, or the use of hunger to ensure loyalty amongst servants, make evident the emphasis which early modern society placed upon hunger as a way to maintain control. Hunger without appetite is rarely revolutionary. Yet the theatre is also significant for the degree to which it probes these connections. In plays such as Massinger's *The Bashful Lover* (1636), Fletcher and Massinger's *The Sea Voyage* or even *2 Henry VI* (1590), hunger emerges as a dangerous means of control which is troubling precisely because it detaches loyalty from a purely ideological social structure, and raises the possibility that undesirable elements such as rebels or malcontents may be able to exert control over the population. Indeed, representations of the appetites of the poor can never wholly eliminate the implied presence of hunger. And this absent cause is particularly powerful in the case of those audience members whose lived experience forces the connections between hunger and appetite to the fore.

The centrality of hunger and appetite in conceptualising processes of social change lends a particular resonance to the representation of women. In the first instance, the portrayal of hunger and appetite provides a means of articulating the ambiguous position of women within early modern society. It enables mediation between the categories of gender and class. At times, hunger is the basis for solidarity between women and the lower class. In *Women Pleased*, the shared deprivation of Isabella and Penurio prompts the awakening of parallel appetites. In *The Bloody Banquet*, the desires of the Young Queen Thetis emerge as a surrogate for the rebellious appetites of the starving populace. Yet hunger and appetite also establish bonds of shared interest between elite men and women, in opposition to the voracious lower classes. In *The Taming of the Shrew*, Katherina is placed in a position of hunger to make her accept her place within the household hierarchy. In *The Sea Voyage*, a young woman is the object of the cannibalistic appetites of upwardly mobile colonists. In *The Bashful Lover*, Maria's resistance to hunger is the mark of her upper-class status, in overt opposition to the rapacious appetites of the lower-class Gothrio. The ambiguous combination of particularity and universality which defines the experience of hunger and appetite lends the depiction of the two drives a pronounced utility for conceptualising the complex position of women within early modern society.

Yet women also played a hugely significant role within the production of food in early modern England. The wide-ranging significance of hunger and appetite consequently has the potential to imbue female characters with a surprising degree of power. In Massinger's *The Picture*, Sophia's control over food enables her to control the actions of first her servant, then two visiting courtiers, and finally her husband. In *The Bloody Banquet*, Thetis deploys her control over food as a strategy of seduction. At the same time, this was a period in which women's productive role was increasingly marginalised. In a material sense, this was undoubtedly a lengthy and complex process. Women in general remained closely connected to the preparation, if not the production of food, and the intrusion of the market into the domestic economy was only partial. Nevertheless, this underlying material process is accentuated within the early modern theatre, where women's productive labour is frequently disregarded. As such, it might be argued that women in the early modern theatre embody a more general shift, whereby women are reconstituted as consumers, rather than producers, of food. At a time when the market could be envisaged as a space dominated by unruly, destabilising appetites, this was a troubling prospect. Indeed, in plays such as *A Woman Killed with Kindness*, these tensions manifest themselves in the spectre of a woman whose commitment to isolation is embodied in the act of self-starvation.

The frequency with which these drives are deployed to interrogate identity is, of course, historically defined. It is a product, in the final instance, of a society in which hunger and appetite were imbued with absolute significance as both the causes and symptoms of major social change. Yet the early modern period is in many ways significant for the extent to which it laid the foundations for a capitalist mode of production which has now become a global phenomenon. The processes which define the representation of hunger and appetite are now visible at a national and international level. Approximately 1 billion people in the world today attempt to survive on less than a dollar a day (Rieff, 2016, p. xiii). In the year preceding the 2008 economic crisis, global prices of corn rose by 31 per cent, rice by 74 per cent, soybeans by 87 per cent and wheat by

130 per cent (cf. Rieff, 2016, p. xii). In the UK, in 2009–10, the Trussell Trust operated food banks in 29 local authorities; by 2013–14, the number had risen to 251 (Loopstra et al., 2015, p. 1). Hunger and appetite remain drives which exert a fundamental influence upon the material base of society. They also retain their significance as the method and matter of political resistance. The twentieth and twenty-first centuries saw hunger strikes in Ireland, America, India, Palestine and Guantanamo, amongst other places. In recent years, rising food prices have been implicated in a wide variety of demonstrations and uprisings, including the Arab revolutions of 2010–11 (Rieff, 2016, p. xii). An understanding of how these now-global dynamics are embodied in the early modern theatre consequently has the potential to provide insights into cultural forms more generally. The work of critics such as David McNally has explored the ways in which supernatural appetites associated with vampires, cannibals and zombies have been deployed from the Renaissance to modern cinema to understand the dynamics of the global capitalist system (McNally, 2012). The potency of hunger as both subject and image of revolt was central to the film theory of Third Worldist practitioners such as the Brazilian film-maker Glauber Rocha, who declared that 'the normal behaviour of the starving is violence' (Rocha, 1995, p. 60). Yet the absolute significance of hunger and appetite as drives which affect both society and its cultural artefacts, remains to be acknowledged by a commensurate degree of scholarly attention.

In particular, scrutiny of the representation of hunger and appetite highlights the role played by need within ideological conflict. Definitions of subjects within the global capitalist system can appear restrained within Adam Smith's definition of man as dominated by the desire to 'truck, barter and exchange', even when they construct this tendency as historically contingent (Smith, 2012, p. 18). An analysis of the role played by hunger in early modern society enables a perspective that privileges need, rather than greed, as the fundamental driving force within society. The ability of a system to satisfy the needs of its subjects emerges as a fundamental requirement for stability. The Renaissance theatre provides a significant example because the power structures of the period were placed under a tremendous amount of strain. In my chapters on service and the food gift, I have explored the effects which polarisation exerted on residual ideologies and practices. The problem, here, emerges not simply from want, but also from excess. Attention to the role played by hunger and need is important not simply for an analysis of the early modern theatre, but also for consideration of more recent ideological structures. Such consideration makes it possible to reject the tendency to understand the central dynamic of the global capitalist system as rooted solely in acquisition and greed, rather than, with regard to the majority of the population, the basic necessity of supporting life.

Moreover, attention to the representation of hunger and appetite also provides a framework for re-evaluating the politics of the early modern theatre. In the first instance, hunger and appetite are striking both for the ubiquity of their use as a tool of political comment, and for the diverse range of political perspectives within which they are implicated. Appetite, for instance, recurs as a way to understand forces of social change. It is associated with a diverse range of causes, and attributed to a wide variety of distinct subjects. The domestic servant embodies an uncontrollable appetite which is explicitly figured as a threat to the status quo. But that appetite is also deployed to critique upper-class hypocrisy and the decline of traditions of service. In other plays, appetite retains many of the same characteristics, but is used to attack the expansive nature of a bourgeoisified elite, or the uncontrolled consumption of a declining aristocracy. The same ambiguity defines the theatre's treatment of moderation. On the one hand, it asserts the need for stability, and attacks the excesses of both an emergent bourgeoisie and the proletarianised lower classes. On the other, it is arguably characteristic of bourgeois ideology, placed in opposition to aristocratic excess. At times, it can also function as an element within lower-class critique, a wish that, as Shakespeare's Gloucester declares, 'distribution should undo excess' (*Lear*, IV.i.73). Want, excess and moderation are defined by their absolute political importance, but also by the absence of specific political content. It is this ambiguity which lends hunger and appetite a certain vitality as the subjects of ideological conflict. They are fundamentally contested concepts, defined by an inherent contradiction which is reminiscent of Valentin Vološinov's discussion of the contested nature of the ideological sign (Vološinov, 1973, p. 23). This is particularly the case in the theatre, where specific instances of these tropes are open to a wide variety of interpretations. The theatre provides a significant example of contemporary political concerns, but attention to the representation of hunger and appetite also makes evident the extent to which the interpretation and interpolation of these concerns were in the final instance decided by struggles which extended beyond the space of the theatre itself. The period considered in this book might, indeed, be considered of particular cultural interest because it is defined by a relatively high level of ideological flux. Hunger and appetite are both prominent and markedly ambiguous in a period in which ideological conflict was waged over the very nature of society. The extent of this conflict can only be understood by acknowledging the dramatic socio-economic changes which were taking place at the time.

Consideration of hunger and appetite also throws light on the relationship of the early modern theatres to praxis. For if literature is political in the sense of engaging with the contradictions of contemporary society and of imagining other systems and solutions, its engagement with specific forms of political activity is frequently far more obscure. Indeed, the relative absence of praxis is one key aspect which differentiates the dramatic form from a political tract. At the same time, the theatre's relationship with forms of practice is frequently implicit, rather than overt. In the revolt plays, for instance, the theatre engages quite extensively with one form of political activity, albeit in an ostensibly critical manner. The representation of the food gift frequently endorses specific forms of hospitable and charitable practice. Yet the representation of hunger and appetite also makes evident the limits inherent in the imagining of new political projects. In the self-starvation of Anne Frankford in *A Woman Killed with Kindness* (1603), the deployment of war as *deus ex machina* in *The Unnatural Combat* (1626) or the tension which surrounds the rewards of service in *The Bashful Lover* (1636), it is possible to discern moments when resolution through a specific form of human activity cannot be imagined. These moments of irresolvable tension might be interpreted as statements of rupture, the product of contradictions in society beyond which literature alone cannot move. In order to understand the politics of the Renaissance stage, it is necessary to acknowledge the extent to which it can both imagine and endorse or critique specific forms of activity, while at the same time recognising that praxis itself generates ideas which might have seemed unthinkable within the confines of creative thought only weeks, months or years before. At these moments of rupture, the ability of the theatre to anticipate political projects is profoundly compromised. The inability of individual plays to conceive of a solution is itself a powerful index of the underlying forces of social change which make the development of new praxis necessary. One might, perhaps, argue that the absence of solutions is itself a powerful invitation to the audience to take both debate and action beyond the space of theatre.

Furthermore, the representation of appetite involves not simply suffering, but also pleasure. Attention to the element of pleasure is significant because this enjoyment is occasionally obscured by critical discussions of the politics of the Renaissance stage. Both eating food and watching a play are implicated in pleasure, even if they cannot be reduced to it. Throughout this book, pleasure has recurred as both an attribute of food and an integral dimension to the theatre. Whether it be the servant's recurrent association with appetence, or the eroticised pleasures implicit in the theatre's elision of culinary and sexual appetites, to consider hunger and appetite is also to consider enjoyment. Pleasure, of course, is also political. Like all the aspects to the representation of hunger and appetite, it is multivalent and ambiguous. Pleasure speaks, in part, to the popular foundations of the Renaissance stage. It is rooted in the popular appetites of carnival and their association with the grotesque. In the theatre, it must also be situated with regard to the emergent capitalist economy of the period. Both food and theatre, in this context, are available only for a price. More widely, pleasure is rooted in envy and resistance, highlighting both the social norms and structures which inhibit it, and the fact that some can consume to excess while others cannot, not simply on the stage, but also in the audience. Lastly, it is rooted in defiance, emerging as the exhilarating pleasure of those who enjoy themselves when they know they should not be allowed to, and embodying therefore the quintessential instance of the theatre's association with transgressive fantasies.

# *Bibliography*

## Primary Sources

### *Manuscripts*

*Norfolk Record Office*
Quarter Session Files, Interrogations and Depositions: 1549–1554 (Case 12A/1a)

*Printed Texts*
S. T. C. refers to the Short Title Catalogue, 2nd ed.


Adams, T. (1619) *The Happines of the Church* (London: Printed by G. P. for Iohn Grismand, S. T. C. 121)

Armin, R. (1610) *Foole Upon Foole, or, Six Sortes of Sottes* (London: Printed for William Ferbrand, S. T. C. 772.5)

Bacon, F. (1985) *The Essays*, ed. John Pitcher (Harmondsworth: Penguin)

Bancroft, T. (1633) *The Gluttons Feauer. Written by Thomas Bancroft* (London: Printed by John Norton, for William Cooke; S. T. C. 1353)

Baxter, N. (1606) *Sir Philip Sydneys Ouránia* (London: Printed by Ed. Allde, for Edward White, S. T. C. 1598)

Bolton, R. (1631) *Instructions for a Right Comforting Afflicted Consciences* (London: Thomas Weaver, S. T. C. 3238)

Boorde, A. (1547) *A Compendious Regiment or a Dietary of Health* (London, S. T. C. 3380)

Bradford, W. (1952) *Of Plymouth Plantation, 1620–1647*, ed. Samuel Eliot Morison (New York: Alfred A. Knopf)

Brathwaite, R. (1630) *The English Gentleman* (London: Printed by John Haviland, S. T. C. 3563)

Bullein, W. (1579) *Bulleins Bulwarke of Defence* (London: Printed by Thomas Marshe, S. T. C. 4034)

Bullein, W. (1595) *The Government of Health* (London: Printed by Valentine Sims, S. T. C. 4042)

Burton, R. (1621) *The Anatomy of Melancholy* (Oxford: John Lichfield and James Short)

*Calendar of State Papers Relating to English Affairs in the Archives of Venice* (1916), ed. Allen B. Hinds, 21 vols (London: Her Majesty's Stationery Office)
Calvin, J. (1561) *The Institution of Christian religion* (London, S. T. C. 4415)
(1577) *The Sermons of M. John Calvin, upon the Epistle of S. Paule too the Ephesians*, trans. Arthur Golding (London, S. T. C. 4448)
Carroll, R., and S. Prickett, eds. (1997) *The Bible: Authorized King James Version* (Oxford: Oxford University Press)
Chapman, G. (1975) *The Widow's Tears*, ed. Akihiro Yamada (London: Methuen)
Chapman, G., Jonson, B., and Marston, J. (1994) *Eastward Ho!*, ed. C. G. Petter (London: A. & C. Black)
*Christmas Lamentation for the Losse of his Acquaintance* (1635) (London, S. T. C. 5203)
Church of England (1571) *The Seconde Tome of Homilees* (London, S. T. C. 13669)
Citois, F. (1603) *A true and admirable historie, of a mayden of Confolens, in the prouince of Poictiers that for the space of three yeeres and more hath liued, and yet doth, vvithout receiuing either meate or drinke* (London: Printed by I. Roberts, S. T. C. 5326)
Cogan, T. (1636) *The Haven of Health* (London: Printed by Anne Griffin, for Roger Ball, S. T. C. 5484)
*The Comedy of George a Green* (1911), ed. F. W. Clarke (Oxford: Malone Society)
Cooper, T. (1580) *A briefe homily wherein the most comfortable and right vse of the Lords Supper, is very plainly opened and delivered, even to the understanding of the unlearned and ignorant* (London: Ralph Newberie; S. T. C. 5684.5)
(1615) *The Art of Giving* (London, S.T.C 5692)
Copely, A. (1595) *Wits Fittes and Fancies* (London, S. T. C. 5738)
Crashaw, W. (1613) 'Epistle dedicatory to Alexander Whitaker', in *Good Newes from Virginia. Sent to the counsel and company of Virginia* (London, S. T. C. 25354)
*A Critical Edition of 'The Life and Death of Jack Straw' 1594* (2002), ed. Stephen Longstaffe (Lewiston: Edwin Mellen)
Crowley, R. (1852) *Select Works of Robert Crowley*, ed. J. W. Cowper (London: Early English Texts Society)
Dasent, J. R., ed. (1902) *Acts of the Privy Council of England, Volume XXVI* (London: Mackie & co.)
Davenant, W. (1673) *The Works of Sr. William Davenant* (London: Henry Herringman, Wing D320)
de Mediolano, J. (1528) *Regimen sanitatis Salerni*, trans. Thomas Paynell (London, S. T. C. 21596)
(1607) *The Englishmans docter. Or, The schoole of Salerne* (London: John Helme, and John Busby Junior, S. T. C. 21605)
Dekker, T. (1602) *Blurt Master-Constable* (London : Edward Allde)
(1618) *Canaans calamitie Ierusalems misery* (London: Thomas Bayly, S. T. C. 6181.2)
(1620) *Dekker his Dreame* (London: printed by Nicholas Okes, S. T. C. 6497)
(1975) *The Shoemaker's Holiday*, ed. D. J. Palmer (London: Ernest Benn Limited)

Donne, J. (1649) *Fifty Sermons* (London: M. F., J. Marriot, and R. Royston, Wing: D1862)

Downame, J. (1616) *The Plea of the Poore* (London: printed by Edward Griffin for Ralph Mabbe, S. T. C. 7146)

Elyot, T. (1539) *The Castle of Health* (London, S. T. C. 7643)

Fletcher, J., and Beaumont, F. (1966–1996) *The Dramatic Works in the Beaumont and Fletcher Canon*, gen. ed. Fredson Bowers, 10 vols (Cambridge: Cambridge University Press)

Ford, J. (1986) *The Selected Plays of John Ford*, ed. Colin Gibson (Cambridge: Cambridge University Press)

Fox, J. (1844) *Fox's Book of Martyrs: The Acts and Monuments of the Church*, ed. John Cumming, 3 vols (London: George Virtue)

*The Geneva Bible: A Facsimile of the 1560 Edition* (2007), ed. Lloyd E. Berry (Peabody, MA: Hendrickson)

Gilpin, B. (1581) *A godly sermon preached in the court at Greenwich* (London: Thomas Man, S. T. C. 11897)

Glapthorne, H. (1874) *The Plays and Poems of Henry Glapthorne* (London: John Pearson)

Gosson, S. (1582) *Playes confuted in five actions* (London: Thomas Gosson, S. T. C. 12095)

Gouge, W. (1631) *Gods Three Arrowes Plague, Famine, Sword, in three treatises* (London: Printed by George Miller for Edward Brewster, S. T. C. 12116)

Greene, R. (1973) *The Scottish History of James IV*, ed. Norman Sanders (Manchester, UK: Revels)

Guazzo, S. (1581) *The Ciuile Conuersation of M. Steeuen Guazzo written first in Italian, and nowe translated out of French by George Pettie* (London: Richard Watkins, S. T. C. 12422)

Gurth, A. (1597) *Most True and More Admirable Newes* (London: Thomas Stirrop, S. T. C. 12531.5)

Hakewill, G. (1635) *An Apologie or Declaration of the Power and Providence of God* (Oxford, S. T. C. 12613)

Hakluyt, R. (1885–1890) *The Principal Navigations, Voyages, Traffiques and Discoveries of the English Nation*, ed. Edmund Goldsmid, 16 vols (Edinburgh: E. and G. Goldsmid)

Hales, J. (1581) *A Compendious or Briefe Examination of Certayne Ordinary Complaints of Divers of Our Country Men* (London: Thomas Marshe, S. T. C. 23133)

Hall, J. (1609) *Discovery of a New World* (London: Ed. Blount. and W. Barrett, S. T. C. 12686.3)

Hamor, R. (1615) *A True Discourse of the Present Estate of Virginia, and the success of the affaires there till the 18 of June. 1614* (London: William Welby, S. T. C. 12736)

Hawkins, J. (1888) 'John Hawkyns to Lord Burleigh', in *Plymouth Armada Heroes: The Hawkins Family*, ed. M. W. S. Hawkins (Plymouth: William Brendon and Son), p. 44

Heywood, T. (2005) *The First and Second Parts of King Edward IV*, ed. Richard Rowland (Manchester: Manchester University Press)

Hitchcock, R. (1580) *A Pollitique Platt for the Honour of the Prince* (London: Jhon Kyngston, S. T. C. 13531)

Hobbes, T. (1981) *Leviathan* (Harmondsworth: Penguin)

'The Hope Contract' (2002) in *Early English Stages: 1300 to 1600*, ed. Glynne Wickham, 5 vols (London: Routledge) vol. 2, pp. 209–11

Hurtado de Mendoza, D. (1598) *The Pleasaunt Historie of Lazarillo de Tormes a Spaniarde* (London: Printed by Abell Jeffes, S. T. C. 15336)

Hutton, M. (1933) 'The Archbishop of York to Robert Cecil', in *Calendar of the Manuscripts of the Marquess of Salisbury*, 24 vols (London: Historical Manuscripts Commission) vol. 16, pp. 220–1

I. M. (1598) *A Health to the Gentlemanly Profession of Seruingmen; or, The Seruingmans Comforts* (London, S. T. C. 17140)

James I (2002) *The Political Works of James I*, ed. C. H. McIlwain (London: The Lawbook Exchange, Ltd.)

Jeninges, E. (1590) *A Briefe Discovery of the Damages that Happen to this Realme by Disordered and Unlawfull Diet* (London: Printed by Roger Ward, S. T. C. 14486)

Jonson, B. (2012) *The Cambridge Edition of the Works of Ben Jonson*, gen. eds. David Bevington, Martin Butler and Ian Donaldson, 7 vols (Cambridge: Cambridge University Press)

Larkin, J., and Hughes, P., eds. (1973) *Stuart Royal Proclamations*, 2 vols (London: Clarendon Press)

Loarte, G. (1594) *The Exercise of a Christian Life Written by G.L.; being the First Ground and Foundaion [Sic], Whence the Two Treatises Appertaining to Resolution, were made and Framed, by R.P* (London: W. Leake; S. T. C. 16644.5)

'A Looking Glasse for Corne-hoorders' (1631) (London: I. Wright, S. T. C. 15225.5)

Lucian (1903) *Misanthropos; or, The Man-Hater [Timon]*, in *Pleasant Dialogues, and Dramma's*, trans. Thomas Heywood, ed. W. Bang, in *Materialien zur Kunde des älteren Englischen Dramas* (Louvain: Uystpruyst)

Lyly, J. (1991) *Campaspe and Sapho and Phao*, ed. G. K. Hunter and David Bevington (Manchester: Manchester University Press)

Markham, G. (1631) *The Good Housewife* (London: Printed by Nicholas Okes for John Harison, S. T. C. 17353)

Marvell, A. (2003) *The Poems of Andrew Marvell*, ed. Nigel Smith (Harlow: Pearson Education)

Massinger, P. (1976) *The Plays and Poems of Philip Massinger*, ed. Philip Edwards and Colin Gibson, 5 vols (Oxford: Clarendon Press)

Mayne, J. (1639) *The City Match* (Oxford: Leonard Lichfield, S. T. C. 17750)

Merbury, F. (1971) *The Marriage Between Wit and Wisdom*, ed. Trevor N. S. Lennam (Oxford: Oxford University Press)

Middleton, T. (2007) *The Collected Works*, gen. ed. Gary Taylor and John Lavagnino (Oxford: Oxford University Press)

Middleton, T., and Shakespeare, W. (2008) *Timon of Athens*, ed. Anthony B. Dawson and Gretchen E. Minton (London: Arden)

Moffett, T. (1655) *Healths Improvement* (London: Printed by Thomas Newcomb for Samuel Thomson, Wing M2382)

Montaigne, M. (1991) *The Complete Essays*, trans. and ed. M. A. Screech (Harmondsworth: Penguin)

Moore, P. (1564) *The Hope of Health* (London: Jhon Kyngston, S. T. C. 18059.5)

Moryson, F. (1617) *An Itinerary Written by Fynes Moryson gent.* (London: J. Beale, S. T. C. 18205)

Munday, A., Chettle, H., Dekker, T., Heywood, T., and Shakespeare, W. (2011) *Sir Thomas More*, ed. John Jowett (London: Arden)

Nashe, T. (1958) *The Works of Thomas Nashe*, 5 vols (Oxford: Oxford University Press)

(1972) *Nashe's Lenten Stuffe*, in *The Unfortunate Traveller and Other Works*, ed. J. B. Steane (Harmondsworth: Penguin)

Neville, A. (1615) *Norfolke Furies, or a view of Ketts campe necessary for the malecontents of our time, for their instruction, or terror* (London, S. T. C. 18480)

*A Notable and Prodigious Historie* (1589) (London, S. T. C. 5678)

Parker, M. (1629) 'Times Alteration: or, The Old Mans Rehearsall' (London: Thomas Symcocke, S. T. C. 19271)

Parr, A., ed. (1995) *Three Renaissance Travel Plays* (Manchester: Manchester University Press)

Peacham, H. (1622) *The Compleat Gentleman* (London: Francis Constable, S. T. C. 19502)

Peckham, G. (1583) *A True Reporte, of the Late Discoueries* (London: John Hinde, S. T. C. 19523)

Percy, G. (1625) *A True Relation of the Proceedings and Occurances of Moment which have Happened in Virginia* (London)

Platter, T. (1937) *Travels in England*, trans. Clare Williams (London: Jonathan Cape)

Purchas, S., ed. (1906) *Hakluytus Posthumus or Purchas His Pilgrimes*, 20 vols (Glasgow: James MacLehose and Sons)

Rawlins, T. (1640) *The Rebellion* (London: Printed by I. Okes, for Daniell Frere, S. T. C. 20770)

*The Records of the Virginia Company of London* (1933), ed. Susan Myra Kingsbury, 4 vols (Washington, DC: Government Printing Office)

Rogers, D. (1642) *Matrimoniall honovr, or, The mutuall crowne and comfort of godly, loyall, and chaste marriage* (London: Printed by Thomas Harper for Philip Nevel, Wing R1797)

Rosselli, G. (1598) *Epulario, or The Italian banquet wherein is shewed the maner how to dresse and prepare all kind of flesh, foules or fishes. As also how to make sauces, tartes, pies, &c. After the maner of all countries. With an addition of many other profitable and necessary things. Translated out of Italian into English* (London: William Barley, S. T. C. 10433)

Ruscelli, G. (1569) *A Verye Excellent and Profitable Booke*, trans. Richard Androse (London, S. T. C. 309)

Sackville, T. and Norton, T. (1970) *Gorboduc or, Ferrex and Porrex*, ed. Irby B. Cauthen (London: Edward Arnold)

Saker, A. (1580) *Narbonus The Laberynth of Libertie* (London, S. T. C. 21593)

Shakespeare, W. (1594) *The First Part of the Contention* (London, S. T. C. 26099)

(1965) *Measure for Measure*, ed. J. W. Lever (London: Arden)

(1991) *The Three-Text 'Hamlet': Parallel Texts of the First and Second Quartos and First Folio*, ed. Paul Bertram and Bernice W. Kliman (New York: AMS Press)

(1995) *King Henry V*, ed. T. W. Craik (London: Arden)

(1995) *Titus Andronicus*, ed. Jonathan Bate (London: Arden)

(1997) *The Two Noble Kinsmen*, ed. Lois Potter (London: Arden)

(1998) *Julius Caesar*, ed. David Daniell (London: Arden)

(1999a) *Henry VI, Part Two*, ed. Ronald Knowles (London: Arden)

(1999b) *King Henry VIII, or All Is True*, ed. Jay L Halio (Oxford: Oxford University Press)

(2004) *The Two Gentlemen of Verona*, ed. William C. Carroll (London: Arden)

(2006) *Antony and Cleopatra*, ed. John Wilders (London: Arden)

(2006) *As You Like It*, ed. Juliet Dusinberre (London: Arden)

(2007) *Shakespeare's Poems*, ed. Katherine Duncan-Jones (London: Arden)

(2008) *Twelfth Night*, ed. Kier Elam (London: Arden)

(2010a) *The Merchant of Venice*, ed. John Drakakis (London: Arden)

(2010b) *The Taming of the Shrew*, ed. Barbara Hodgdon (London: Arden)

(2011) *The Tempest*, ed. Alden T. Vaughan and Virginia Mason Vaughan (London: Arden)

(2013) *Coriolanus*, ed. Peter Holland (London: Arden)

Shakespeare, W. and Fletcher, J. (2000) *Henry VIII*, ed. Gordon McMullan (London: Arden)

Shakespeare, W. and Wilkins, G. (2014) *Pericles*, ed. Suzanne Gossett (London: Arden)

Smith, J. (1986) *The Complete Works of Captain John Smith (1580–1631)*, ed. Philip L. Barbour, 3 vols (Chapel Hill: University of North Carolina Press)

Smith, T. (1583) *De Republica Anglorum* (London: Printed by Henrie Midleton for Gregorie Seton, S. T. C. 22857)

Smythe, J. (1590) *Certain Discourses, Written by Sir John Smythe, Knight: Concerning the Formes and Effects of Diuers Sorts of Weapons* (London: Richard Johnes, S. T. C. 22883)

Spenser, E. (1997) *A View of the Present State of Ireland*, ed. Andrew Hadfield and Willy Maley (Oxford: Blackwell)

St. Bernard (1614) *Saint Bernard his Meditations* (London: Francis Burton, S. T. C. 1919a)

Stanley, W. (1588) *A Briefe Discouerie of Doctor Allens Seditious Drifts* (London: Francis Coldock, S. T. C. 6166)

Stephens, J. (1615) *Satyrical Essayes Characters and Others* (London: Roger Barnes, S. T. C. 23249)

Stubbes, P. (1583) *The Anatomie of Abuses* (London: Richard Jones, S. T. C. 23377)

*A Students Lamentation that hath sometime been in London an apprentice for the rebellious tumults lately in the citie hapning* (1595) (London: William Blackwall, S. T. C. 23401.5)

'The Supplication of the Blood of the English Most Lamentably Murdered in Ireland, Cryeng Out of the Yearth for Revenge (1598)' (1995), ed. Willy Maley, in *Analecta Hibernica*, 36, pp. 1–77

Tawney, R. H. and Power, E., eds. (1924) *Tudor Economic Documents: Being Select Documents Illustrating the Economic and Social History of Tudor England*, 3 vols (London: Longmans)

Taylor, J. (1868) *The Works of John Taylor the Water Poet*, 4 vols (Manchester: Spenser Society)

Twine, L. (1966) 'The Pattern of Painful Adventures', in *Narrative and Dramatic Sources of Shakespeare*, ed. Geoffrey Bullough, 8 vols (New York: Columbia University Press) vol. 6, pp. 423–82

Vaughan, W. (1608) *The Golden-Groue Moralized in Three Bookes* (London: Richard Serger, and Iohn Browne, S. T. C. 24611)

(1612) *Approved directions for health, both naturall and artificiall deriued from the best physitians as well moderne as auncient* (London: Roger Jackson, S.T.C. 24615)

Venner, T. (1620) *Via Recta* (London: Printed by Edward Griffin for Richard Moore, S. T. C. 24643)

Virginia Company (1610) *A True Declaration of the estate of the Colonie in Virginia* (London: William Barret, S. T. C. 24833)

Vives, J. L. (1541) *A Very Fruteful and Pleasant Boke Callyd the Instruction of a Christen Woman*, trans. R. Hyrde (London, S. T. C. 24858)

*A Warning-piece for Ingroosers of Corne* (1643) (London: William Gilbertson, Wing W926)

Whitaker, A. (1613) *Good Newes from Virginia* (London: Printed by Felix Kyngston for William Welby, S. T. C. 25354)

Wiggins, M., ed. (2008) *A Woman Killed with Kindness and Other Domestic Plays* (Oxford: Oxford University Press)

Williams, R. (1643) *A Key into the Language of America* (London: Printed by Gregory Dexter, Wing W2766)

Wilson, T. (1936) *The State of England, Anno Dom. 1600*, ed. Frederick Jack Fisher (London: Camden Miscellany)

Wither, G. (1628) *Britain's Remembrancer* (London, S. T. C. 25899)

Wood, T. (1611) *The Protestants and Iesuites up in armes in Gulicke-land* (London: Nicholas Bourne, S. T. C. 20449)

(1634) *New Englands Prospect* (London: Printed by Thomas Cotes, for John Bellamie, S. T. C. 25957)

Wyatt, Sir Francis (1926) 'Letter of Sir Francis Wyatt, Governor of Virginia, 1621–1626', *The William and Mary Quarterly*, 6.2, 114–21

## Secondary Sources

Adelman, J. (1992) *Suffocating Mothers: Fantasies of Maternal Origin in Shakespeare's Plays, 'Hamlet' to 'The Tempest'* (London and New York: Routledge)

Agnew, J.-C. (1986) *Worlds Apart: The Market and the Theatre in Anglo-American Thought, 1550–1750* (Cambridge: Cambridge University Press)

Akhimie, P. (2009) 'Travel, Drama, and Domesticity: Colonial Huswifery in John Fletcher and Philip Massinger's *The Sea Voyage*', *Studies in Travel Writing*, 13.2, 153–66

Albala, K. (2002) *Eating Right in the Renaissance* (Berkeley, Los Angeles and London: University of California Press)

(2003) *Food in Early Modern Europe* (Westport, CT: Greenwood)

(2007) *The Banquet: Dining in the Great Courts of Late Renaissance Europe* (Urbana and Chicago: University of Illinois Press)

(2011) 'The Ideology of Fasting in the Reformation Era', in *Food and Faith in Christian Culture*, ed. Ken Albala and Trudy Eden (New York: Columbia University Press), pp. 41–58

Allen, R. C. (1992) *Enclosure and the Yeoman* (Oxford: Oxford University Press)

Anderson, B. (2006) *Imagined Communities: Reflections on the Origin and Spread of Nationalism* (London: Verso)

Anderson, L. (2005) *A Place in the Story: Servants and Service in Shakespeare's Plays* (Newark: University of Delaware Press)

Anderson, P. (1975) *Lineages of the Absolutist State* (London: New Left Books)

(1992) *English Questions* (London: Verso)

Angel-Perez, E. and Poulain, A., eds. (2008) *Hunger on the Stage* (Newcastle: Cambridge Scholars Publishing)

Angel-Perez, E. and Poulain, A. (2008) 'Introduction', in *Hunger on the Stage*, ed. Elisabeth Angel-Perez and Alexandra Poulain (Newcastle: Cambridge Scholars Publishing), pp. ix–xii

Appelbaum, R. (2004) *Literature and Utopian Politics in Seventeenth-Century England* (Cambridge: Cambridge University Press)

(2006) *Aguecheek's Beef, Belch's Hiccup, and Other Gastronomic Interjections: Literature, Culture and Food among the Early Moderns* (Chicago: University of Chicago Press)

(2010) 'Food', in *Ben Jonson in Context*, ed. Julie Sanders (Cambridge: Cambridge University Press), pp. 314–21

Appleby, A. (1978) *Famine in Tudor and Stuart England* (Liverpool: Liverpool University Press)

Arab, R. (2005) 'Ruthless Power and Ambivalent Glory: The Rebel-Labourer in *2 Henry VI*', *Journal for Early Modern Cultural Studies*, 5.2, 5–36

Archer, I. W. (1991) *The Pursuit of Stability: Social Relations in Elizabethan London* (Cambridge: Cambridge University Press)
Archer, J. E., Turley, R. M. and Thomas, H. (2014) *Food and the Literary Imagination* (Basingstoke: Palgrave Macmillan)
Arens, W. (1979) *The Man-Eating Myth: Anthropology and Anthropophagy* (Oxford: Oxford University Press)
Arnold, O. (2007) *The Third Citizen: Shakespeare's Theater and the Early Modern House of Commons* (Baltimore, MD: Johns Hopkins University Press)
Aston, T. H. and Philpin, C. H. E., eds. (1985) *The Brenner Debates: Agrarian Class Structure and Economic Development in Pre-Industrial England* (Cambridge: Cambridge University Press)
Bailey, A. (2004) 'Livery and Its Discontents: "Braving It" in *The Taming of the Shrew*', *Renaissance Drama*, 33, 87–135
Bakhtin, M. (1984) *Rabelais and His World*, trans. Helene Iswolsky (Bloomington, IN: Indiana University Press)
Behre, K. S. (2018) '"Look What Market She Hath Made": Women, Commerce, and Power in *A Chaste Maid in Cheapside* and *Bartholomew Fair*', *Early Theatre: A Journal associated with the Records of Early English Drama*, 21.1, 127–44.
Beier, A. L. (1985) *Masterless Men: The Vagrancy Problem in England, 1560–1640* (London: Methuen)
Bell, R. (1985) *Holy Anorexia* (Chicago: University of Chicago Press)
Bellamy, L. (2019) *The Language of Fruit: Literature and Horticulture in the Long Eighteenth Century* (Philadelphia: University of Pennsylvania Press)
Belsey, C. (1985) *The Subject of Tragedy: Identity and Difference in Renaissance Drama* (London: Methuen)
Berking, H. (1999) *Theory, Culture and Society: Sociology of Giving* (London: Sage Publications Ltd)
Bernthal, C. A. (2002) 'Jack Cade's Legal Carnival', *SEL Studies in English Literature 1500–1900*, 42.2, 259–74
Bevington, D. and Smith, D. L. (1999) 'James I and *Timon of Athens*', *Comparative Drama*, 33.1,. 56–87
Biet, C. (2008) 'Child Pasties and Devoured Hearts: Anthropophagous Feasts and Theatrical Cruelty in England and France (Late 16th – Early 17th Centuries)', in *Hunger on Stage*, ed. Elisabeth Angel-Perez and Alexandra Poulain (Newcastle: Cambridge Scholars Publishing), pp. 56–76
Blits, J. H. (1981) 'Caesarism and the end of Republican Rome: *Julius Caesar*, Act I, scene i', *The Journal of Politics*, 43.1, 40–55
Bloch, E. (1995) *The Principle of Hope*, trans. Neville Plaice, Stephen Plaice and Paul Knight, 3 vols (Cambridge, MA: The MIT Press)
Bly, M. (2000) *Queer Virgins and Virgin Queans on the Early Modern Stage* (Oxford: Oxford University Press)
Boehrer, B. T. (1997) *The Fury of Men's Gullets: Ben Jonson and the Digestive Canal* (Philadelphia: University of Pennsylvania Press)
Boling, J. (1999) 'Fletcher's Satire of Caratach in Bonduca', *Comparative Drama*, 33.3, 390–406

Bourdieu, P. (1977) *Outline of a Theory of Practice*, trans. Richard Nice (Cambridge: Cambridge University Press)

(1984) *Distinction: A Social Critique of the Judgement of Taste*, trans. Richard Nice (Cambridge, MA: Harvard University Press)

(1993) *The Field of Cultural Production: Essays on Art and Literature* (Cambridge: Polity Press)

(2005) 'Taste of Luxury, Taste of Necessity', in *The Taste Culture Reader: Experiencing Food and Drink*, ed. Carolyn Korsmeyer (Oxford), pp. 72–8

Bowsher, J. and Miller, P. (2009) *The Rose and the Globe: Playhouses of Tudor Bankside, Southwark Excavations, 1988–91* (London: Museum of London Archaeology)

Braudel, F. (1992) *Civilisation and Capitalism, 15th–16th Century, Volume I: The Structures of Everyday Life: The Limits of the Possible*, trans. from the French by Miriam Kochan, revised by Siân Reynolds (Berkeley, Los Angeles and London: University of California Press)

Brenner, R. (1985a) 'Agrarian Class Structure and Economic Development in Pre-Industrial Europe', in *The Brenner Debates: Agrarian Class Structure and Economic Development in Pre-Industrial England*, ed. T. H. Aston and C. H. E. Philpin (Cambridge: Cambridge University Press), pp. 10–63

(1985b) 'The Agrarian Roots of European Capitalism', in *The Brenner Debates: Agrarian Class Structure and Economic Development in Pre-Industrial England*, ed. T. H. Aston and C. H. E. Philpin (Cambridge: Cambridge University Press), pp. 213–310

(1993) *Merchants and Revolution: Commercial Change, Political Conflict and London's Overseas Traders, 1550–1653* (Cambridge: Cambridge University Press)

Brewer, J. (1990) *The Sinews of Power: War, Money, and the English State, 1688–1783* (Cambridge, MA: Harvard University Press)

Bristol, M. (1985) *Carnival and Theatre: Plebeian Culture and the Structure of Authority in Renaissance England* (London: Methuen)

Bromley, L. (1986) 'Domestic Conduct in *A Woman Killed with Kindness*', *Elizabethan and Jacobean Drama*, 26.2, 259–76

Brotton, J. (1998) '"This Tunis, sir, was Carthage": Contesting Colonialism in *The Tempest*', in *Post-Colonial Shakespeare*, ed. Ania Loomba and Martin Orkin (London and New York: Routledge), pp. 23–42

Brown, P. (1994) '"This thing of darkness I acknowledge mine": *The Tempest* and the Discourse of Colonialism', in *Political Shakespeare: Essays in Cultural Materialism*, ed. Jonathan Dollimore and Alan Sinfield (2nd ed.) (Manchester: Manchester University Press), pp. 48–71

Brown, P. A. (2003) *Better a Shrew than a Sheep: Women, Drama, and the Culture of Jest in Early Modern England* (Ithaca: Cornell University Press)

Bruster, D. (1992) *Drama and the Market in the Age of Shakespeare* (Cambridge: Cambridge University Press)

(2002) 'The Dramatic Life of Objects in the Early Modern Theatre', in *Staged Properties in Early Modern English Drama*, ed. Jonathan Gil

Harris and Natasha Korda (Cambridge: Cambridge University Press), pp. 67–98

Burgess, G. (1990) 'On Revisionism: An Analysis of Early Stuart Historiography in the 1970s and 1980s', *The Historical Journal*, 33.3, 609–27

(1996) *Absolute Monarchy and the Stuart Constitution* (New Haven and London: Yale University Press)

Burke, P. (2009) *Popular Culture in Early Modern Europe* (Farnham: Ashgate)

Burnett, M. T. (1995) '"Fill gut and pinch belly": Writing Famine in the English Renaissance', *Explorations in Renaissance Culture*, 21, 21–44

(1997) *Masters and Servants in English Renaissance Drama and Culture: Authority and Obedience* (Basingstoke: Palgrave)

Butler, M. (1984) *Theatre and Crisis, 1632–1642* (Cambridge: Cambridge University Press)

Bynum, C. W. (1987) *Holy Feast and Holy Fast: The Religious Significance of Food to Medieval Women* (Berkeley, Los Angeles and London: University of California Press)

Byres, T. J. (2006) 'Differentiation of the Peasantry under Feudalism and the Transition to Capitalism: In Defence of Rodney Hilton', *Journal of Agrarian Change*, 6.1, 17–68

Cahn, S. (1987) *Industry of Devotion: The Transformation of Women's Work in England, 1500–1660* (New York: Columbia University Press)

Camporesi, P. (1980) *Bread of Dreams: Food and Fantasy in Early Modern Europe*, trans. David Gentilcore (Cambridge: Polity Press)

(1996) *The Land of Hunger*, trans. Tania Croft-Murray (Cambridge: Polity Press)

Caputi, C. (2017) '"A Whore You Are, Madam" or, the Binary That Wasn't: Female Dyads and Doubling in John Fletcher's *The Chances* and *Women Pleased*', *Early Modern Literary Studies*, 27, 1–15

Carroll, W. C. (1996) *Fat King, Lean Beggar: Representations of Poverty in the Age of Shakespeare* (Ithaca: Cornell University Press)

Cartelli, T. (1991) *Marlowe, Shakespeare and the Economy of Theatrical Experience* (Philadelphia: University of Pennsylvania Press)

Cavell, S. (1983) '"Who Does the Wolf love?" Reading *Coriolanus*', *Representations*, 3, 1–20

Celovsky, L. (2009) 'Ben Jonson and Sidneian Legacies of Hospitality', *Studies in Philology*, 106.2, 178–206

Cockayne, E. (2007) *Hubbub: Filth, Noise and Stench in England, 1600–1770* (New Haven and London: Yale University Press)

Coddon, K. S. (1993) '"Slander in an Allow'd Fool": *Twelfth Night*'s Crisis of the Aristocracy', *Studies in English Literature, 1500–1900*, 33.2, 309–25

Cohen, W. (1985) *Drama of a Nation: Public Theatre in Renaissance England and Spain* (Ithaca: Cornell University Press)

(2001) 'The Undiscovered Country: Shakespeare and Mercantile Geography', in *Marxist Shakespeares*, ed. Jean E. Howard and Scott Cutler Shershow (London and New York: Routledge), pp. 128–58

Coleman, D. C. (1966) 'The "Gentry Controversy" and the Aristocracy in Crisis, 1558–1641', *History*, 51.172, 165–78

Cook, A. J. (1981) *The Privileged Playgoers of Shakespeare's Audience* (Princeton, NJ: Princeton University Press)

Corrigan, P. and Sayer, D. (1985) *The Great Arch: English State Formation as Cultural Revolution* (Oxford: Basil Blackwell)

Coward, B. (1982) 'A "Crisis of the Aristocracy" in the Sixteenth and Early Seventeenth Centuries? The Case of the Stanleys, Earls of Derby, 1504–1642', *Northern History*, 18.1, 54–77

Craig, H. (2009) 'The Three Parts of Henry VI', in *Shakespeare, Computers and the Mystery of Authorship*, ed. Hugh Craig and Arthur F. Kinney (Cambridge: Cambridge University Press), pp. 40–77

Crawford, J. (1999) 'Fletcher's *The Tragedie of Bonduca* and the Anxieties of the Masculine Government of James I', *Studies in English Literature 1500–1900*, 39.2, 357–81

Cunningham, A. and Grell, O. P. (2000) *The Four Horsemen of the Apocalypse: Religion War, Famine and Death in the Reformation* (Cambridge: Cambridge University Press)

Daileader, C. (1998) *Eroticism on the Renaissance Stage: Transcendence, Desire and the Limits of the Visible* (Cambridge: Cambridge University Press)

Davies, K. M. (1977) 'The Sacred Condition of Equality – How Original Were Puritan Doctrines of Marriage?', *Social History* 5, 563–80

Davis, N. (1965) *Society and Culture in Early Modern France* (Stanford: Stanford University Press)

Davis, N. Z. (2000) *The Gift in Sixteenth-Century France* (Oxford: Oxford University Press)

Dawson, A. B. and Minton, G. E. (2008) 'Introduction', in *Timon of Athens*, ed. Anthony B. Dawson and Gretchen E. Minton (London: Arden), pp. 1–145

Derrida, J. (1992) *Given Time: I. Counterfeit Money*, trans. Peggy Kamuf (Chicago: University of Chicago Press)

Diehl, H. (1997) *Staging Reform, Reforming the Stage: Protestantism and Popular Theater in Early Modern England* (Ithaca and London: Cornell University Press)

Dillon, J. (2000) *Theatre, Court and City, 1595–1610: Drama and Social Space in London* (Cambridge: Cambridge University Press)

(2002) 'Elizabethan Comedy', in *The Cambridge Companion to Shakespearean Comedy*, ed. Alexander Leggatt (Cambridge: Cambridge University Press), pp. 47–63

Dobb, M. (1963) *Studies in the Development of Capitalism* (London and New York: Routledge)

Dobson, M. (2009) '"His Banquet is Prepared": Onstage Food and the Permeability of Time in Shakespearean Performance', *Shakespeare Jahrbuch*, 145, 62–73

Dolan, F. (1994) *Dangerous Familiars: Representations of Domestic Crime in England, 1550–1700* (Ithaca: Cornell University Press)

Doty, J. (2013) 'Shakespeare and Popular Politics', *Literature Compass*, 10.2, 162–74

Douglas, M. (1984) *Food in the Social Order: Studies of Food and Festivities in Three American Communities* (New York: Russell Sage Foundation)

Douglas-Fairhurst, R. (2008) 'Tragedy and Disgust', in *Tragedy in Transition*, ed. Sarah Brown and Catherine Silverstone (Oxford: Blackwell), pp. 58–77

Dowd, M. (2009) *Women's Work in Early Modern English Literature and Culture* (Basingstoke: Palgrave)

Drouet, P. (2008) '"I speak this in hunger for bread": Hunger in *King Lear* and *Coriolanus*', in *Hunger on the Stage*, ed. Elisabeth Angel-Perez and Alexandra Poulain (Newcastle: Cambridge Scholars Publishing), pp. 2–16

Eagleton, T. (1989) 'Base and Superstructure in Raymond Williams', in *Raymond Williams: Critical Perspectives*, ed. Terry Eagleton (Cambridge: Polity Press), pp. 165–75

(1992) 'Value: *King Lear, Timon of Athens, Anthony and Cleopatra*', in *Shakespearean Tragedy*, ed. John Drakakis (London and New York: Routledge), pp. 76–89

Edwards, P., and Gibson, C. (1976) '*The Unnatural Combat: Introduction*', in *The Plays and Poems of Philip Massinger*, ed. Philip Edwards and Colin Gibson, 5 vols (Oxford: Clarendon Press), vol. 2, pp. 181–94

Egan, G. (2004) *Shakespeare and Marx* (Oxford: Oxford University Press)

Elias, N. (2000) *The Civilising Process: Sociogenetic and Psychogenetic Investigations*, trans. Edmund Jephcott (Oxford: Basil Blackwell)

Elton, G. (1974) *Studies in Tudor and Stuart Politics and Government, Volume II: Parliament and Political Thought* (Cambridge: Cambridge University Press)

Erskine-Hill, H. (1996) *Poetry and the Realm of Politics: Shakespeare to Dryden* (Oxford: Clarendon Press)

Evett, D. (2005) *Discourses of Service in Shakespeare's England* (New York: Palgrave Macmillan)

(2007) 'The Year's Work in Service Studies: Shakespeare, 2005', *Modern Philology*, 104.3, 412–29

Fitter, C. (2012) *Radical Shakespeare: Politics and Stagecraft in the Early Career* (London and New York: Routledge)

Fitzpatrick, J. (2007) *Food in Shakespeare: Elizabeth Culinary Culture and the Plays* (Aldershot: Ashgate Publishing Ltd)

(2010) '"I must eat my dinner": Shakespeare's Foods from Apples to Walrus', in *Renaissance Food from Rabelais to Shakespeare: Culinary Readings and Culinary Histories*, ed. Joan Fitzpatrick (Aldershot: Ashgate), pp. 127–43

(2011) *Shakespeare and the Language of Food: A Dictionary* (London: Continuum)

Forse, J. H. (1993) *Art Imitates Business: Commercial and Political Influences in Elizabethan Theatre* (Bowling Green, OH: Bowling Green State University Press)

Fouassier, F. (2008) '"I have a punk after supper, as good as a roasted apple": The Cannibal Relationship of Prostitutes and their Clients on the English

Renaissance Stage', in *Hunger on the Stage*, ed. Elisabeth Angel-Perez and Alexandra Poulain (Newcastle: Cambridge Scholars Publishing), pp. 30–44
Gair, R. (1982) *The Children of Paul's: The Story of a Theatre Company, 1553–1608* (Cambridge: Cambridge University Press)
Garwood, S. (2009) '"The Skull Beneath the Skin": Women and Self-Starvation on the Renaissance Stage', *Shakespeare Jahrbuch*, 145, 106–23
Gasper, J. (2007) 'Introduction to *The Bloody Banquet: A Tragedy*', in *Thomas Middleton: The Collected Works*, gen. ed. Gary Taylor and John Lavagnino (Oxford: Oxford University Press), pp. 637–69
George, D. (2000) 'Plutarch, Insurrection, and Dearth in *Coriolanus*', *Shakespeare Survey*, 53, 63–72
Ghose, I. (2008) *Shakespeare and Laughter: A Cultural History* (Manchester: Manchester University Press)
Gilbert, A. H. (1918) 'Virginia in *Eastward Ho*', *Modern Language Notes*, 33.3, 183–4
Goldstein, D. (2013) *Eating and Ethics in Shakespeare's England* (Cambridge: Cambridge University Press)
Goldstein, D. and Tigner, A., eds. (2016) *Culinary Shakespeare: Staging Food and Drink in Early Modern England* (Pittsburgh: Duquesne University Press)
Goldstein, D., Tigner, A. and Wall, W. (2016) 'Introduction', in *Culinary Shakespeare: Staging Food and Drink in Early Modern England* (Pittsburgh: Duquesne University Press), pp. 1–17
Goldstone, J. (1991) *Revolution and Rebellion in the Early Modern World* (Berkeley: University of California Press)
Gossett, S. (2014) 'Introduction', in *Pericles*, ed. Suzanne Gossett (London: Arden), pp. 1–163
Graham, V. E. (1962) 'The Pelican as Image and Symbol', in *Revue de Littérature Comparée*, 36.2, 235–44
Gramsci, A. (1971) *Selections from the Prison Notebooks of Antonio Gramsci*, trans. Quintin Hoare and Geoffrey Nowell-Smith (Cambridge, MA: MIT Press)
Greaves, R. L. (1981) *Society and Religion in Elizabethan England* (Minneapolis, MN: University of Minnesota Press)
Green, R. (2005) 'Open Ears, Appetite, and Adultery in *A Woman Killed with Kindness*', *English Studies in Canada*, 31.4, 53–74
Greenblatt, S. (1988) 'Murdering Peasants: Status, Genre and the Representation of Rebellion', in *Representing the English Renaissance*, ed. Stephen Greenblatt (Berkeley, Los Angeles and London: University of California Press), pp. 1–30
(1994) 'Invisible Bullets: Renaissance Authority and Its Subversion, Henry IV and Henry V', in *Political Shakespeare: Essays in Cultural Materialism*, ed. Jonathan Dollimore and Alan Sinfield (2nd ed.) (Manchester: Manchester University Press), pp. 18–47
Greenfield, P. (2009) 'Touring', in *The Oxford Handbook of Early Modern Theatre*, ed. Richard Dutton (Oxford: Oxford University Press)
Gregory, C. A. (1982) *Gifts and Commodities* (London: Academic Press)
Gurr, A. (1987) *Playgoing in Shakespeare's London* (Cambridge: Cambridge University Press)

(2009) *The Shakespearean Stage, 1574–1642* (Cambridge: Cambridge University Press)

Gutierrez, N. A. (2003) *'Shall She Famish Then?' Female Food Refusal in Early Modern England* (Aldershot: Ashgate Publishing)

Habakkuk, H. J. (1958) 'The Economic History of Modern Britain', *The Journal of Economic History*, 18.4, 486–501

Hadfield, A. (2005) *Shakespeare and Republicanism* (Cambridge: Cambridge University Press)

Harbage, A. (1941) *Shakespeare's Audience* (New York: Columbia University Press)

(1952) *Shakespeare and the Rival Tradition* (New York: Palgrave Macmillan)

Harman, C. (2008) *A People's History of the World* (London: Verso)

Haslem, L. S. (1995) '"Troubled with the Mother": Longings, Purgings, and the Maternal Body in Bartholomew Fair and The Duchess of Malfi', *Modern Philology*, 92.4, 438–59

Heal, F. (1984) 'The Idea of Hospitality in Early Modern England', *Past and Present*, 102, 66–93

(1990) *Hospitality in Early Modern England* (Oxford: Clarendon Press)

(2008) 'Food Gifts, the Household and the Politics of Exchange in Early Modern England', *Past and Present*, 199.1, 41–70

(2014) *The Power of Gifts: Gift-Exchange in Early Modern England* (Oxford: Oxford University Press)

Heinemann, M. (1980) *Puritanism and Theatre: Thomas Middleton and Opposition Drama under the Early Stuarts* (Cambridge: Cambridge University Press)

(1993) 'Drama and Opinion in the 1620s: Middleton and Massinger', in *Theatre and Government Under the Early Stuarts*, ed. J. R. Mulryne and Margaret Shewring (Cambridge: Cambridge University Press), pp. 237–65

Helgerson, R. (1992) *Forms of Nationhood: The Elizabethan Writing of England* (Chicago: Chicago University Press)

(2003) 'Shakespeare and Contemporary Dramatists of History', in *A Companion to Shakespeare's Works: The Histories*, ed. Richard Dutton and Jean Howard (Oxford: Blackwell), pp. 26–7

Heller, H. (2011) *The Birth of Capitalism: A Twenty-First-Century Perspective* (London: Pluto Press)

Herrmann, R. B. (2011) 'The "Tragicall Historie": Cannibalism and Abundance in Colonial Jamestown', *The William and Mary Quarterly*, 68.1, 47–74

Hill, C. (1967) *Reformation to Industrial Revolution: A Social and Economic History of Britain, 1530–1780* (London: Weidenfeld & Nicolson)

(2002) *Century of Revolution* (London and New York: Routledge)

Hilton, R., ed. (1978) *The Transition from Feudalism to Capitalism* (London: Verso)

Hindle, S. (2008) 'Imagining Insurrection in Seventeenth-Century England: Representations of the Midland Rising of 1607', *History Workshop Journal*, 66, 21–61

Hobgood, A. (2014) *Passionate Playgoing in Early Modern England* (Cambridge: Cambridge University Press)

Hodgson, E. (2009) '"A Fine and Private Place": Chapman's Theatrical Widow', *Medieval & Renaissance Drama in England*, 22, 60–77

Holbrook, P. (2003) 'Class X: Shakespeare, Class, and the Comedies', *in A Companion to Shakespeare's Works: The Comedies*, ed. Richard Dutton and Jean Howard (Oxford: Blackwell), pp. 67–89

Holstun, J. (2000) *Ehud's Dagger: Class Struggle in the English Revolution* (London: Verso Books)

(2004) 'The Spider, the Fly, and the Commonwealth: Merrie John Heywood and Agrarian Class Struggle', *English Literary History*, 71.1, 53–88

Horn, J. (2005) 'The Conquest of Eden Possession and Dominion in Early Virginia', in *Envisioning an English Empire: Jamestown and the Making of the North Atlantic World*, ed. Robert Appelbaum and John Sweet (Philadelphia: University of Pennsylvania Press), pp. 25–48

Horn, J., Kelso, W., Owsley, D. and Straube, B. (2013) *Jane: Starvation, Cannibalism, and Endurance at Jamestown* (Williamsburg, VA: Colonial Williamsburg Foundation and Preservation)

Houlbrooke, R. (1984) *The English Family 1450–1700* (London: Taylor and Francis)

Hulme, P. (1998) 'The Cannibal Scene', in *Cannibalism and the Colonial World*, ed. Francis Barker, Peter Hulme and Margaret Iverson (Cambridge: Cambridge University Press, 1998)

Hutson, L. (1994) *The Usurer's Daughter: Male Friendship and Fictions of Women in Sixteenth-Century England* (London: Routledge)

James, M. E. (1986) *Society, Politics and Culture* (Cambridge: Cambridge University Press)

Jameson, F. (1991) *Postmodernism, or, the Cultural Logic of Late Capitalism* (London: Verso)

(2002) *The Political Unconscious: Narrative as a Socially Symbolic Act* (London and New York: Routledge)

Jones, E. L. (1965) 'Agriculture and Economic Growth in England, 1660–1750: Agricultural Change', *Journal of Economic History*, 25.1, 1–18

Jorgensen, P. (1956) *Shakespeare's Military World* (Berkeley, Los Angeles and London: University of California Press)

Jowett, J. (2003) 'Middleton and Debt in Timon of Athens', in *Money and the Age of Shakespeare: Essays in New Economic Criticism*, ed. Linda Woodbridge (Basingstoke: Palgrave MacMillan), pp. 219–35

(2011) 'Introduction', in *Sir Thomas More*, ed. John Jowett (London: Arden), pp. 1–129

Jowitt, C. (2003) 'Colonialism, Politics, and Romanization in John Fletcher's Bonduca', *Studies in English Literature 1500–1900*, 43.2, 475–94

(2006) '"I am Another Woman": The Spanish and French Matches in Massinger's *The Renegado* (1624) and *The Unnatural Combat* (1624–5)', in *The Spanish Match*, ed. Alexander Samson (Aldershot: Ashgate), pp. 151–72

Kahn, C. (1987) '" Magic of bounty": Timon of Athens, Jacobean Patronage, and Maternal Power', *Shakespeare Quarterly*, 38.1, 34–57

Karim-Cooper, F. (2013) 'Touch and Taste in Shakespeare's Theatres', in *Shakespeare's Theatres and the Effects of Performance*, ed. Farah Karim-Cooper and Tiffany Stern (London: Bloomsbury Publishing), pp. 214–36

Kerridge, E. (1967) *The Agricultural Revolution* (London: Allen and Irwin)

Kesson, A. (2014) 'Was Comedy a Genre in English Early Modern Drama?' *British Journal of Aesthetics*, 54.2, 213–25

Khamphommala, V. (2008) '"Food of Love": Hunger and Desire in Shakespeare's Comedies', in *Hunger on the Stage*, ed. Elisabeth Angel-Perez and Alexandra Poulain (Newcastle: Cambridge Scholars Publishing), pp. 17–29

Kiefer, F. (1986) 'Heywood as Moralist in A Woman Killed with Kindness', *Medieval and Renaissance Drama in England*, 3, 83–98

Kishlansky, M. (1979) *The Rise of the New Model Army* (Cambridge: Cambridge University Press)

Knights, L. C. (1962) *Drama and Society in the Age of Jonson* (London: Chatto & Windus)

Knowles, K. (2009) 'Appetite and Ambition: The Influence of Hunger in Macbeth', *Early English Studies*, 2, 1–20

Knutson, R. L. (1991) *The Repertory of Shakespeare's Company 1594–1613* (Fayetteville: University of Arkansas Press)

(2009) 'Adult Playing Companies 1593–1603', in *The Oxford Handbook of Early Modern Theatre*, ed. Richard Dutton (Oxford: Oxford University Press)

Korda, N. (2011) *Labors Lost: Women's Work and the Early Modern English Stage* (Philadelphia: University of Pennsylvania Press)

(2012) *Shakespeare's Domestic Economies: Gender and Property in Early Modern England* (Philadelphia: University of Pennsylvania Press)

Korsmeyer, K. (2005) 'Perspectives on Taste', in *The Taste Culture Reader: Experiencing Food and Drink*, ed. Carolyn Korsmeyer (Oxford: Berg), pp. 1–9

Kupperman, K. O. (2005) 'Foreword', in *Envisioning an English Empire: Jamestown and the Making of the North Atlantic World*, ed. Robert Appelbaum and John Sweet (Philadelphia: University of Pennsylvania Press), pp. xi–xv

Lacan, J. (1977) *Écrits: a Selection*, trans. Alan Sheridan (London: Tavistock)

LaCombe, M. (2012) *Political Gastronomy: Food and Authority in the English Atlantic World* (Philadelphia: University of Pennsylvania Press)

Lapavitsas, C. (2003) *Social Foundations of Markets, Money and Credit* (London and New York: Routledge)

Laslett, P. (1965) *The World We Have Lost* (London: Methuen)

Leggatt, A. (1988) *Shakespeare's Political Drama: The History Plays and the Roman Plays* (London and New York: Routledge)

Lee, H. L. (2006) 'The Devil or the Physician: The Politics of Cooking and the Gendering of Cooks in Jonson and Massinger', *English Literary Renaissance*, 36.2, 250–77

Leites, E. (1982) 'The Duty to Desire: Love, Friendship, and Sexuality in some Puritan Theories of Marriage', *Journal of Social History*, 15.3, 383–408

Lennartz, N. (2012) 'Introduction', in *The Pleasures and Horrors of Eating: The Cultural History of Eating in Anglophone Literature*, ed. Marion Gymnich and Norbert Lennartz (Bonn: Bonn University Press), pp. 9–22

Levin, R. (1989) 'Women in the Renaissance Theatre Audience', *Shakespeare Quarterly*, 40.2, 165–74

Lévi-Strauss, C. (1978) *The Raw and the Cooked* (London: Cape)

Linebaugh, P. and Rediker, M. (2000) *The Many-Headed Hydra: Sailors, Salves, Commoners and the Hidden History of the Revolutionary Atlantic* (Boston, MA: Beacon Press)

Loomba, A. and Orkin M. (1998) 'Introduction: Shakespeare and the Post-Colonial Question', in *Post-Colonial Shakespeare*, ed. Ania Loomba and Martin Orkin (London: Routledge), pp. 1–20

Loopstra, R., Reeves, A., Taylor-Robinson, D., Barr, B., McKee, M. & Stuckler, D. (2015) 'Austerity, Sanctions, and the Rise of Food Banks in the UK', *BMJ*, 350, 1–6

MacLean, S. B. (2009) 'Adult Playing Companies 1583–1593', in *The Oxford Handbook of Early Modern Theatre*, ed. Richard Dutton (Oxford: Oxford University Press)

Maitra, E. (2013) 'Toward an Ethical Polity: Service and the Tragic Community in Timon of Athens', *Renaissance Drama*, 41, 173–198

Malinowski, B. (2002) *Argonauts of the Western Pacific: An Account of Native Enterprise and Adventure in the Archipelagoes of Melanesian New Guinea* (London and New York: Routledge)

Malthus, T. (1959) *Population: The First Essay* (Ann Arbor: University of Michigan Press)

Mandrou, R. (1975) *Introduction to Modern France, 1500–1640: An Essay in Historical Psychology* (London: Arnold)

Mann, D. (2008) *Shakespeare's Women: Performance and Conception* (Cambridge: Cambridge University Press)

Manning, R. (1976) *The English People and the English Revolution, 1640–1649* (London: Heinemann Educational)

Manning, R. B. (1988) *Village Revolts: Social Protest and Popular Disturbances in England, 1509–1640* (Oxford: Clarendon Press)

(1993) *Hunters and Poachers: A Social and Cultural History of Unlawful Hunting in England, 1485–1640* (Oxford: Clarendon Press)

Marx, K. and Engels, F. (1975–2004) *Collected Works*, 50 vols (London: Lawrence and Wishart)

Mathur, M. (2007) 'An Attack of the Clowns: Comedy, Vagrancy, and the Elizabethan History Play', *Journal for Early Modern Cultural Studies*, 7.1, 33–54

Mauss, M. (2002) *The Gift*, trans. W. D. Halls (London: Routledge)

Maxwell, B. (1926) 'The Hungry Knave in the Beaumont and Fletcher Plays', *Philological Quarterly*, 5, 299–306

McBride, K. (2001) *Country House Discourse in Early Modern England: A Cultural Study of Landscape and Legitimacy* (Aldershot: Ashgate)

McEachern, C. (2008) 'Why Do Cuckolds Have Horns?' *Huntington Library Quarterly*, 71.4, 607–31

McKee, L. (2013) 'Giving and Serving in Timon of Athens', *Early Modern Literary Studies*, 16.3, 1–22

McMillin, S. and Maclean, S.-B. (1998) *The Queen's Men and Their Plays* (Cambridge: Cambridge University Press)

McMullan, G. (1994) *Politics of Unease in the Plays of John Fletcher* (Amherst: University of Massachusetts Press)

McNally, D. (2012) *Monsters of the Market: Zombies, Vampires and Global Capitalism* (Chicago: Haymarket Books)

McQuade, P. (2000) '"A Labyrinth of Sin": Marriage and Moral Capacity in Thomas Heywood's A Woman Killed with Kindness', *Modern Philology*, 98.2, 231–50

Meads, C. (2001) *Banquets Set Forth: Banqueting in English Renaissance Drama* (Manchester: Manchester University Press)

Mennell, S. (1985) *All Manners of Food: Eating and Taste in England and France from the Middle Ages to the Present* (Oxford: Basil Blackwell)

Mészáros, I. (1989) *The Power of Ideology* (Brighton: Harvester Wheatsheaf)

Moisan, T. (1991) '"Knock me here soundly": Comic Misprision and Class Consciousness in Shakespeare', *Shakespeare Quarterly*, 42.3, 276–90

Montrose, L. (1989) 'Professing the Renaissance: The Poetics and Politics of Culture', in *The New Historicism*, ed. H. Aram Veeser (London and New York: Routledge), pp. 15–36

Moran, A. (2015) 'An Emetic upon St. Bartholomew's Day: Purging, Stripping, and Reclothing the Pauline Body in Bartholomew Fair', *Ben Jonson Journal*, 22.1, 23–40

Mukherjee, A. (2015) *Penury into Plenty: Dearth and the Making of Knowledge in Early Modern England* (London and New York: Routledge)

Mullaney, S. (2013) '"All that Monarchs Do": The Obscured Stages of Authority in *Pericles*', in *Shakespeare: The Late Plays*, ed. Kiernan Ryan (London and New York: Routledge), pp. 88–106

Munro, L. (2005) *Children of the Queen's Revels: A Jacobean Theatre Repertory* (Cambridge: Cambridge University Press)

Neiberg, L. K. (2013) 'Death's Release: Comedy and the Erotics of the Grave in The Widow's Tears', *Shakespeare Studies*, 41, 177–90

Neil, K. (2014) 'The Politics of Suicide in John Fletcher's Tragedie of Bonduca', *Journal for Early Modern Cultural Studies*, 14.1, 88–114

Neill, M. (2000) *Putting History to the Question: Power, Politics and Society in English Renaissance Drama* (New York: Columbia University Press)

Neuss, P. (1973) 'Active and Idle Language: Dramatic Images in *Mankind*', in *Medieval Drama*, ed. Neville Denny (London: Edward Arnold), pp. 41–67

Noble, L. (2003) '"And Make Two Pasties Of Your Shameful Heads": Medicinal Cannibalism and Healing the Body Politic in Titus Andronicus', *English Literary History*, 70.3, 677–708

Norbrook, D. (2002) *Poetry and Politics in the English Renaissance* (Oxford: Oxford University Press)

Nunn, H. (2013) 'Playing with Appetite in Early Modern Comedy', in *Shakespearean Sensations: Experiencing Literature in Early Modern England*, ed. Katharine A. Craik and Tanya Pollard (Cambridge: Cambridge University Press), pp. 101–17

Oates, M. and Baumol, W. (1972) 'On the Economics of the Theater in Renaissance London', *The Swedish Journal of Economics*, 74.1, 136–60

Ornellas, K. de (2007) '"Fowle Fowles"? The Sacred Pelican and the Profane Cormorant in Early Modern Culture', in *A Cultural History of Animals in the Renaissance*, ed. Bruce Boehrer (Oxford: Berg), pp. 27–52

Palmer, D. W. (1992) *Hospitable Performances: Dramatic Genre and Cultural Practices in Early Modern England* (West Lafayette: Purdue University Press)

Panek, J. (1994) 'Punishing Adultery in *A Woman Killed with Kindness*', *Studies in English literature, 1500–1900*, 34.2, 357–78

Pannen, I. (2012) '"I would not Taste of Such a Banquet": Ill-f (l) avoured Consumption in The Bloody Banquet', *Actes des congrès de la Société française Shakespeare*, 29, 93–104

Parr, A. (1995) 'Introduction' in *Three Renaissance Travel Plays*, ed. Anthony Parr (Manchester: Manchester University Press), pp. 1–56

Paster, G. K. (1993) *The Body Embarrassed: Drama and the Disciplines of Shame in Early Modern England* (Ithaca: Cornell University Press)

Patterson, A. (1989) *Shakespeare and the Popular Voice* (Oxford: Basil Blackwell)

Perret, M. (1983) 'Petruchio: The Model Wife', *Studies in English Literature, 1500–1900*, 23.2, 223–35

Perry, C. (2006) *Literature and Favoritism in Early Modern England* (Cambridge: Cambridge University Press)

Pettet, E. C. (1947) 'Timon of Athens: The Disruption of Feudal Morality', *The Review of English Studies*, 23.92, 321–36

Pincombe, M. (1996) *The Plays of John Lyly: Eros and Eliza* (Manchester: Manchester University Press)

Pleij, H. (1997) *Dreaming of Cockaigne: Medieval Fantasies of the Perfect Life* (New York: Columbia University Press)

Porter, R. (1980) 'Preface', in *Bread of Dreams: Food and Fantasy in Early Modern Europe* by Piero Camporesi, trans. David Gentilcore (Cambridge: Polity Press), pp. 1–16

Purkiss, D. (2010) 'Crammed with Distressful Bread? Bakers and the Poor in Early Modern England', in *Renaissance Food from Rabelais to Shakespeare: Culinary Readings and Culinary Histories*, ed. Joan Fitzpatrick (Aldershot: Ashgate), pp. 11–24

Rackin, P. (1990) *Stages of History: Shakespeare's English Chronicles* (London and New York: Routledge)

(1997) 'Historical Difference / Sexual Difference', in *Privileging Gender in Early Modern England*, ed. Jean R. Brink (Kirkville: Sixteenth-Century Journal Publishers), pp. 37–64

Regan, P. C. and Atkins, L. (2006) 'Sex Differences and Similarities in Frequency and Intensity of Sexual Desire', *Social Behavior & Personality: An International Journal*, 34.1, 95–101

Ribner, I. (1965) *The English History Play in the Age of Shakespeare* (London and New York: Routledge)

Rice, R. (2004) 'Cannibalism and the Act of Revenge in Tudor-Stuart Drama', *Studies in English Literature 1500–1900*, 44.2, 297–316

Rieff, D. (2016) *The Reproach of Hunger: Food, Justice and Money in the Twenty-First Century* (London: Verso)

Rivlin, E. (2012) *The Aesthetics of Service in Early Modern England* (Evanston: Northwestern University Press)

(2015) 'Service and Servants in Early Modern English Culture to 1660', *Journal of Early Modern Studies*, 4, 17–41

Rocha, G. (1995) 'An Esthetic of Hunger', in *Brazilian Cinema*, ed. Randal Johnson and Robert Stam (New York: Columbia University Press), pp. 69–71

Rochester, J. (2010) *Staging Spectatorship in the Plays of Philip Massinger* (Aldershot: Ashgate Publishing, Ltd.)

Rollins, H. E. (1921) 'Notes on Some English Accounts of Miraculous Fasts', *The Journal of American Folklore*, 34.134, 357–76

Saccio, P. (1969) *The Court Comedies of John Lyly: A Study in Allegorical Dramaturgy* (Princeton: Princeton University Press)

Sanchez, M. (2008) 'Seduction and Service in The Tempest', *Studies in Philology*, 105.1, 50–82

Sartre, J.-P. (2004) *Critique of Dialectical Reason, Volume One: Theory of Practical Ensembles*, trans. Alan Sheridan-Smith (London: Verso)

Sawday, J. (1995) *The Body Emblazoned: Dissection and the Human Body in Renaissance Culture* (London and New York: Routledge)

Schalkwyk, D. (2008) *Shakespeare, Love and Service* (Cambridge: Cambridge University Press)

Schoenfeldt, M. C. (1999) *Bodies and Selves in Early Modern England: Physiology and Inwardness in Spenser, Shakespeare, Herbert, and Milton* (Cambridge: Cambridge University Press)

Scott, J. C. (1990) *Domination and the Arts of Resistance: Hidden Transcripts* (New Haven and London: Yale University Press)

Sears, T. A. (2010) 'Beyond Hunger: The Alimentary Cultural Code in Lazarillo de Tormes', in *The Lazarillo Phenomenon: Essays on the Adventures of a Classic Text*, ed. Reyes Coll-Tellechea and Sean McDaniel (Lewisburg, PA: Bucknell University Press), pp. 98–119

Segarra, S., Eisen, M., Egan, G. and Ribeiro, A. (2016) 'Attributing the Authorship of the Henry VI Plays by Word Adjacency', *Shakespeare Quarterly*, 67.2, 232–56

Sharp, B. (1980) *In Contempt of All Authority: Rural Artisans and Riot in the West of England, 1586–1660* (Berkeley, Los Angeles and London: University of California Press)

Sharpe, J. A. (1997) *Early Modern England: A Social History, 1550–1760* (London: Arnold)

Sharpe, K., ed. (1978) *Faction and Parliament: Essays on Early Stuart History* (London: Taylor & Francis)

Slack, P. (1979) 'Mortality Crises and Epidemic Disease in England, 1485–1610', in *Health, Medicine and Mortality in the Sixteenth Century*, ed. Charles Webster (Cambridge: Cambridge University Press), pp. 50–1

Smith, A. (2012) *The Wealth of Nations* (Ware: Wordsworth Editions)

Soler, J. (1997) 'The Semiotics of Food in the Bible', in *Food and Culture: A Reader*, ed. Caroline Counihan and Penny Van Esterik (London: Routledge), pp. 55–66

Stallybrass, P. (1991) 'Reading the Body and the Jacobean Theatre of Consumption', in *Staging the Renaissance: Reinterpretations of Elizabethan and Jacobean Drama*, ed. David Scott Kastan and Peter Stallybrass (New York: Routledge), pp. 210–20

Stallybrass, P. and White, A. (1986) *The Politics and Poetics of Transgression* (Ithaca: Cornell University Press)

Steggle, M. (2007) *Laughing and Weeping in Early Modern Theatres* (Aldershot: Ashgate Publishing Limited)

Stone, L. (1972) *The Causes of the English Revolution, 1529–1642* (New York: Harper & Row)

(1977) *The Family, Sex and Marriage in England, 1500–1800* (New York: Harper and Row)

Sweet, J. (2005) 'Introduction: Sea Changes', in *Envisioning an English Empire: Jamestown and the Making of the North Atlantic World*, ed. Robert Appelbaum and John Sweet (Philadelphia: University of Pennsylvania Press), pp. 1–21

Tassi, M. (2005) *The Scandal of Images: Iconoclasm, Eroticism and Painting in Early Modern English Drama* (Selinsgrove: Susquehanna University Press)

Taylor, G. (2001) 'Gender, Hunger, Horror: The History and Significance of *The Bloody Banquet*', *Journal for Early Modern Cultural Studies*, 1.1, 1–45

Templeman, S. (2013) '"What's This? Mutton?": Food, Bodies, and Inn-Yard Performance Spaces in Early Shakespearean Drama', *Shakespeare Bulletin*, 31.1, 79–94

Thompson, E. P. (1971) 'The Moral Economy of the English Crowd in the Eighteenth Century', *Past & Present*, 50, 76–136

(1995) *The Poverty of Theory and Other Essays* (London: The Merlin Press Ltd)

Thong, T. (2007) '"Quality Food, Honestly Priced": Traders and Tricksters in Ben Jonson's *Bartholomew Fair*', in *Food and Morality: Proceedings of the Oxford Symposium on Food and Cookery*, ed. Susan R. Friedland (Totnes: Prospect Books), pp. 288–97

Tilley, M. P. (1950) *A Dictionary of the Proverbs in England in the Sixteenth and Seventeenth Centuries: A Collection of the Proverbs Found in English Literature and the Dictionaries of the Period* (Ann Arbor: University of Michigan Press)

Underdown, D. (1985) *Revel, Riot and Rebellion: Popular Politics and Culture in England, 1603–1660* (Oxford: Oxford University Press)

Vandereycken, W. and van Deth, R. (1994) *From Fasting Saints to Anorexic Girls: The History of Self-Starvation* (London: Athlone Press)

Vickers, B. (2011) 'Shakespeare and Authorship Studies in the Twenty-First Century', *Shakespeare Quarterly*, 62.1, 106–42

Vogel, L. (2013) *Marxism and the Oppression of Women: Toward a Unitary Theory* (Chicago: Haymarket Books)

Vološinov, V. A. (1973) *Marxism and the Philosophy of Language*, trans. Ladislav Matejka and I. R. Titunik (London: Seminar Press)

Wall, W. (2002) *Staging Domesticity: Household Work and English Identity in Early Modern Drama* (Cambridge: Cambridge University Press)

Walsham, A. (1999) *Providence in Early Modern England* (Oxford: Oxford University Press)

Walter, J. (1991) 'The Social Economy of Dearth in Early Modern England', in *Famine, Disease and the Social Order in Early Modern Society*, ed. John Walter and Roger Schofield (Cambridge: Cambridge University Press), pp. 75–128

(2006) *Crowds and Popular Politics in Early Modern England* (Manchester: Manchester University Press)

Walter, J. and Schofield, R. S. (1991) 'Famine, Disease and Crisis Mortality in Early Modern Society', in *Famine, Disease and the Social Order in Early Modern Society*, ed. John Walter and Roger Schofield (Cambridge: Cambridge University Press), pp. 1–74

Walters, T. (2002) '"Such Stowage as These Trinkets": Trading and Tasting Women in Fletcher and Massinger's *The Sea Voyage*', in *Consuming Narratives: Gender and Monstrous Appetite in the Middle Ages and the Renaissance*, ed. Liz Herbert McAvoy and Teresa Walters (Cardiff: University of Wales Press), pp. 67–80

Weil, J. (2005) *Service and Dependency in Shakespeare's Plays* (Cambridge: Cambridge University Press)

Weimann, R. (1987) *Shakespeare and the Popular Tradition in the Theatre: Studies in the Social Dimension of Dramatic Form and Function* (Baltimore, MD: Johns Hopkins University Press)

Weinrich, H. (2004) *Lethe: The Art and Critique of Forgetting* (Ithaca and London: Cornell University Press)

Wheatley, E. (2014) 'Rereading the Story of the Widow of Ephesus in the Middle Ages and the Renaissance', *Comparative Literature Studies*, 51.4, 627–43

Whittle, J. (2000) *The Development of Agrarian Capitalism: Land and Labour in Norfolk, 1440–1580* (Oxford: Oxford University Press)

Whitney, C. (2006) *Early Responses to Renaissance Drama* (Cambridge: Cambridge University Press)

Wiggins, M. (2012–2015) *British Drama, 1533–1642: A Catalogue*, 6 vols (Oxford: Oxford University Press)

Wiles, D. (2005) *Shakespeare's Clown: Actor and Text in the Elizabethan Playhouse* (Cambridge: Cambridge University Press)

Williams, G. (1994) *A Dictionary of Sexual Language and Imagery in Shakespearean and Stuart Literature*, 3 vols (London: The Athlone Press)

Williams, R. (1975) *The Country and the City* (Oxford: Oxford University Press)
(1977) *Marxism and Literature* (Oxford: Oxford University Press)
(2005) *Culture and Materialism: Selected Essays* (London: Verso)
Wilson, R. (1993) *Will Power: Essays on Shakespearean Authority* (London: Harvester Wheatsheaf)
Wood, A. (2001) *Riot, Rebellion and Popular Politics in Early Modern England* (Basingstoke: Palgrave Macmillan)
(2007) *The 1549 Rebellions and the Making of Early Modern England* (Cambridge: Cambridge University Press)
Wood, E. M. (2002) *The Origin of Capitalism: A Longer View* (London: Verso)
Woodbridge, L. (2001) *Vagrancy, Homelessness and English Renaissance Literature* (Urbana and Chicago: University of Illinois Press)
(2010) *English Revenge Drama: Money, Resistance, Revenge* (Cambridge: Cambridge University Press)
Wrightson, K. (1982) *English Society 1580–1680* (London and New York: Routledge)
(2000) *Earthly Necessities: Economic Lives in Early Modern Britain* (New Haven and London: Yale University Press)
Žižek, S. (2008) 'The Secret Clauses of the Liberal Utopia', *Law Critique*, 19, 1–18

# *Index*

Lightning Source UK Ltd.
Milton Keynes UK
UKHW021102230721
387631UK00004B/112

9 781108 832069